The Great American
Bathroom Reader

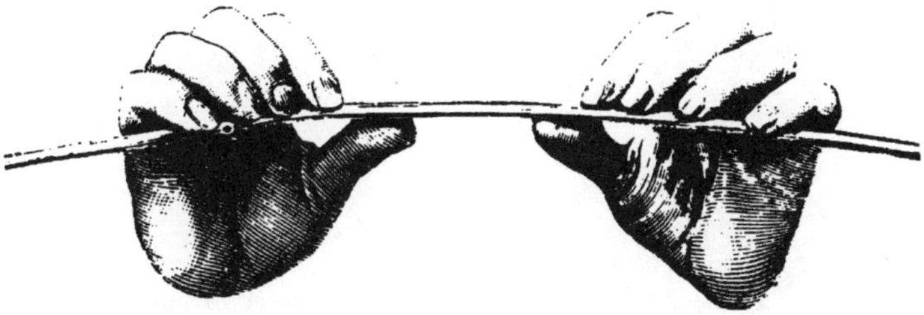

Mark B. Charlton

BARNES
&NOBLE
BOOKS
NEW YORK

This edition published by Barnes & Noble, Inc.,
by arrangement with James Charlton Associates

1997 Barnes & Noble Books

ISBN 1-5661-9404-0 *trade paperback*
ISBN 0-7607-2042-8 *casebound*

Text design by Sisco & Evans, New York

Printed and bound in the United States of America

00 01 02 03 MC 9 8 7 6 5 4 3 2
00 01 02 03 MP 9 8 7 6 5 4 3 2 1

RRD-H

Contents

The LITTLEST ROOM

☛ In Hot Water

According to archaeological discoveries, the first bathrooms were built in the Orkney Islands off the coast of Scotland some 10,000 years ago. Indoor facilities dating back to 3000 B.C. have been excavated in what were private homes in what is now Pakistan and India. However, the bathrooms unearthed in the palaces of Crete from 2000 B.C. show amazing ingenuity, with indoor plumbing and flush toilets.

While bathing took on religious significance with ancient Hindus, Egyptians, and Jews, ancient Romans made it a social phenomenon. The baths, more like modern spas, featured extravagant health and beauty treatments, exercise areas, and gourmet foods. Bathers could get scented, rubbed, oiled, clipped, and curled and then stroll over to shops, gardens, libraries, or lecture rooms for a little socializing.

Originally the sexes enjoyed separate facilities, but later it became fashionable for women and men to go to the baths together. This practice was preferred until the Catholic Church condemned it. Perhaps because of the ban, baths in operation during the early Renaissance in Europe were less concerned with bathing than copulating. In fact, at the time, an Italian word for "bath" was also used for "brothel."

The luxurious baths of Rome thrived from the second century B.C. through the fall of the Roman Empire—around A.D. 500. From then on, for many centuries to come, bathing, cleanliness, and plumbing were not a top priority in Europe. Rampant plagues and devastating epidemics were sad proof of people's fear of personal hygiene and public sanitation.

Although whole-body bathing in ancient Egypt in 1500 B.C. was a sacred rite, in 17th-century Spain the act of immersing oneself in water with the express purpose of using soap was thought to be a heathen practice. Historians believe Louis XIV never washed in water. (Rather begs the question...if he did freshen up from time to time, with what?)

We think Benjamin Franklin was the first to own a bathtub in the colonies. The first indoor bathroom in the United States was probably the one installed in the New York home of George Vanderbilt in 1855.

When a horrific cholera epidemic in the 1830s decimated the population of London, English authorities finally instituted modern sanitation on a large scale.

Of historical note, during World War II the ever-practical British royals did their part to conserve water. All the tubs in Buckingham Palace had a high-water mark of five inches. During his time in the White House, William Taft had to have a specially made bathtub installed for him (he weighed over 300 pounds).

☛ Commode Over

The modern flush toilet is descended from the one patented by Alexander Cumming in 1775 in England, but Queen Elizabeth I had a "privy" designed and installed for her in 1596.

It was the brainchild of one of the queen's godsons, Sir John Harrington, who was, appropriately, from Bath. Although a commanding bit of workmanship, the little room fell into disfavor when Harrington wrote a book about the queen's privy and so enraged her, she kicked him out of the palace.

Thomas Crapper, who helped develop the modern toilet bowl, has had his name become synonymous—actually eponymous—with the facility. Millions of American servicemen in World War I used his contraption and brought the nickname home with them. Crapper's name, however, is just an unlucky coincidence. The Dutch word *krappe* (or "scraps") has been used for centuries when referring to excrement.

The noblewomen of Versailles popularized bidets. The first models, inventive blends of art and architecture, were enclosed in small marquetry closets. The Marquise de Pompadour, a favorite of Louis XV and one of history's most famous courtesans, is said to have had an elaborate one with a lid made of rosewood, while Marie Antoinette's accompanied her to prison.

☛ Paper Products

The habit of reading while on the commode (a habit, incidentally, the authors wholeheartedly approve of, support, and encourage) can be traced back to the first toilet paper. American businessman Joseph Gayetty introduced store-bought paper in 1857 under the name "Gayetty's Medicated Paper—a perfectly pure article for the toilet and for the prevention of piles." It was sold in packets of single sheets and his name was watermarked on every one.

Gayetty's paper didn't last. People were just as happy using what they always had (store catalogues, fliers, newspapers, advertisements, pamphlets, notices, and any paperlike product). And you could actually entertain yourself with it during your private moments, something you couldn't do with Gayetty's blank toilet paper.

Edward and Clarence Scott, brothers and business partners in a fledgling paper business, figured out the allure of a roll of perforated sheets. It was the 1880s when they started trying to market their idea, just when indoor plumbing was becoming popular and growing urban areas were building public waterworks and sewer systems. Having their factory in Philadelphia proved serendipitous, because the city had more fully plumbed bathrooms than any other city at the time, and nearby New York was putting up tenements for newly arrived immigrants as fast as humanly possible. ScotTissue was born, marketed as "soft as old linen."

☛ Soft Soap

Soap in various forms was used by ancient Hittites, Sumerians, and Phoenicians and was unearthed in the archaeological digs of Pompeii. However, it wasn't until the medical establishment realized that bacteria and infection were related to dirt that soap became a product with mass appeal.

Soap hasn't changed very much from the ancient Phoenician recipe developed in 600 B.C. The trick then was to boil animal fat, water, and wood ash together. The liquid evaporated and left behind a waxy solid—soap. Plant or animal oil was applied after a scrubbing to counteract the roughness of the wood ash.

Perfumes and dyes were added by the first century to make the soap fragrant and attractive, and the stuff was first fashioned into handy bar shapes. To this day, most soaps are derived from fat and grease mixed with lye (an alkali made from good old wood ash), scents, and softeners.

For shampoo, we have the Gauls to thank. Two thousand years ago, they came up with a shampoo made from combining wood ash with animal fat.

☛ Pure as the Beaten Soap

A factory accident at Procter and Gamble resulted in one batch of soap being beaten into an airy froth. Tossing it out would have been wasteful, so it was processed and cut into bars. The extra air bubbles allowed the soap to float. When Ivory Soap was put on the market in 1879, consumers snapped it up in a lather of excitement.

The 99 and 44/100 percent line? It came from a report analyzing the soap's chemistry. A lab technician wrote that the soap had few impurities—56/100 of 1 percent, to be precise. Harley Procter liked the purity angle so much, he used it in his advertising efforts.

Good Scents

Scents, perfumes, fresheners, and incense have been used for thousands of years. The word *perfume* is based on the Latin "through smoke," which is how incense works. Sweet-smelling oil was daubed on burning animal sacrifices to mask the stink. Eventually, just the fragrant smoke was offered up as a symbolic, sacred gift. (Two of the three Wise Men gave frankincense and myrrh. Frankincense, by the by, is a sweet-smelling gum that is burned as incense; myrrh is a sort of gum resin used in perfume and medicine.)

Different scents became highly prized and international commodities. Ancient Egyptian women and Greek men were perfume aficionados, using different scents on different parts of their bodies. Cleopatra, for example, prized floral oils for her hands and almond, honey, orange blossom, and cinnamon creams for her feet.

Roman soldiers wore special perfumes into battle and their interest in scents took root in the lands they conquered. During the heyday of the Holy Roman Empire, entire homes were regularly perfumed. Nero so adored the smell of roses, he invested a fortune in rose water.

After a hiatus in popularity, exotic scents were brought back from the East by the Crusaders. Four, coming for the first time to the West, were animal secretions from unlikely suspects: ambergris, from the stomach of sperm whales; castor, compliments of a type of beaver, also from an abdominal sac; civet, a glandular secretion unique to civet cats; and musk, from a sac in the abdomen of a Chinese deer. These four are the highly prized, fundamental essences of modern perfume, although cheaper, synthetic versions have been devised.

When and where bathing was frowned upon, people who could afford them were understandably fond of perfumes. Elizabeth I took time to scent her clothes, shoes, and gloves. Her private blend was made with eight grains of musk and sugar stirred into rose water and damask water. The concoction had to boil for five hours and then be strained. (At least *something* was swished about in hot water.)

Some Elizabethan women wore an aromatic accessory in the form of a necklace of scented beads. A recipe for a "perfumed necklace for ladies" included musk, civet, and rose water rolled into a paste and formed into small balls. Before they hardened, the sweet-smelling paste balls were strung like beads into a necklace. Ladies of the Elizabethan court also concocted a recipe to be rubbed into the coats of their lap dogs before taking the pets to call on friends.

What is the difference between perfume, toilet water, and cologne? Perfume is a blend of ethyl alcohol with at least 25 percent of one or some combination of essential oils (ambergris, castor, civet, and musk). Toilet water is ethyl alcohol with approximately 5 percent essential oils. Cologne is about 3 percent essential oils. Some of the most expensive perfumes on the market have high concentrations of essential oils that are literally worth their weight in gold.

☛ Word of Mouth

For centuries, false teeth were made of bone, ivory, or wood, and occasionally gold. Sometimes good teeth were extracted from those willing to sell them or, somewhat ghoulish though it may seem, from those unable to object: the dead.

Precursors to modern false teeth were developed by the French. Pierre Franchard made them from enamel and gold borrowed from a jeweler. Dentures made from porcelain were developed by Nicolas Dubois de Chemant, a dentist, in the late 1780s. He secured a patent in England with a paste specially created for his dentures used by Wedgwood, the fine china company.

Porcelain teeth set into rubber plates were developed in the latter part of the 19th century. Dentures were at last becoming more comfortable, and dentistry, thanks to modern hygiene and anesthetics, was becoming less painful. Modern dentures and plates use new and improved plastics.

☛ All Manner of Manners

Since Elizabethans figure into so much of this section, a word on their less than refined manners. One book of etiquette published during this era advised gentlemen to refrain from using the fireplace as a urinal because of the ghastly stench.

Things hadn't come very far since the scholar Erasmus (d. 1536), best known for his humanistic treatises, wrote a kind of etiquette book and wisely cautioned against engaging someone in conversation who was in the middle of urinating or defecating.

In Victorian times, things had improved a tad. English debutantes were warned against eating cheese or game because of their unfortunate effect on a young woman's breath...a far cry from using the andirons as a toilet.

In his day, Napoleon was thought to be extremely odd because he opted to change his undergarments daily. It was Beau Brummel who made cleanliness desirable by making it chic in the early 19th century. The man whose name is eponymous for any fellow who's meticulously attentive to fashionable attire is also credited with popularizing personal hygiene and pristine linens. He sent his undergarments and bed sheets to be washed and dried on Hampstead Heath so, one assumes, they'd be infused with clean, floral-scented air. Adamantly anti-grunge, Brummel kept three hairdressers in his employ to arrange his coiffure and wigs. It was said he did not tip his hat to ladies for fear of mussing his "do."

☛ Bathroom Banter

"I refuse to endanger the health of my children in a house with less than three bathrooms."

—Myrna Loy, in *Mr. Blandings Builds His Dream House*

"In my experience, if you have to keep the lavatory door shut by extending your left leg, it's modern architecture."

—Nancy Banks-Smith

"The only country where the money falls apart and you can't tear the toilet paper."

—Billy Wilder on France

"Separate bedrooms and separate bathrooms."

—Bette Davis on the secret of a good marriage

"Who invented the brush they put next to the toilet? That thing hurts!"

—Andy Andrews

"'There won't be any revolution in America,' said Isadore. Nitkin agreed. 'The people are all too clean. They spend all their time changing their shirts and washing themselves.... You can't feel fierce and revolutionary in a bathroom.'"

—Eric Linklater

"When you consider how indifferent Americans are to the quality and cooking of the food they put into their insides, it cannot but strike you as peculiar that they should take such pride in the mechanical appliances they use for its excretion."

—H. L. Mencken

"I am sitting in the smallest room in my house. I have your review in front of me. Soon it will be behind me."

—German composer Max Reger, writing to a critic

"Was it Eliot's toilet I saw?"

—Palindrome allegedly uttered by an American publisher after paying his first visit to the London firm of Faber & Faber, T. S. Eliot's publisher

"The classes that wash most are those that work least."

—G. K. Chesterton

"If the father of our country, George Washington, was Tutankhamened tomorrow and, after being aroused from his tomb, was told that the American people today spend two billion dollars yearly on bathing material, he would say, 'What got 'em so dirty?'"

—Will Rogers

"Beer is not a good cocktail party drink, especially in a home where you don't know where the bathroom is."

—Billy Carter

"Show me a nation whose national beverage is beer, and I'll show you an advanced toilet technology."

—Paul Hawkins

CLOTHES *Call*

Under Statements

Catherine de Medici, who was fond of horseback riding, discovered a problem. That is, if her skirts flew skyward when her horse jumped or when the wind was blowing, she became a party to a crime. It was against the law for anyone other than her husband to see the "private" parts of her anatomy revealed by an indelicate lift of her hem. She had special garments sewn called "calcons" or knickers. One critic of the time railed, "Women should leave their buttocks uncovered under their skirts, they should not appropriate a masculine garment but leave their behinds nude as is suitable for them."

Bloomers are named in honor of activist Amelia Jenks Bloomer (1818–1894), who championed the rights of women in her magazine, *The Lily*. The publication was one of the first women's-interest magazines in this country. One of her causes was that women should feel free to dress more comfortably. When she encountered the fashion of a skirt worn over baggy pantaloons, she applauded the design in print.

Pantaloons got their name from a stock character, Pantaleone. In 16th-century traveling theater companies, the popular figure wore leggings. The word, which eventually came to mean any kind of long trousers, has long since been shortened to plain old *pants.*

Designer Labels

Necessity has driven many to become clothes designers who lent their names to their creations. The collarless sweater, for example, was named for the seventh Earl of Cardigan because he fancied the garment. He earned his reputation while serving in the English army in the Crimean War as head of the legendary Light Brigade. Raglan sleeves are in honor of the first Baron of Raglan, a British army commander. He popularized the style when he became famous for his exploits at the Battle of Waterloo.

Waterloo spawned all sorts of practical duds still in popular use. Wellingtons (or wellies, as they are known fondly by the British) are named for the Duke of Wellington, who wore to-the-knee riding boots during his daring exploits in the battle. Present-day wellies tend to be made of rubber and are the preferred footwear of farmers, fisherfolk, and rainy-day people.

Another military man, Dwight David Eisenhower, popularized the Eisenhower jacket. Ike wore the standard-issue army jacket when he served as theater commander during World War II in Europe. The name is still invoked for relatively tailored, snug-fitting jackets that come to the waist.

Yet a different jacket style can be traced to Jawaharlal Nehru, the prime minister of India from 1947 until his death in 1964. The traditional short, up-turned collar he wore briefly enjoyed fad-dom in the 60s.

Although she had nothing to do with its design, "Mae West" was a military nickname for an inflatable life preserver, which fit like a jacket and gave one (anyone) a busty profile reminiscent of the remarkably bosomed actress. Members of the Royal Air Force are credited with coming up with the moniker in the 30s when Mae West was enjoying her heydey.

Other famous namesakes:

- Acrobat Jules Léotard lent his name to a tight-fitting bodysuit.

- Scientist Charles Macintosh patented the first practical waterproof fabric. "Macintosh" now refers to any old raincoat.

• A tailored topcoat is named for the man who popularized it, a 19th-century Earl of Chesterfield. His original was single-breasted and featured concealed buttons.

• Edward VIII (the Windsor who abdicated the throne of England to be with his true love, Mrs. Simpson) tied his tie in such a way as to inspire the knot named for him.

• A Victorine, a scarf-like garment of fur (also known as a "tippey") with long, dangly ends, is named for Queen Victoria.

Cowboy Duds

The wild, wooly, dusty West inspired several famous refinements on basic designs. John Batterson Stetson was a milliner in New Jersey before he headed toward the Rockies around the time of the Civil War. He based his design for the essentially practical hat on what he believed the true westerner needed and wanted from headgear. But as much as we identify Stetsons as an icon of the American West, the chapeaus were made in a factory in Philadelphia.

Levi's, perhaps the most recognized "designer" clothing item in the world, are named for their Bavarian-American originator, Levi Strauss (1829–1902). Young Levi left New York for San Francisco during the height of the Gold Rush. His plan was to make money selling dry goods to miners and settlers. When he saw that men out west led a rough-and-tumble life and needed resilient trousers, he refashioned tent material into rugged pants. A tailor named Jacob Davis helped him work out the idea of using copper rivets to reinforce stress points.

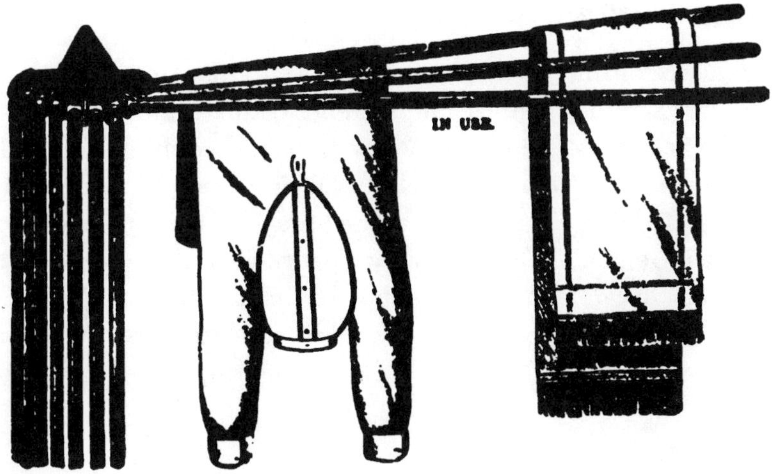

Practical Dresser

• If your zipper gets stuck, take a bar of soap and rub it over the zipper teeth. You're on your own getting the soap out of the zipper. Sometimes the lead of a pencil has the same effect.

• When a drawstring gets pulled out, wet the string and put it in your freezer for five minutes. Now you can thread the stiffened string neatly.

• Need an emergency repair on a hem? Try masking tape or a stapler.

• Pesky buttons keep popping off? First, if color matching is not an issue, try using dental floss instead of thread. It lasts longer. Also, if it's a four-hole button, sew and knot two holes at a time separately. Then, if one thread breaks, the button is still attached thanks to the second thread.

• No time to shine? Spraying hair spray on freshly polished shoes helps extend the life of the shine.

• Black patent leather pumps looking a little shabby? With a chamois, rub in a tiny dab of petroleum jelly. Cracks a problem? Use a black felt-tipped laundry marker.

Toga Party

Togas were the outerwear favored by the citizens of the Roman Empire when they ventured into public. While today's hearty-partying college students rely on cotton blend bed sheets, original togas were made from woolen cloth. The garment was cut from a single piece of fabric and worn around the torso and across the shoulder. Generals and emperors wore toga pictas, decorated with gold stars, to commemorate a victory or similar occasion. Toga praetexta (with a purple border) was worn by children. However, upon reaching the age of 15, boys switched to toga virilis ("manly"), the plain, undyed fabric worn by most men.

Airing the Laundry

Who do we have to thank for the concept of laundry? Eli Whitney. Whitney's engine or "gin," introduced at the turn of the 19th century, was responsible for increasing cotton production and making fabric available and affordable.

In the 17th century, most folks owned a few articles of clothing made from heavy felt or wool. These items were rarely if ever washed and were replaced only when they could no longer be mended.

But with the gin, women no longer needed to spin wool. Instead, those who could afford to bought bolts of cotton ready for sewing. The irony here is that we often assume our forebears had a rougher time in the olden days. Life was hard. But truth is, besides having little laundry (perhaps one summer outfit and one winter outfit), colonials tended to have one pot on the fire. Whatever was in the pot was served for months on end. No pesky supermarket forays or menu planning.

The problem was, these new-fangled cotton clothes needed laundering. Washing required filling kettles of water, heating the water, soaping, rubbing, rinsing, toting, hanging, collecting, folding, ironing, and putting away. Doing the laundry became a time-consuming, back-breaking, and dreaded task for 19th-century women. It's no wonder Europeans traveling in the States wrote about the sickly pallor and stooped shoulders of the housewives they encountered.

Clean clothes quickly became a symbol of status. If your family turned up consistently in fresh, washed clothes, it meant you could afford to pay for cotton cloth as well as a laundress. In 1844, Harriet Beecher Stowe wrote to her husband, Calvin, "The arranging of the whole house…the cleaning…the children's clothes and the baby have seemed to press on my mind all at once. Sometimes it seems as if anxious thought has become a disease with me from which I could not be free." In spite of the fact that Stowe was a wealthy woman and employed servants, the author keenly felt the pressures of running a household and minding her family. Some things, alas, never change.

Hair's to You

Hair fashions have also been named for the people who first sported them. A gravity-defying upswept hairdo takes its name from the Marquise de Pompadour, the officially acknowledged mistress of Louis XV who wielded enormous influence on both the king and his court (Voltaire was among her admirers).

The style of beard known as a Vandyke is named for the Flemish portrait painter who popularized it, Anthony Van Dyck (1599–1641). Sideburns were popularized by Ambrose Burnside, a Union general in the Civil War who would later serve as a governor of, and then senator from, Rhode Island. Aside from his natty facial hair, Burnside achieved moderate fame for his rifle designs, too.

GESTURES *of* GOOD WILL

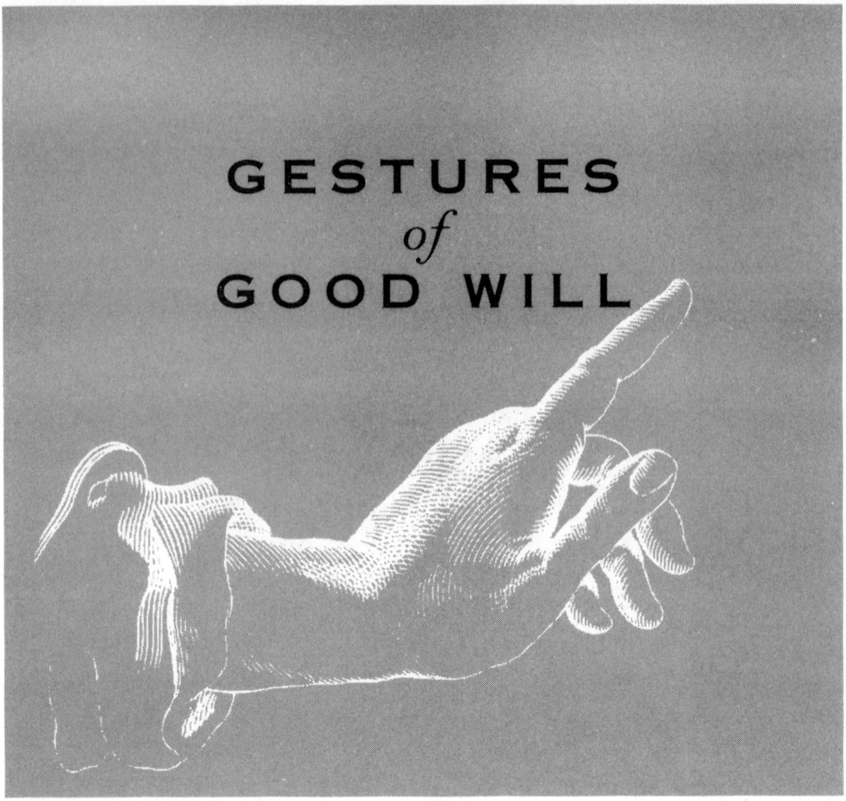

➢ Cross Your Fingers

How did the gesture of crossing one's fingers originate? The sign was not always a safe one to give. When Christians were being persecuted and fed to lions, who could blame them for making the sign of the cross covertly behind their backs? And it's likely they may have told a lie or two to protect themselves from the consequences of having their religion discovered. The finger-crossing gesture, then, came to be a way to protect oneself when telling a lie.

In Mediterranean countries, a cross is formed with the forefingers of both hands held perpendicular to one another. "Back, you vampire!"

South Americans tend to use the thumb and forefinger of one hand, with the thumb the upright "timber" and the first two joints of the forefinger the "crosstimber." Kissing the crossed fingers turns the gesture into an oath or pledge that one is telling the truth.

In North America and certain other northern European cultures, when the forefinger is crossed by the middle finger tightly wound around it, the gesture signifies a lie is being told.

At Rest

The placement of the hands after death is subject to fascinating rules and customs in different cultures.

In Ethiopia, the placement of the hands signifies the deceased's religious status. Laypeople, for example, are buried with their arms meeting at the abdomen, thumbs tied together with white string. A monk, priest, or once-married nun is buried with arms across the chest, and a celibate monk or virgin nun rests with the arms folded over so that the fingers can rest in the mouth.

Among the Annang tribe in Nigeria, the right hand of a deceased first-born son is raised and held up by a string tied to the ceiling of the hut in which he lies in state.

Native Americans of the Dakotas painted a hand in black over the lower part of the face of a great warrior.

In Poland, the hands are placed over the heart, and in Hungary, money is put into the deceased's hands. These traditions presumably deal respectively with the fear of vampires and the cost of safe passage to the next world.

In the United States, hands folded on the stomach are most common, followed by hands at the sides and, rarely, hands crossed over the chest.

Judaic law has many instructions concerning the treatment of the body after death, but only an indirect reference to the hands: the "limbs should be straightened." Thus the arms and hands are generally laid at the sides. Catholics are often buried with a rosary held between clasped hands.

A bizarre funeral custom flourished in Europe and America in the 19th century. It became fashionable to be buried in a coffin equipped with a pull-chain, which was attached through a copper tube to a little bell above ground. Coffins so equipped offered the only-seeming-to-be-dead a chance to be resurrected. Imagine hearing the sound of a little bell tinkling in a deserted churchyard?

That Nails It

When you next invest time and money into building, buffing, and polishing your fingernails only to have one break or chip moments later, remember that the fashion of long, manicured nails developed among the rich—the idle, knee-deep-in-servants rich.

The Chinese developed a cult of the nail, with the ladies of the imperial court encasing their long nails in silver or gold sheaths to protect them. The Mandarins gilded their nails to indicate rank. (Nail painting was originally practiced to guard the fingers and hands from evil spirits—choose your color carefully.)

In many parts of the world, one fingernail is grown long to show that one doesn't perform manual labor. In the Philippines it's the thumbnail, while in Greece it's the little fingernail.

The little fingernail was also grown long by 17th-century courtiers, but for a different reason. It was necessary because no one was allowed to knock at the door of royalty or dignitaries; rather, petitioners were instructed to scratch softly.

A small number of Indian gentlemen with long-suffering wives have taken to getting their names in the *Guinness Book of World Records* by growing the longest fingernails. This is usually done with one hand, leaving the other hand free to take care of business.

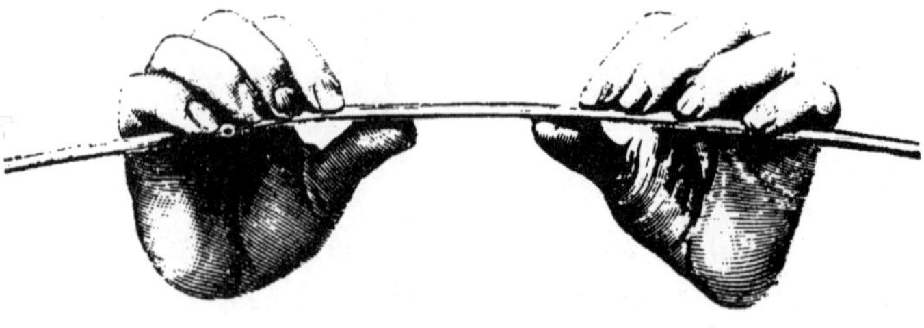

When in Rome

Personal advisors, tutors, and even on-line computer databases provide globe-trotting wheeler-dealers with a comprehensive overview of the protocol and customs of different countries and cultures. While most people worldwide recognize an upturned thumb as a gesture meaning "all's well" or "well done" and a downturned thumb as "not good," refrain from twirling your upturned thumb in Saudi Arabia unless you actually mean, "f— off." Forewarned is forearmed.

• In Germany, it's advisable to keep your hands above the table as opposed to resting in your lap. This dates back to when ill-mannered guests passed secret messages and weapons under the table. Notes like "Let's depose Wolfgang.... Siegfried's dagger is in the potato salad."

• In Iceland, Ireland, Norway, or Sweden, it's bad form to joke about elves. Uttering anything negative about the little guys makes you a target for their mischief-making.

• In Algeria, Morocco, and Tunisia, it's thought to be a slap in the face if you refuse a request to scrub someone's back in the public baths.

• In Saudi Arabia, the left hand is routinely used to administer bathroom hygiene. Therefore, avoid the sinister tendency to eat or to pass something with your left hand. Also, resist asking a Saudi man how his wife is doing. That's a no-no.

• In Finland, a visit to the sauna is a popular way to entertain both friends as well as business colleagues. Finns tend to go in naked but understand the modesty of non-Finns. Drape a towel.

- In parts of the Middle East and Asia, exposing the soles of your feet to someone is akin to saying that person is but dust under your feet to you. This is a serious breach.

- In China, the custom is to offer a guest of honor or visitor the choicest parts of the meal. Refusing them is rude. So, pass the fish lips.

- In Hong Kong, sending flowers can be a risky business. There are specific flowers for specific events and specific lunar months. And never turn your fish over on your plate—it's a curse on the country's fishermen.

- In Brazil, pass the salt but set it down on the table for the next person to use. It's thought to be bad luck to hand it directly to someone.

- In England, never ask members of the royal family a question or have them repeat themselves. Never initiate conversation at a royal occasion. If you do, quickly slap the back of your hand. This means, "Egad, sorry, old chap, I've made a dreadful mistake."

- In Greece, don't be tempted to mimic Zorba by throwing crockery and smashing your glass. It can mean jail and a fine.

- In South Korea, belch at dinner and slurp your soup. It compliments your host and signals that you're enjoying the food.

- In Colombia, if you "saw" your right index finger over the left, you are discussing a bribe and saying that you'll split the profits.

Head of the Class

Before Commodore Perry sailed his ships through the silk curtain, Japan was an elaborately hierarchical feudal society, unchanged for centuries. The ruling class, the shoguns, answered to the emperor who was revered as divine. Below the shoguns were the soldiers (samurai), farmers, artisans, and traders. Within each class there were many subtle gradations.

But how to tell whether an approaching stranger was gold or mud? Sumptuary laws helped. For example, the Shogun Ieyasu dictated the following sumptuary law in 1615: "All costumes and ornaments are to be appropriate to the wearer's rank, and not extravagant in color or

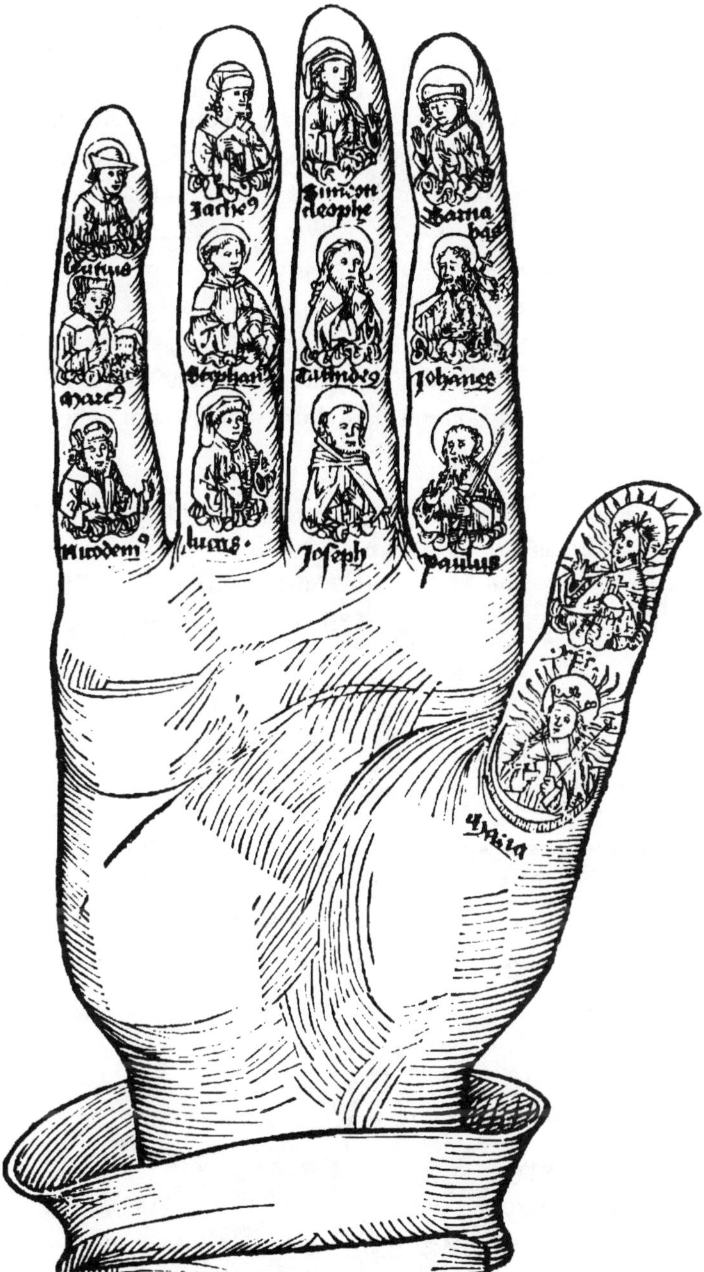
lucas
Joseph
Paulus

pattern. Common people are not to ride in palanquins without permission. Exception is made for physicians, astrologers, aged persons, and invalids."

Sumptuary laws have been widely used for eons. In Olde England, only a member of the royal family was permitted to hunt with a falcon. In Victorian England, class lines began to blur (bother!) when a new level, a middle class, was evolving. But the Victorians, ever fond of class distinctions, came up with a system of classifying working men. From top to bottom: military officers; professionals; employers or managers; junior professionals; clerks; retailers; skilled laborers; semi-skilled laborers; unskilled laborers; and soldiers and sailors. Gentlemen, the chaps who didn't need to hold a job, outranked them all.

The fez (called the "tarboosh" by Moroccans), once outlawed by Ataturk in 1925 as a royalist symbol, is still worn by young men in Morocco who are members of the court of King Hassan II. Staff members at the palace wear conical-shaped versions that denote their status.

The elite in Poland centuries ago set themselves apart by favoring elaborately curlicue-toed slippers. After all, if you were well-to-do, why would you need practical shoes?

Class consciousness inspired many regulations in the New World, too. For example, in 1634, the Massachusetts general court limited the right to wear high-crowned beaver hats to those who held property worth 200 pounds or more.

True COLORS

➵ Earth Tones

The first paints and pigments used by cave painters, such as those who decorated the caves of Lascaux in France around 12,000 B.C., were derived from chalks, char, ashes, and soil. Eventually, dyes were extracted from plants, animals, and minerals. The mineral extractions lasted longer and were more vibrant.

The ancient Egyptians experimented with colors made from processing various chemicals. They pulverized malachite to form a specific green color to represent the Nile. Ancient Chinese ground cinnabar (mercuric sulfide) to make a precious vermilion red. The Romans discovered "Tyrian purple," which was made from shellfish harvested in the Mediterranean at Tyre. The purple was so pure, it came to represent great wealth and/or imperial strength.

Some paints were treasured and hugely expensive because, like Chinese cinnabar, they were made from precious metals or rare stones. Ultramarine blue, for example, was prized by early Italian painters. It got its name, meaning "from across the seas," because it was made from lapis lazuli mined in Afghanistan and transported west. The color was reserved for depicting Christ and the Virgin Mary.

Paints have been made by grinding the extracts into dust and then mixing them with an organic binder (such as egg, beeswax, tree resin, or gum) that allows them to adhere to various surfaces. This process, still in use, can be traced back thousands of years.

For Artists' Sake

The only painting Vincent van Gogh ever sold himself (for about $75) was called *The Red Vineyard.* He said of his painting *The Night Cafe,* "I have tried to express the terrible passions of humanity by means of red and green."

Pablo Picasso's "blue" period is so called not just because of the preponderance of blue but because of the somber mood evident in the works.

The Russian painter Wassily Kandinsky wrote, "Color is the keyboard, the eyes are the harmonies, the soul is the piano with many strings. The artist is the hand that plays, touching one key or another, to cause vibrations of the soul."

Of his famous painting *The Scream,* Edvard Munch wrote, "I sensed a scream passing through nature. I painted…the clouds as actual blood. The color shrieked."

The German writer Johann Wolfgang von Goethe was also a painter, who wrote about color and color theory, and even created color wheels.

The Impressionist painter Claude Monet wrote, "When you go out to paint, try to forget what objects you have before you, a tree, a house, a field, whatever. Merely think: here is a little square of blue, here an oblong of pink, here a streak of yellow, and paint it just as it looks to you…until it gives your own naive impression of the scene before you."

Edouard Manet incorporated remarkable variations of black in his paintings. He made "ivory black" by blending black with red, cobalt blue, and orange.

"When I paint green, it doesn't mean grass; when I paint blue, it doesn't mean sky," offered French artist Henri Matisse.

Paul Klee waxed, "Color possesses me. I no longer have to pursue it. It will possess me always. I know it. This is the meaning of this happy hour. Color and I are one. I am a painter."

Put Up the Shades

• Scientists believe that the human eye can distinguish more than 7,295,000 shades of color.

• Ski resorts rate the difficulty of their trails with green circles (for beginners), blue squares (intermediate skiers), black diamonds (experts), and double black diamonds (experts with excellent medical insurance).

• Barbershop poles are red and white because some barbers (mercifully, many decades ago) doubled as dentists. The red and white stripes, representing blood-soaked bandages, advertised the dentist was in. (An inch off the top and the molar from the back, please.)

• Pick your flowers carefully in Japan. Sending white flowers to newlyweds is a serious faux pas. Presenting someone with yellow blossoms means you wish to end your friendship.

• The Four Horsemen of the Apocalypse are associated with colors: Conquest rides a white horse, Slaughter red, and Famine black. Death rides a pale horse.

• The first illuminated neon tubes were developed in 1907. The first neon sign was created in France, and a Packard dealership in Los Angeles erected the first neon sign in America in 1923. Now, colorful neon signs, particularly from the 1930s and 1940s, are considered collectibles, and the business of repairing and recharging old ones is booming.

• The "pink for girls and blue for boys" custom is a relatively new one. For centuries, Catholic cultures favored blue for both boy and girl babies (because blue was associated with the Virgin Mary), while white was a popular secular choice. Interestingly, in 1918, a publication stressed that pink, "a stronger color," was better suited for boys and "delicate and dainty" blue was better for girls. The reversal started inexplicably in the late 1930s and had caught hold by the early 1950s.

• The ancient Japanese had only five words to describe color: *akane* (orange), *hanada* (turquoise), *kariyasu* (yellow), *kuro* (black), and *shiro* (white). It's believed that these were the only color names because only dyes of those five colors could be extracted from local plants.

Dark Days

Black Saturday, for you trivia hounds, refers to September 10, 1547, when the English wiped out the Scots at the Battle of Pinkie near Edinburgh.

Black Friday refers to several disastrous historic events that have occurred on Fridays. However, the most memorable was Friday, September 24, 1869, when Jay Gould and James Fisk Jr. precipitated the infamous Wall Street Panic (a catastrophic first back then). A similar event on May 11, 1966, earned the name Black Friday when bankers Overend, Gurney, and Company stopped all payments and created havoc.

Black Tuesday is in honor of October 29, 1929, when the stock market, after days of trouble, crashed. Over 17 million shares were sold on the New York Stock Exchange. Banks closed their doors, and companies folded overnight. This set off the Great Depression, the aftershocks of which were felt around the world.

Black Monday, in English schoolboy slang, was the day school resumed after vacation.

Black Sabbath is the annual midnight get-together for witches, warlocks, demons, and sorcerers with the devil presiding.

The title of Fats Domino's 50s hit **"Blue Monday,"** came to characterize an emotion associated with being back on the job after a weekend off.

Made in the Shade

According to a survey by DuPont Automotive, the company that supplies paint to the Big Three automakers, the color green has made a considerable comeback among new-carbuyers.

White is still the most popular choice in the sport/compact car and truck/van categories, but green is now the preferred color for luxury and full/intermediate cars. Nearly 20 percent of all vehicles bought in 1994 and 1995 were green (including varieties of teal and aqua), a dramatic rise from 1992. Light browns and muted shades have also become favored picks, especially for luxury and full-size carbuyers. Purple, a dark horse for years, appeared on the charts in 1994 for the first time as a top 12 color choice.

A spokesperson for DuPont offered the opinion that "people who select green are socially well-adjusted, civilized, and suburban." How so? DuPont tracks color trends by analyzing color research in other hue-dependent fields such as fashion, graphic arts, and home and commercial furnishings. New colors are added to the company's palette as tastes change. The hot colors projected for the next millennium are earth tones such as golds, browns, beiges, and greens.

Color Wards

• According to the U.S. Postal Service, more than 160 places in the country incorporate "green" in their names. "Green" derives from the same ancient Indo-European root as "grow." After all, "chlorophyll," the word for the pigment that makes plants green and helps them grow, means "green leaf" in Greek.

• That distinctive yellow for school buses, introduced in 1950, has been a standard color in this country since 1971 and is actually called National School Bus Chrome Yellow. It was originally designated by the General Services Administration and approved for nationwide use by the Occupational Safety and Health Administration.

• Sailors wearing navy blue dates back to the 18th century. The uniforms of officers in the British navy were navy by order of King George II, who, it was said, was influenced by a dark-blue-and-white riding habit worn by the Duchess of Bedford. By 1857, Parliament made it official.

• Garnet derives from the word *pomegranate*, the seed color of which it resembles. Garnets have long been credited with having special powers including healing the sick, giving off light, and generating heat. Some ancients believed they came from dragons and called them dragon stones.

• Carrots contain carotene, an orange pigment. Therefore, if you drink enough carrot juice or eat enough carrots, your skin will take on an orange cast. However, if you overdose on orange food, you may

actually suffer from carotene poisoning. It's carotene in a flamingo's diet (found in algae and small mollusks) that keeps it flamingo-colored.

• Gold was considered the only true color by Japanese artists of the 18th century because of its subtle qualities. Specifically, it was prized because it suggested surfaces, through luster and sheen, rather than defining them.

• Black holes are not, as Captain Kirk may have once suggested, rips in space. Rather, they are amalgams of, well, stuff and have a remarkably strong gravity. Because light can't escape the pull, they are invisible. They are the result of gigantic stars that have broken up but retain their superheaviness.

• *Auburn* originally meant "white" (from the Latin *alburnus*) but was cast about Europe in the 16th century and transformed into *a-broun*—a reddish brown. The word *album* is also derived from the Latin word for "white." In ancient Rome, an album was a plain, white tablet made of stone. Public notices were etched onto it.

Crayon Box

Edwin Binney and C. Harold Smith formed a partnership in 1885 to manufacture printing ink and, later, slate pencils. Binney & Smith is still making crayons and kindergarten memories.

Eight crayon colors were retired by Crayola in 1990 to make room for bolder, brighter colors in their box of 64: blue gray, green blue, lemon yellow, maize, orange red, orange yellow, raw umber, and violet blue. But don't feel blue. They were inducted into the Crayola Hall of Fame in Easton, Pennsylvania. You can visit them there.

The perky little replacement colors are cerulean, dandelion, fuchsia, jungle green, royal purple, teal blue, wild strawberry, and vivid tangerine.

The year the 64-pack was introduced with that winning sharpener was 1958. The first eight-box of crayons Crayola issued in 1903 sold for a nickel and contained brown, red, orange, yellow, green, blue, violet, and black.

Up THE GARDEN PATH

And a Pinch of Pansy

Various parts of plants have been used as medical therapies since ancient times. Homeopathy and herbalism are enjoying a renaissance as people look toward natural treatments for their maladies. Before administering any drug (plant-derived or over-the-counter), be sure you know what you are doing.

ajuga—The sap of the ajuga contains tannin, which helps stop bleeding. So if you ever happen to cut yourself shaving while in your garden, you can avail yourself of this all-natural styptic pencil.

althea,* or *hollyhock—*Althaea* is Greek for "that which heals." The plant althea (also known as hollyhock) has been used both as an insect repellent and as a soothing treatment for insect bites. It was once a common ingredient in cough syrups and was also thought to work wonders for sore throats, upset stomachs, and vaginal infections.

alyssum,* or *basket of gold—Alyssum was used to treat mental illness. Indeed, its name is from the Greek meaning "without madness." The superstitious believed that a posy of this flower would keep people from becoming angry with you.

columbine—Once one of the most important of the medicinal plants, columbine was used to treat, among other things, measles and smallpox.

coneflower—Long used for medicinal purposes, scientists have now isolated chemicals within the coneflower that are effective in treating certain viral infections.

dahlia—Dahlia roots have an extremely high sugar content. Before the discovery of insulin, they were used to treat diabetics.

echinacea—A popular product in herb shops today, echinacea extracts are touted as immune-system builders.

gentian—Used since ancient times to kill intestinal worms and treat other digestive disorders, gentian is still used today externally on insect stings.

hyacinth—Ancient Greeks used hyacinths to treat dysentery and poisonous spider bites. Potions made from the plant were also said to prevent the change of voice that occurs when boys reach puberty.

iberis,* or *candytuft—A popular plant among herbalists, iberis was once widely used as a treatment for rheumatism.

impatiens—The sap of one common variety of impatiens has been proven effective in the treatment of poison ivy. It was traditionally used as a salve for skin conditions by several Native American tribes.

iris—The iris was one of the flowers most widely cultivated and used for an astounding variety of medicinal purposes. Fevers, chills, coughs, colds, epilepsy, headaches, and snakebites are just some of the conditions that were treated with concoctions made from the iris flower and roots.

marigold—The leaves of the marigold were used to treat wounds and to get rid of warts.

pansy—Pansy leaves were typically used to brew love potions, but Nicholas Culpeper, the famous 17th-century herbalist and writer, believed they were more useful in combating one of the more unpleasant aftereffects of unsafe sex. He claimed that a syrup made from pansies could cure venereal disease.

spiderwort—Spiderwort is currently of great interest to scientists because of its extreme sensitivity to pollution and radiation. When exposed to these toxins, even at low levels, the stamens of the spiderwort undergo changes in color that are quite reliable indicators.

verbena—Verbena was used to treat rabies, asthma, rheumatism, and epilepsy. It was also considered an aphrodisiac.

Desert Blooms

The wily cactus survives in the desert because it conserves water so cleverly. The entire plant is designed to hold moisture in. The clusters of prickles, called areoles, hold an insulating layer of air snug against the plant. They also cool the plant by catching dew and whatever rainfall occurs. While there are succulents in many deserts around the world, cacti grow exclusively in New World deserts.

The majestic saguaro is found in the Sonora Desert. Like snowflakes, each has a different pattern, but they tend to be tall (upwards of 40 feet) with "arms" that stretch out from a center trunk. Each one may contain several tons of water. By boring holes into the trunks, several types of small desert birds find cool havens and protection from predators.

The prickly pear (resembling a cluster of ping-pong paddles) is among the most hardy of the cacti. While the pear-shaped fruit is edible, glochids (fine hairs on the outside of the pear) get under your skin (literally) and cause infection as well as pain.

The cholla is perhaps the prickliest of all cacti. It grows in a wide variety of shapes and there are as many names as types (pencil, teddy bear, and staghorn, for example). The jumping cholla is so named because of its spines, which seem to "jump" onto passersby and hold on tenaciously.

The barrel cactus, fat with water, is the one parched cowboys look for. Moisture can be chewed from the pulp.

Plant Life

• *Sub rosa* means, literally, "under the rose." In ancient times, a rose was suspended from the ceiling of council chambers as an indication that everyone in attendance was expected to keep silent about the proceedings.

• Mistletoe was a sacred plant to ancient Celtic and Teutonic tribes, who used it in ceremonies and hung it from their ceilings to ward off evil spirits. Druids credited the plant with maintaining family happiness.

• Why is a four-leaf clover considered lucky? Because it is an anomaly (most clovers have only three leaves). Ancient Druids (Celtic for "oak-wise"), who lived and worshipped in the British Isles several hundred years B.C., saw the discovery of a rare four-leaf clover as a positive sign during their tree-worshipping ceremonies. Although horticulturalists developed a four-leaf clover seed in the 1950s and so now they are anyone's for the picking, it's still exciting (and lucky) to find one in a patch of three-leafers.

• The word *baccalaureate* is Latin for "laurel berry" because laurel, an ancient symbol of victory, was once conferred upon those who had received a bachelor's degree.

• Ancient Greeks and Romans enjoyed violets in their food and drinks, and cooks in 14th-century England turned the tiny purple blossoms into jelly and fritters. Violets can be boiled or dipped in a syrup made of sugar dissolved in water. Also dipped in granulated sugar, they crystallize into edible sugar flowers and can be used as decorations on cakes and as elaborate sweets. (The same thing is sometimes done with tiny rosebuds or rose petals.) Crème de violette is an amethyst-colored Dutch liqueur made from violets. Please, eat the daisies!

Days of Roses

• In honor of President William McKinley's fondness for carnations, January 29, his birthday, was declared Carnation Day. Carnations, incidentally, take their name from the Latin *carnis*, meaning "flesh" as in fleshy-pink-colored. "Carnation red" refers to the distinctive brilliant red of some varieties. The popular flower is also the state flower of Ohio. Some 50 varieties of carnations were cultivated during the reign of Charles I because his queen so loved them.

• On Geranium Day, held in April in England, stickers are sold to benefit the Greater London Fund for the Blind. Why geraniums? Probably because in the language of flowers they signify consolation. Rose emblems (for Queen Alexandra Rose, wife of Edward VII) are sold in June to benefit London hospitals.

• Poppy Day began in World War I. During the war, poppies were sold on street corners to benefit the war orphans of France and Belgium. To commemorate the 1918 signing of the armistice, they are sold on November 11 by the British Legion to benefit veterans and charities. Since 1922, the Veterans of Foreign Wars in the United States have sold them on that day to benefit disabled and needy American vets. Poppies grew in Flanders, an infamously bloody battlefield in World War I, and have long been associated with eternal sleep.

• October 6 is Ivy Day, the anniversary of the death of Irish statesman Charles Stewart Parnell in 1891. Ivy was chosen to represent the Parnellites because it was an evergreen, like the emerald isle, and a perfect contrast to British prime minister Benjamin Disraeli's emblem, the primrose. Primrose Day is April 19, the day Disraeli died in 1881. The Primrose League was formed after Disraeli's death to promote his brand of Conservative principles.

- Instead of May Day, Hawaiians celebrate Lei Day on May 1. There are contests for the most original floral garlands.

- Perhaps the grandest tribute is paid the venerable rose at the Tournament of Roses (a century-old tradition) held New Year's Day in Pasadena, California. Every inch of each floral float featured in the two-hour parade must be covered with flowers or other natural materials such as bark, leaves, or seeds. Volunteers spend days gluing and wiring flowers in place. The most delicate blossoms are placed in individual vials of water and set into the floats one at a time. The average float is decked with more flowers than the average florist goes through in a year. The first Rose Bowl was held in 1902 when Stanford University played the University of Michigan. Stanford gave up in the third quarter when the score reached 49–0. Chariot races replaced football until 1916. The stadium doors to the Rose Bowl, named by the Tournament's press agent Harlan "Dusty" Hall, opened on January 1, 1923.

Posy Poetry

During Victorian times, it was the rage to send and receive "talking" bouquets called tussie-mussies (a phrase that dates back to the Middle Ages). Lovers could discreetly exchange floral posies in which each blossom (and, in some cases, herb or fruit) was code for a message, sign, compliment, rebuff, or sentiment. Flower dictionaries became best-sellers, and young women delighted in poring over them with the nosegay from an admirer in hand. Bouquets became subtle love letters.

A typical tussie-mussy might have been a combination of baby's breath (pure heart), azaleas (first love), primroses (youth, innocence, and gaiety), blue violets (faithfulness), and a China rose (beauty always new). The grape hyacinth, probably not as popular in romantic exchanges, signified usefulness.

A young lady could respond to an admirer's message by wearing his tussie-mussy in public. Pinned in her hair meant, basically, "slow down, hombre." Tucked into her cleavage signaled friendship. However, if she wore the flowers next to her heart, this was a green light to love.

Vernal Verbiage

Medieval painters used flowers and fruits to represent various aspects of the sacred. Lily of the valley stood for purity, for example, and strawberries for spiritual fruits that come from good deeds. Shakespeare tipped his hand to his Elizabethan audience by draping the dead Ophelia in a garland. Crowflowers stood for a "fair maid," nettles for "stung," daisies for "true," and long purples for "cold hand of death."

So next time you order flowers, suit the blossom to the occasion. Herewith, a sampling of the floral dictionary.

anemone *expectation*
aster *elegance*
arbor vitae *constancy in friendship*
camellia *excellence*
carnation *admiration*
cherry blossom *duplicity, false hopes*
clover *fertility*
cypress *mourning*
daisy *innocence*
fern *fascination*
forget-me-not *forget me not (no surprise there)*
foxglove *insincerity*
holly *good wishes*
hyacinth *sport or play*
iris *hope or faith*
ivy *faithfulness*
laurel *glory or victory*
lily *purity*
marigold *sorrow*
narcissus *conceit*
peony *healing*
primrose *youth*
rosemary *remembrance*
snowdrop *hope or consolation*
sunflower *devotion or loyalty*
sweet William *gallantry*
thistle *defiance*
tulip *passionate love*
violet *steadfastness*
yew *resurrection or faith*
zinnia *thoughts of faraway friends*

ANIMAL *Tales*

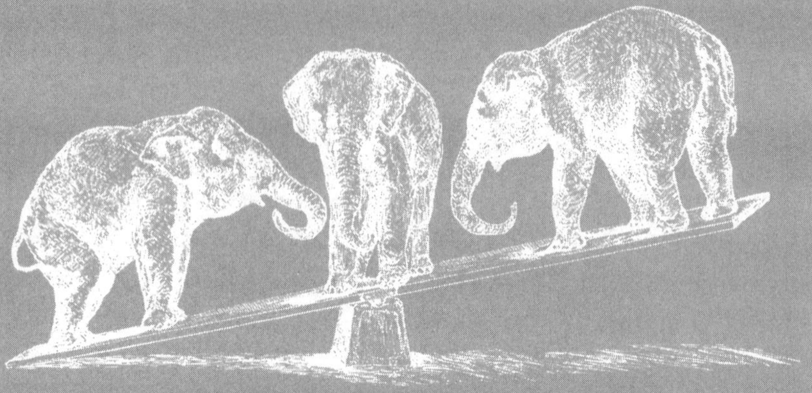

➤ Fake Fur

On the occasion of British National Pet Week in 1991, the Royal Society for the Prevention of Cruelty to Animals polled some 400,000 children in England and Wales to establish a Top 10 list of pet names. Snowy appeared in just about every category and was the number-one pick for rabbits. Tintin's dog, in the English versions of the wonderful adventures of the globe-trotting comic book character, is Snowy. Snowbell, the family cat, barely tolerates Stuart Little in E. B. White's classic tale about an adventurous mouse.

The dandelion comes by its name via France. *Dent de lion* means "lion's tooth" and refers to the jagged edge of the flower and leaves.

Before finally deciding upon Huckleberry Hound, Hanna-Barbera tossed around Alfalfa Hound, Cactus Hound, and Dingy Dog.

Winnie-the-Pooh got his name from a bear cub in the London Zoo named Winnipeg and a swan, Pooh, who lived on a lake near A. A. Milne's home.

Piggy banks, while often made in the shape of swine, are named for pygg, a kind of earthenware clay once widely used in western Europe for crockery. People often squirreled away money in a pygg jar. Eventually, potters made pygg pigs.

While Goldilocks now gets top billing, the original story (written by British poet laureate Robert Southey in 1837) was titled "Story of the Three Bears." His original heroine was a bad-tempered old biddy who ransacked the bears' neat-as-a-pin home. Sweet, little, flaxen-haired Goldilocks inexplicably evolved over time.

➤ Spider Bytes

Tarantulas, of which there are several species around the world, are fascinating critters with a bad reputation. They can spin seven different kinds of webs, and some are capable of producing a web as strong as steel. They have leg spans of up to seven inches and can weigh as much as an ounce.

While some people run in horror from tarantulas (found in hot, desert climes), the big boy of spiderdom is not aggressive. If you had the inclination to look over your shoulder during your speedy escape, you'd notice the tarantula scooting in the opposite direction.

Tarantulas save their attacks for food, jumping on edible insects and injecting venom through their fangs. While they will display their fangs to would-be predators and try to temporarily blind them by blowing a dust made from their fur at the predators' eyes, it's all smoke and bluster. It may work occasionally, but a hungry lizard, desert rodent, tarantula hawk (a kind of wasp), snake, or bird will eat it anyway.

Female tarantulas may live up to 25 years. The males rarely get beyond 10 because, once they mate at 10 years old, the female devours them. And not to worry if one does bite you. It hurts but it's not fatal. It's the bite of a black widow spider that packs a bigger punch than rattlesnake venom.

How do spiders find their way up flights of stairs and come to rest in bathtubs, scaring the dickens out of people who live in apartment buildings? The eggs of common local spiders are cocooned in webs, which are blown through the air into our homes, where they hatch.

➤ What's the Diff?

Why are deer *and* antelope home on the range? Chances are the lyricist meant pronghorns. There are many examples throughout the animal kingdom of animals being confused for one another.

bison/buffalo—Actually, there are no buffalo wandering the American plains. They are bison. In 1900, there were fewer than 100 left in this country, but the numbers are steadily climbing.

porpoise/dolphin—Both are members of the cetacean (whale) family, but dolphins live in coastal waters close to land, while porpoises prefer deep coastal waters and the open sea. Physically, dolphins have a prominent beak sharply demarcated from the forehead. Porpoises have no real beak. Dolphins have conical teeth while porpoises have flattened teeth that expand at the tip. An orca ("killer whale") is actually a kind of porpoise.

alligator/crocodile—Alligators are the more common in the swamps and rivers throughout the South and are thought to be less cranky than crocs. They have wider snouts, and the teeth usually disappear when the gator's mouth is closed. Crocodiles hang out in southern Florida (and, yes, Australia) and have narrower snouts, and the fourth tooth on each side of the lower jaw hangs out of their closed mouths. Alligators get their name from the Spanish explorers who ventured to Florida. They named the critter *el lagarto* or "*the* lizard" (to differentiate it from any little old lizard). Caimans, a type of alligator, have a shorter, broader mouth. Finally, the gavial, which belongs to the crocodilian group, has a smaller head and a long, slender, pointy mouth with sharp teeth.

hedgehog/porcupine—The word *porcupine* comes from the Italian words for "pig" (*porco*) and "spine" (*spino*). Porcupines are vegetarians and can be found in the western and northeastern United States and in Canada. Members of the rodent family, they climb up head

first and climb down tail first. They can weigh up to 30 pounds and reach 2½ feet in length. Hedgehogs are much smaller and nibble on insects. Inhabiting the hedgerows of Europe, they have about 8,000 quills (an adult porcupine can have over 30,000), which tend not to come out. An Australian marsupial similar in many ways to the hedgehog is called an echidna.

crane/heron—A crane has a patch of red on its face and flies with its neck extended. Herons fly with their heads tucked in by their shoulders.

turtle/tortoise—The interesting little detail here is that the sex of hatchlings is determined by the water temperature in which they're born. If it's chilly, 82° or below, it's a brood of boys. If it's warmer, in the 90s, it's a gathering of girls. Of the 200 different species, there are marked differences between turtles and tortoises. While turtles have thin, flat legs, webbing, and flop around water, tortoises sport thick, round legs, are webless, and prefer life on land. Their shells also give a clue. Turtles have rounded, flat shells, and tortoises have high domes. Finally, if you're still not sure, count the toesies on their rear feet: turtles have five, and tortoises have but four.

frog/toad—Toads are the water lovers, while frogs live on land. Toads have rough warty-looking skin that is dry, while frogs are smooth and moist. And one rarely sees toad legs on the menu, because the poor dears have short legs. Frogs have long, meaty ones.

chrysalis/cocoon—A butterfly transforms inside a chrysalis, while a moth metamorphoses from within a cocoon.

centipede/millipede—Centipedes have between 28 and 354 legs, depending upon the species. Each segment of its body has two legs. Millipedes have been recorded as having up to 750 feet (a Caribbean specimen) but never an even 1,000. Each body segment of a millipede has four legs. Also, millipedes add legs and segments as they mature.

horn/antler—Horns are hollow, while antlers are solid. An animal with horns keeps them its whole life long, while a critter with antlers sheds them annually. Horns are single-pronged, while antlers branch. According to Cherokee lore, Rabbit and Deer decided to race to see who was faster. Owl spied Rabbit cheating before the race had even begun and reported him. Deer was given antlers as a reward.

venomous/nonvenomous snakes—Not that you are going to want to get close enough to run down this entire checklist, but a venomous snake will tend to have elliptical pupils, a head much wider than its neck, a single anal plate, and single scales on the underside of its tail. A nonvenomous snake will typically have round pupils, a head slightly wider than its body, a divided anal plate, and a double row of scales on the underside of its tail.

➤ Creature Curiosities

• Kangaroos aren't the only pocketed critters in the Outback. Koalas have pouches, too. They take their liquid refreshment from the one to two pounds of eucalyptus leaves they munch every day. They never drink water (*koala* is an aboriginal word meaning "no water"). They only go for about a dozen different species of eucalyptus (there are over 100). Koala mums give birth to one or two babies at a time. At birth, koalas are less than an inch long. They travel up to the pouch by following a trail of their mother's saliva. They stay tucked inside for about six months and until they are some six inches long. They'll then spend their days hanging out (literally, on mama's back) and their nights in her pocket for another few months.

- When armadillos give birth, the babies in litters of four are either all male or all female, never a combination.

- Oysters are wonderfully changeable things. They alter their sex every year. They are able to spawn in either male or female form depending upon the salt content and the temperature of the water. And when they spawn, they spawn—releasing a million eggs at a time. It takes five to seven months for an oyster to produce a pearl.

- Seahorses have an interesting arrangement. Like horseshoe crabs, they mate when the moon is full. Females release eggs into a pouch on the male's abdomen. He fertilizes and nourishes the eggs and will bear 50 young (seafoals) at a time. To avoid detection by predators, a seahorse can change colors.

- A chameleon can extend its tongue a distance equal to the animal's length.

Animal Myths

- Neither bats nor moles are blind.

- Elephants are not scared of mice.

- Bears do not hug their prey. They effectively swat with their forepaws.

- Cobras cannot be "charmed" by the tune of a flute.

- Rattlesnakes often strike without a single shake of their rattles.

- The last straw will not break a camel's back—if the load is too heavy, a camel will not stand up with it.

- Lemmings do not commit mass suicide by following one another to a cliff and hurling themselves into the briny deep. They do, on occasion, swim out of their depth and drown.

- Ostriches do not bury their heads in the sand.

• Bulls do not become enraged upon seeing the color red. They are color-blind. They do get riled when someone waves something in front of their faces and then tries to stick them between the shoulder blades.

• Crocodiles don't shed tears as a form of intentional fakery. Rather, when they choke down big chunks of food, they tend to gasp for air and when this happens, their tear glands discharge "tears." Also, they don't smile. They do like to bask in the sun with their mouths open, though. It helps them muster energy so they can hunt in the cool of the evening.

➤ Animal Behavior

Ever wonder when horses relax? They never seem to kick back. They rarely lie down—except when sick, foaling, or rolling around for fun. Horses can stand for days and weeks at a time by locking their knees and sleeping standing up. Flamingos do it one-legged, which is even more impressive.

Goats don't really eat tin cans. Rather, they chew them to suck the glue holding the labels in place. Yummy!

Possums really do play possum. However, it's not cleverness or brilliant acting. It's simply a natural reaction to being threatened. A possum doesn't have the brain power to fake death. Rather, if hissing and showing its 50 teeth doesn't intimidate a would-be predator, and running away doesn't work, the marsupial will go limp with its eyes wide open and may stay that way for several hours.

An adult porcupine doesn't shoot quills like arrows but, rather, slaps them into its victim. Each quill is loaded with scales that work like barbs. A baby porcupine is born with soft quills that harden in a matter of minutes.

Few animals mate 'til death do them part. Canadian geese, beavers, loons, swans, and wolves are among the select group.

The word *amphibian* is Greek for "having a life of two kinds." One life is spent as a larva or tadpole, breathing through gills underwater. The other is spent on land, breathing through lungs. Newts actually have three lives—as a larva, an eft, and a full-grown newt.

Endangered Species

Descriptions of equine creatures with a single horn appear in the Scriptures and in the Roman catacombs, and white unicorns were frequently used in medieval literature and art as emblems of virtue and purity.

In heraldry, the unicorn had the head and body of a horse, the tail of a lion, the legs and hooves of a stag, and a twisted horn emerging from its forehead. It symbolized physical strength and moral virtue. James III of Scotland had unicorns printed on coins—known as unicorns. Queen Jane Seymour adopted them as one of her emblems. When James VI of Scotland ascended to the English throne as James I, the unicorn first appeared on the royal arms of England. The battles between the lion and the unicorn in Spenser's allegory *The Faerie Queen* represent the historical animosity between England and Scotland.

Other heraldic creatures include the hydra, wyvern, chimera, gorgon, cockatrice, basilisk, and gryphon. Take note, Scrabble players.

Calendar Pets

- The dog days, July 3 through August 11, get their name from the rising of the Dog Star.
- Groundhog Day is aligned with Candlemas, February 2. A German old wives' tale claims that if the fuzzy fellow emerges and sees his shadow, six more weeks of winter are in store. However, the groundhogs of Punxsutawney have only been accurate about a quarter of the time.
- Bunnies have been associated with Easter since the ancient Anglo-Saxons worshipped the goddess Eastre, who was in turn symbolized by the hare.

At Bat

Although bats suffer a bad rap, they provide one especially valuable service. A single bat can devour 600 mosquitoes in one hour. One bat cave in Texas boasts a population of some 30 million bats, which consume 250 tons of mosquitoes every night.

Another nifty feature of batdom is that bats are the only mammal that truly flies. The bony bits in their wings are actually their fingers, with their thumbs making the little clawlike appendages at the tip of each wing.

And you should know that bats, while they do roost upside down, do not fly at people—enrapt on getting enwrapped in hair. Using a kind of radar system called echolocation, they avoid slamming into any object, except perhaps a cloud of skeeters. As some species of bats (there are 40 or so species in North America) are endangered, it's best not to disturb their roosts. If you find a bat in your house, open the windows so it can fly out and flap its way home.

➤ Such a Honey

Shakespeare wrote, "...for so work the honey bees, / Creatures that by a rule in nature teach / The act of order to a peopled kingdom." Indeed, honeybees are a nifty little society. The members of a hive are divided into three classes: the queen, drones, and workers. There is only one queen per colony. She doesn't exactly rule the roost, but she is revered and catered to as the mother of all the eggs in the hive. She's busy as, well, a bee, and so she isn't expected to chip in on the hivework. Any female bee can be chosen as queen, to be coddled from egghood by her worker bees.

Worker bees are exclusively female and can do anything except reproduce. Only the queen has this special capacity. Young workers tend to the hive until they are ready to take short flights out into the world. Some remain as guards, while others begin a life of foraging for nectar.

Drones are exclusively male. Their superior vision and wing strength help propel them toward the queen in order to reproduce. Once they have performed this, their sole function, they are killed. (So much for parental bonding with the beelets.)

Ants, as class-conscious as bees, divide themselves into workers and soldiers who follow their allegiance to their queen. As in a beehive, every ant colony has a queen mum. Workers are the queen's daughters; if not infertile, they are less fertile than their mother. Their duty is to collect food to feed the queen and the colony's larvae (who obviously must have a particular craving for deviled eggs, ham sandwiches, and crumbs found around the kitchen sink). The soldiers use their large heads to block entrances to the colony when it's threatened. They defend the home front and are expert diggers. Workers tend to stay close to the colony shoving those grains of sand and dirt clods around. Cozy.

Baby Names

A baby deer is a fawn, and a baby duck is a duckling, but what is a baby moose? Like a baby cow or buffalo, it's a calf. Other baby names include kit (beaver), porcupette (porcupine), kit or pup (fox), owlette (owl), kitten (cat or rabbit), gosling (goose), tadpole (frog), and cygnet (swan).

Doggin' It

The most popular dog breeds are tracked through registration numbers maintained by the American Kennel Club. However, it's a list that shifts from year to year depending upon changes in taste and fashion. Certain breeds appear on the list one year and drop off the next. A breed might become popular after, say, a certain dog becomes a spokeshound for a product, is featured in a film, or attracts a lot of attention at the Westminster Dog Show. These are among the most consistently popular breeds:

Labrador retrievers
Rottweilers
German shepherds *(Alsatians)*
Golden retrievers
poodles
cocker spaniels
beagles
dachshunds
dalmatians
Pomeranians
Chinese shar-peis *(only recognized by the AKC since 1992)*

On the subject of dogs, it's interesting to note that while proper names such as Lucy, Tess, Ben, and Max rank among the most popular names for pooches in the United Kingdom, American dog owners favor Lady, King, Duke, Prince, and Princess.

All MAPPED OUT

☛ All the Presidents' Names

Presidents have lent their names to hotels, landmarks, dams, bridges, and universities. But who has the most American towns named for him?

President James Madison edges out George Washington 27 to 26. Monroe rates 22, Andrew Jackson and Thomas Jefferson each boast 20, and Grover Cleveland comes in with 19.

The most popular place-name in the country, however, goes to never-was-president Benjamin Franklin. The statesman, writer, and inventor is honored with 28 Franklins. Interestingly, there are also 26 Clintons, all named well before Bill took office.

While certainly respectful of the Oval Office, the good folk of Ismay, Montana (there are 22 by last count), voted to rename their town Joe. President Joe? No. Rather, the honor goes to famed quarterback Joe

Montana. The change is only good through the football season, however, and reverts to Ismay after the Super Bowl.

From Sea to Shining Sea

The derivations of other American cities and towns honor celebrities, the landscape, home turf, totems, and landmarks. For example:

Abilene *Hebrew for "grassy plain"*

Akron *Greek for "summit"*

Albuquerque *Spanish for "white oak"*

Alcatraz *Spanish for "pelican"*

Baton Rouge *French for "red staff"*

Berkeley *in honor of Irish philosopher George Berkeley (1685–1753)*

Boise *French for "woody"*

Carlsbad *for Karlsbad, Bohemia*

Cheyenne *Dakota for "people of a foreign language"*

Chicago *Algonquin for "place of wild onions"*

Detroit *French for "narrows"*

El Paso *Spanish for "the pass" or "the gap," for the canyon carved out by the Rio Grande*

Kalamazoo *Ojibwa meaning "otter tail"*

Milwaukee *Algonquin for "good land" or "council place"*

Nantucket *a local tribe's word for "its useless soil tempts no one"*

Omaha *Sioux for "upstream people"*

Palo Alto *Spanish for "tall logs," for the giant redwoods*

Pasadena *Ojibwa meaning "crown of the valley"*

Pensacola *a Native American word meaning "hairy people"*

Pueblo *Spanish for "village"*

Roanoke *Native American word for "smooth shells" or money*

Santa Fe *Spanish for "holy faith"*

Spokane *Salish for "children of the sun"*

Tallahassee *Creek for "old village"*

Tampa *Calusa for "nearby"*

Terre Haute *French for "high land"*

Topeka *Kansa for "potato"*

Truth or Consequences *named for the game show in 1950 (formerly Hot Springs)*

Tucson *Pima for "black creek"*

Wheeling *Delaware for "head of the river"*

Westward, Oh!

Keeping American maps up to date in the last half of the 19th century was a full-time job. While Arkansas (in 1836), Louisiana (1812), and Missouri (1821) had achieved statehood, the American West in the 1840s was either uncharted, Native American, or claimed by other countries. By the turn of the century, many factors had forever changed the country, including the extraordinary number of settlers heading west and the completion of the transcontinental railroad in 1869.

On the path to statehood, a territory would first have to amass 5,000 free male voters to elect its own assembly and send a nonvoting representative to Congress. When the population numbered 60,000, the assembly could petition Congress for admission to the Union and, depending upon the political winds blowing in the capital, be admitted sooner or later. The profile of the American frontier changed every few years after the admittance of Texas in 1845.

Iowa in 1846
California in 1850
Minnesota in 1858
Oregon in 1859
Kansas in 1861
Nevada in 1864
Nebraska in 1867
Colorado in 1876
Washington, Montana, North Dakota, and South Dakota in 1889
Idaho and Wyoming in 1890
Utah in 1896
Oklahoma in 1907
Arizona and New Mexico in 1912
Alaska and Hawaii in 1959

In Name Only

In 1870, the founders of Modesto, California, had wanted to name the town for financier W. C. Ralston. He demurred. Hence the name Modesto as in a modest guy.

Anaheim was named by German-speaking settlers. It's a combination of Santa Ana River and *heim*—German for "home."

Portland, Oregon, was named by the winner of a coin toss for Portland, Maine. Had the other flipper, from Massachusetts, won, it would have been Boston, Oregon.

Around New York, Coney Island was so named because of the numerous rabbits that once frolicked there. *Koenig* is German for "rabbit." The Bronx's name comes from Jonas Bronck, a Dane, who owned a large farm north of Manhattan. Brooklyn was named "broken land" by its Dutch settlers in honor of a town in the Netherlands.

Langtry, Texas, was named by Judge Roy Bean, who was besotted by English actress Lillie Langtry.

Gary, Indiana, is named for Judge Elbert H. Gary, a chairman of the board of U.S. Steel. The city was planned and built by the steel industry.

☛ Being Counted

- There are only 46 states in the United States. Massachusetts, Pennsylvania, Virginia, and Delaware are commonwealths.

- Eleven states seceded from the Union between 1860 and 1861. They were Alabama, Arkansas, Florida, Georgia, Louisiana, Mississippi, North Carolina, South Carolina, Tennessee, Texas, and Virginia.

- Six Flags amusement parks adapted their name from Texas history. At various points, six flags flew over the Lone Star State: Spain (from 1519 to 1685 and again from 1690 to 1812); France (from 1685 to 1690); Mexico (from 1821 to 1836); the Republic of Texas (from 1836 to 1845); the Confederacy (from 1861 to 1865) and the United States (from 1845 to 1861 and 1865 until today). Long may they wave.

- The Baby Bells are seven major providers of local phone services. They are NYNEX (New York and New England), Pacific Telesis (California and Nevada), U.S. West (ranging from Washington state east to Minnesota and south to Arizona and New Mexico), BellSouth (serving much of the South), Southwestern Bell Corporation (parts of Arkansas through Texas and parts of Missouri), Ameritech (around the Great Lakes), and Bell Atlantic (serving most of the eastern seaboard).

Far Afield

Seven European nations have patron saints. They are England (Saint George), Ireland (Saint Patrick), Scotland (Saint Andrew), Wales (Saint David), France (Saint Denys), Italy (Saint Anthony), and Spain (Saint James).

While the founding fathers of Pakistan had long been busy, the official founding of the country was delayed until 1947, just after World War II. *Pakistan* is an acronym for several regions: the *p* is for Punjab, *a* for Afghan border states, *k* for Kashmir, *s* for Sind, and *tan* for Baluchistan. *Pak* is also an Urdu word for "pure, holy," and *stan* is an Urdu suffix for "land." (The *i* must be for euphonic effect.)

Vatican City, an independent state of just under 110 acres in the middle of Rome, has its own currency, flag, ruler (the pope), and postage stamps. For years, each airmail stamp issued had a picture of an angel on it.

Botany Bay in New South Wales, Australia, was so named because Joseph Banks and Dr. Solander, who sailed there with Captain Cook aboard the *Endeavour*, collected so many plant species they'd never before seen.

The A to Zed on addressing a note to a pal in England: United Kingdom is composed of England, Scotland, Northern Ireland, and Wales plus all the bitty coastal islands dotting the sea. Great Britain is the main island—England, Scotland, and Wales only. England is a single country inhabited by the English.

A Sand Paper

Most sand dunes, sculpted from sand and wind in wide open spaces, fall into one of six distinct categories.

Transverse dunes only get to be about six feet high with a ridge along the top. Wind carves the ridge and helps sand accumulate on the windblown side. They sometimes resemble ocean waves, one line following the next.

Barchan dunes occur where there is not as much sand, and rocks and plant life conspire to block the wind. Sand collects around these sorts of blockers, covering them completely. Crescent-shaped hills form with the inner curve facing away from the wind. **Parabolic dunes** are moon-shaped, like barchans, but face in the opposite direction.

Star dunes result when the wind comes from several directions. From a bird's eye view, the sandy mounds look like stars.

Longitudinal dunes, found most often in the Sahara, arrange themselves parallel to the direction of the wind. They may extend for up to 200 miles in jagged waves. **Whaleback dunes** are similar to these but have rounded crests.

• The Sahara, the world's largest desert (with approximately the same square mileage as the United States), has its own specialized vocabulary. For example, an "erg" is a sea of sand. "Yermosols" are the shallow layers of soil that blanket an underlayer of gravel (the basis of more than 50 percent of Saharan soils). The stretches of land where wind has swept over the North African bedrock are "hammadas." "Regs" are plains of loose gravel and small stones.

• Desert winds have also inspired singular words. They are called "jeggos" in the American Southwest, "sirocco" in Algeria, "khamsin" in Egypt, "harmatten" in the southern Sahara, and "shamal" in Arabia.

• Dry channels formed by rushing water once cutting through rock are called "dry washes" or "arroyos." However, in the Middle East, they are known as "wadis." In the Gobi Desert they are "sal," and in the Kalahari they are referred to as "laagtes."

• Colorado's Great Sand Dunes National Monument boasts an 800-foot dune, the highest in North America. Jockey's Ridge, found on North Carolina's Outer Banks, is arguably the biggest on the eastern seaboard.

☛ Running Hot and Cold

The Sahara wins the Biggest Temperature Drop in a Single Day Award. In the course of 24 hours, the temperature bottomed out at 26° from 126°. The record for the hottest day was noted in September 1922 in the Sahara—136.4°.

Not to be outdone, the Arabian Desert is believed to have the most sand, while Chile's Atacama Desert only gets an average of 4/100ths of an inch of rain a year (making it the driest desert in the world).

Going to the other extreme, some 48 million square miles of the earth's surface are covered year-round with snow and ice. The snowiest spot in the United States is Ranier Paradise in Washington state, where a total of 1,122 inches of snow fell in the winter of 1971–72. The deepest snow measured in the United States was 451 inches at Tamarack, California, in March 1911.

But there are much colder places than the American Rockies in winter. Take Siberia (please!). It can get so cold that boiling water poured from a kettle will freeze before it hits the ground. Bolshoi cold. Oddly, the interior of Antarctica and the Sahara do have something in common. The annual precipitation in both places is less than two inches.

Head for the Borders

The folks who manufacture sashes for Miss Universe pageants must keep on their toes, geographically speaking. There are always countries in the process of redrawing borders somewhere on the globe. Nations that have already undergone name changes in this century include:

Basutoland to ***Lesotho***
Bechuanaland to ***Botswana***
Belgian Congo (the Congo) to ***Zaire***
British Honduras to ***Belize***
Burma to ***Myanmar***
Ceylon to ***Sri Lanka***
Dahomey to ***Benin***
Dutch Guiana to ***Suriname***
French Soudan to ***Mali***
Gold Coast to ***Ghana***
New Hebrides to ***Vanuatu***
Northern Rhodesia to ***Zambia***
Persia to ***Iran***
Rhodesia to ***Zimbabwe***
Tanganyika to ***Tanzania***
Transjordan to ***Jordan***
Urundi to ***Burundi***

Don't Know Much 'Bout Geography

- The northernmost point of the United States is Point Barrow, Alaska, and the southernmost is Ka Lae (South Cape) on the island of Hawaii. Within the 48 contiguous states, the northernmost point is Northwest Angle, Minnesota, and the southernmost is Key West, Florida.

- The eastern most U.S. city is Eastport, Maine, but the eastern most point is, technically, Semisopochnoi Island in Alaska because the Aleutian Islands tip into the Eastern Hemisphere. The western most city is Atka, Alaska.

- According to the United States Geologic Survey, the geographic center of the United States (including Alaska and Hawaii) is in Butte County, North Dakota. The center of the 48 contiguous states is outside Lebanon, Kansas. The geographic center of the continent of North America is in Pierce County, North Dakota.

• In the U.S. the lowest point is Death Valley in California, and the highest is Mount McKinley in Alaska. The deepest lake is Crater Lake in Oregon.

• The highest U.S. waterfall is Yosemite Falls, which is in three sections: Upper Yosemite Fall, Cascades, and Lower Yosemite Fall.

• Of the country's national parks, Yellowstone National Park in Wyoming, Montana, and Idaho is the oldest (1872), and Wrangell–St. Elias in Alaska is the largest (13,018 square miles). The largest national monument is Death Valley in California and Nevada. The most frequently visited is the Great Smoky Mountains National Park, which straddles North Carolina and Tennessee, followed by Grand Canyon National Park and Yosemite.

• Anchorage, Alaska has the distinction of being the American city with the greatest number of square miles (1,697.7), followed by Jacksonville, Florida, and Oklahoma City.

• The most popular American place-names are Midway, Fairview, Oak Grove, Five Points, Pleasant Hill, Centerville, Mount Pleasant, Riverside, Bethel, and New Hope.

• U.S. Bureau of the Census reports reveal that the most highly populated metropolitan areas in America are, in descending order, New York, Los Angeles, Chicago, San Francisco, Philadelphia, and Miami. New York's over 14 million ranks fifth in the world behind Tokyo (including Yokohama), Mexico City, São Paulo, and Seoul.

☛ It's a Helluva Town

New York, New York. Ya hate it or ya love it. But consider its distinctions:

New York is the fifth most highly populated city in the world and, after Mexico City, the most populous in North America, with over 7 million. And it is the largest city in the world that is not a national capital.

It was the most highly populated city in the United States in 1900, too, with over 3 million. It is the most densely populated city in the nation, followed by Paterson, New Jersey, and San Francisco.

With 624, it has more historic spots (as recorded in the *National Register of Historic Places*) than any other city in the country. Philadelphia has 470, while Washington, D.C., has 336.

It accommodates the second-tallest habitable building in the United States, the World Trade Center. Only the Sears Tower in Chicago is taller. Still, the twin towers sport the higher public observation deck (1,360 feet).

The city has more skyscrapers (over 130) than any other city in the world. Chicago, in second place, has 47. The first modern skyscraper was the city's Woolworth Building, completed in 1913.

New York is *not* in the Top 10 list of cities with the highest number of crimes per capita.

The New York Yankees, one of the city's two baseball teams, has won more World Series (23) than any other team. The team plays in the Bronx at Yankee Stadium, the ballpark that was the first to be called a stadium. Before it opened in 1923, all other venues were called fields or parks.

The longest bridge in the nation is the Verrazano Narrows Bridge, a suspension bridge that connects Brooklyn and Staten Island, and the fourth longest is the George Washington Bridge linking New Jersey to the city. The city is also home to three of the ten largest tunnels in the country: the Brooklyn-Battery, the Holland, and the Lincoln.

The Jacob Javits Convention Center is the sixth largest convention center in the country.

The city has the busiest Amtrak station in the United States. Penn Station handled over 5.8 million boardings in 1994. Only Union Station in Washington, D.C., came close, with over 3.3 million. And while D.C.'s Metro system has more track, the New York subway system has many more station stops (461 compared to 86).

It is home to three of the ten most visited art museums in the country: the Metropolitan Museum of Art, the Museum of Modern Art, and the Whitney.

☛ New York Accents

"A car is useless in New York, essential everywhere else. The same with good manners."
—Mignon McLaughlin

"Being a New Yorker means never having to say you're sorry."
—Lily Tomlin

"In New York crime is getting worse. I was there the other day. The Statue of Liberty had both hands up."
—Jay Leno

"New York: where everyone mutinies but no one deserts."
—Harry Hershfield

"The nation's thyroid gland."
—Christopher Morley

"Skyscraper National Park."
—Kurt Vonnegut

"When it's 5 below in New York, it's 78 in Los Angeles, and when it's 110 in New York, it's 78 in Los Angeles. There are 2 million interesting people in New York, and only 78 in Los Angeles."
—Neil Simon

"If a day goes by and I haven't been slain, I'm happy."
—Carol Leifer

"New York: the only city where people make radio requests like 'This is for Tina—I'm sorry I stabbed you.'"
—Carol Leifer

"New York Taxi Rules: 1. Driver speaks no English. 2. Driver just got here two days ago from someplace like Senegal. 3. Driver hates you."
—Dave Barry

"When we moved to New York we had to get rid of the children. Landlords didn't like them and, in any case, rents were so high. Who could afford an apartment big enough to contain children?"
—Russell Baker

"New York is the only city in the world where you can get deliberately run down on the sidewalk by a pedestrian."
—Russell Baker

"If you live in New York, even if you're Catholic, you're Jewish."
—Lenny Bruce

"New York now leads the world's great cities in the number of people around whom you shouldn't make a sudden move."
—David Letterman

"Traffic signals in New York are just rough guidelines."
—David Letterman

"A marriage, to be happy, needs an exterior threat. New York provides that threat."
—Garrison Keillor

It's ABOUT TIME

In the Beginning

According to Genesis, on the first day, God created light. On the second, the firmament (and so, too, water); on the third, dry land and vegetation; on the fourth, the sun, moon, and stars; on the fifth, the creatures of the sea and of the air; on the sixth, creatures of the earth and man. On the seventh day, God rested.

On the Calendar

The basic problem folks had establishing an accurate calendar lay in the conflict between the synodic (lunar) and tropical (solar) year. Months are based on lunar calculations, the length of time it takes for the moon to travel through a complete cycle. The year, however, is based on the length of time it takes the earth to orbit the sun (though, of course, early astronomers, who had different ideas about what orbited what, merely observed and measured the time between equinoxes). When you multiply the length of a lunar month by 12, you come up shy of a full solar year by about 11 days. To make a calendar, some type of intercalation (the practice of adding days to the calendar at appropriate intervals) was necessary.

Tarquinius, a Roman king, believing he had a solution, decreed that an extra month be added between February 23 and 24 every two years. But for a variety of reasons (incompetence, neglect, and politics), the additional month was added irregularly.

By 46 B.C., with the matter of a fixed calendar still unresolved, Julius Caesar stepped in. He fixed the length of the year at 365¼ days and introduced the leap year of 366 days every fourth year. He based his calendar on the calculations and observations made by the Greek astronomer Sosigenes. The months alternated between 30 and 31 days, with February, then the last month of the year, having 29 (30 in the leap year). Never one to be shy about such things, he named July after himself.

Fast forward a few decades, to A.D. 46 and the reign of Augustus. No slouch in the ego department himself, he decided it was only right and fair that he should have his name on a month as well. Thus the month following July became August. But that didn't prove satisfactory. Because of the alternating cycle of 30 and 31 days per month, August

didn't have as many days as July. What's an emperor to do? He swiped a day from February, leaving it with 28 days, and gave August a 31st.

The Julian calendar (sorry about that, Augustus) held for about 1,600 years. But as brilliant as Sosigenes' work had been, he had made an error in calculating the length of the year that amounted to about 11 minutes and 14 seconds annually. By 1545, the minutes snowballed into a discrepancy of 10 full days.

Pope Gregory XIII commissioned a study in 1572 and, 10 years later, issued an edict that October 5, 1582, would become October 15, 1582, eliminating those pesky 10 days. To prevent a recurrence of the problem, it was decided that centennial years would not be leap years unless they were divisible by 400. This Gregorian calendar also set January as the first month of the year. Although it was a number of years before most of the world accepted it, it is the calendar still in use through much of the world today.

Once in a Blue Moon

It is those intercalated days, by the way, that make possible the phenomenon of the "blue moon." Usually there is just one full moon per month, but should it fall in the first three days of a 31-day month or the first two days of a 30-day month, you can have two full moons in one month; the second is the one known as the blue moon.

This generally happens only once a year, giving rise to the expression "once in a blue moon," meaning a rare occurrence. Even more unusual is to have two blue moons in one year, something that happens only if the first full moon of the year falls on January 1. So if something is as rare as hen's teeth, better say, "twice in blue moons."

Just a Second

Sixty seconds in a minute and 60 minutes in an hour. Coincidence? Nah. The magic number 60 comes from the ancient Babylonians, who seemed to have a special fondness for the number (probably because it was easily and evenly divisible by a slew of smaller numbers).

What about 24 hours to a day? The most likely explanation is that 12 was an ancient mystical number. So was seven, the number of days in a week. It's also a prime number.

And what is the connection between time and the taking of notes during a meeting? The minutes of a meeting have nothing to do with the clock. Rather, the Latin root is *minutus*, or "small," and refers to the brevity of the record.

Remains of the Day

The length of a day is determined by the length of time it takes for the earth to make a complete revolution on its axis. But how that length of time is divided and measured is actually quite arbitrary.

Days are measured from midnight to midnight; however, as recently as 1925, some astronomers clocked the day from noon to noon. Native American tribes measured the day from sunrise to sunrise, while other civilizations, such as the Jews, marked days from sunset to sunset—the system still used in their religious calendar.

The ancient Greeks, Romans, and Egyptians followed a 24-hour clock, but since they divided their day into 12 hours of daylight and 12 hours of darkness, the actual length of the hours depended upon the season. Squeezing in 12 hours of daylight on December 21, the winter solstice, meant that the hours on that day were very short.

It was not until the invention of the mechanical clock in the late Middle Ages that it became important to set an hour of specific and unvarying length.

A postscript—as a family name, Day is not derived from the 24-hour (well, actually, 23 hours, 56 minutes, and 4.9 seconds) period. Rather, Day is an occupational name for a *dey* or female servant. The word comes from the Old Norse word for "maid" and is from the same root as *lady*.

Time Zones

Standard time was established in 1883 when a meridian was drawn through Greenwich, England, at zero longitude. This became known

as the prime meridian, and Greenwich Mean Time became Universal Time, used throughout the world for science and navigation. From that point, meridians were then drawn at every 15° of longitude, creating 24 different time zones around the world, each zone differing from the one before and after by one hour.

Politics, religion, and national boundaries do, of course, play havoc with this system from time to time. Clocks in Israel, for religious reasons, are set about two hours earlier than in the rest of that time zone. China operates on only one time zone for the entire country, even though its land mass stretches through 11 different time zones. Our government made a similar arbitrary decision in 1983, when it placed all of Alaska (except the Aleutians) into one time zone (Alaska Standard Time) instead of the four it had operated under previously.

And if you've ever vacationed at a Club Med, you are probably familiar with Club Med time. In order to give their guests more daylight hours in which to enjoy themselves, "villages" operate their own version of Daylight Savings Time, simply setting their resort clocks back one hour. Counselors at sleepaway camps are often invested with the power to indulge in this kind of time manipulation as well. Lights out.

Time Travels

A jubilee, a special celebration commemorating a special anniversary, comes from Jewish history. Once every 50 years, fields went untended, Hebrew slaves were freed and ram's horns were blown (in Hebrew, *jubilee* means "ram"). In Latin, *jubilare* means "to proclaim in exultation."

For the last several centuries, a jubilee has been associated with jubilation. In the Roman Catholic Church, a year of jubilee occurred every 100 years (later every 50 years, and more recently every 25). This was when the faithful could make a pilgrimage to Rome for a remission of sins.

Roamin' Holidays

Ever wonder why Easter moves around on the calendar? Because the Christian Church learned not to compete with ancient pagan celebrations that were tied to the harvest and the phases of the moon. Church fathers decided it made better sense to merge religious ceremonies with the relics of pre-Christian holy days. Easter is celebrated with the first full moon after the spring equinox.

Salad Days

The calendar is sweetly flavored with culinary references. For example:

- Pancake Tuesday, also known as Doughnut Day, Fat Tuesday, and Mardi Gras, is Shrove Tuesday, the final feasting day before Lent. The custom of gobbling pancakes dates back to 16th-century England. Some cities still celebrate Shrove Tuesday with pancake races, in honor of a woman who purportedly heard the confession bell and raced to church flipping pancakes as she went.

• Carnival, interestingly, is from the Latin "flesh, farewell," for the season of merrymaking before Lent and abstinence.

• Although rarely heard anymore, Fig Sunday was once another name for Palm Sunday. Religious folks ate figs, a practice that derives from Christ's cursing a barren fig tree.

• Garrison Keillor claims there's a Toast 'n' Jelly Day celebrated each year in Lake Wobegon, Minnesota.

• Why salad days? In William Shakespeare's *Antony and Cleopatra*, Cleopatra looks back scornfully on the love she felt for Caesar in her youth, "my salad days, / when I was green in judgment, cold in blood." Therefore, salad days are those of youthful inexperience, hardly worthy of nostalgia. With maturity, one can enjoy one's just desserts.

On Holiday

Among fascinating holidays celebrated around the world:

• On Saint David's Day, every March 1, the Welsh wear leeks in honor of their patron saint.

• April Fool's Day has been traced back to the 17th century in Great Britain. The trick was to tell someone a fib and send him off on a silly errand. Scots called the victim an "April Gowk," which, though suspiciously onomatopoetic, actually means "cuckoo."

• Children's Day in Japan is celebrated on May 5. Kids take to the parks to fly kites decorated with pictures of carp. The fish symbolize strength, persistence, courage, and success.

• In Western Samoa, an annual high point lands on the second Sunday of October, called Lotu-a-Tamaita or White Sunday. Children, dressed in white, lead church services, enjoy specially prepared goodies, and receive gifts.

But we needn't go too far afield. These United States have enough oddball holidays on record to require *Chase's Annual Events*. For instance:

• Sadie Hawkins Day, November 4, is a classic example. Popularized by Al Capp's "Li'l Abner" cartoon strip, it is the one day of the year girls and women may take the initiative with their sweethearts up to and including proposals of marriage—usually after a spirited chase. Once an Appalachian phenomenon, it's now a favorite theme for high school dances everywhere. Another tradition—that in a leap year, on February 29, a woman may ask a man to marry her—dates back to the 13th century when the Scottish parliament voted that any man who refused a proposal on this date would be fined a pound.

- The last Saturday in January is big doings in Whigham, Georgia—Rattlesnake Roundup Day. Snakes are hunted, held, and consumed.

- Evacuation Day still commands a following on March 17 in Boston and Suffolk County, Massachusetts. It is celebrated to honor the day in 1776 when British troops hightailed it out of Boston.

- The Betty Picnic is held in Tom Pierce Park in Oregon on June 17 to celebrate all the glories of Betty. Anyone named Betty is welcome.

- Elvis International Tribute Week is held mid-August in Memphis for obvious reasons.

Making Dates

Contrary to what you were taught, our founding fathers did not actually declare independence from King George on July 4. It was July 2, 1776, when the Continental Congress in Philadelphia said, "Whoa." Why the discrepancy? Thomas Jefferson's manuscript was adopted on the fourth and, when published as a document, bore that date. As copies of the Declaration made their way around the rest of the infant nation, people rejoiced (or lamented) when they heard the news—some many months after the fact.

Another historical fallacy revolves around Columbus Day (also known as Discovery or Discoverers' Day). October 12 was designated a general holiday by President Harrison in 1892. While Columbus happened upon the Bahamas (not the United States) on October 12, 1492, the holiday of America's "discovery" has since been rounded off to the second Monday in October. Of the event, Mark Twain wrote, "It was wonderful to find America, but it would have been more wonderful to miss it." John Updike bemoaned the "municipal headache of the Columbus Day parade."

It Must Be a Sign

Some 2,000 years ago, the astronomer Hipparchus watched the sun travel the same course among the stars every 12 months. This course is now called an ecliptic, and it contains as well the apparent courses of the moon, earth, and other planets. The area on each side of the ecliptic is the zodiac, and each section of 30 degrees represents a different sign.

The signs are named for the 12 constellations positioned within the zodiac noted by Hipparchus. As time passed, the 30-degree sections have moved backward. Aries now sits in the constellation that is Pisces. In the middle of the 26th century, there will be another shift as the vernal equinox moves out of Pisces and into Aquarius. So, what's your sign?

Aries the Ram (March 21–April 19) is confident, impulsive, and independent.

Taurus the Bull (April 20–May 20) is stubborn, devoted, and determined.

Gemini the Twins (May 21–June 21) is bright, impulsive, and ambitious.

Cancer the Crab (June 22–July 22) is sensitive, sympathetic, and impressionable.

Leo the Lion (July 23–August 22) is charitable, temperamental, and enthusiastic.

Virgo the Virgin (August 23–September 22) is intellectual, calm, and methodical.

Libra the Scales (September 23–October 23) is sociable, just, and orderly.

Scorpio the Scorpion (October 24–November 21) is loyal, philosophical, and willful.

Sagittarius the Archer (November 22–December 21) is practical, imaginative, and grounded.

Capricorn the Goat (December 22–January 19) is persistent, candid, and dedicated.

Aquarius the Waterbearer (January 20–February 18) is idealistic, unselfish, and generous.

Pisces the Fish (February 19–March 20) is cautious, sympathetic, and emotional.

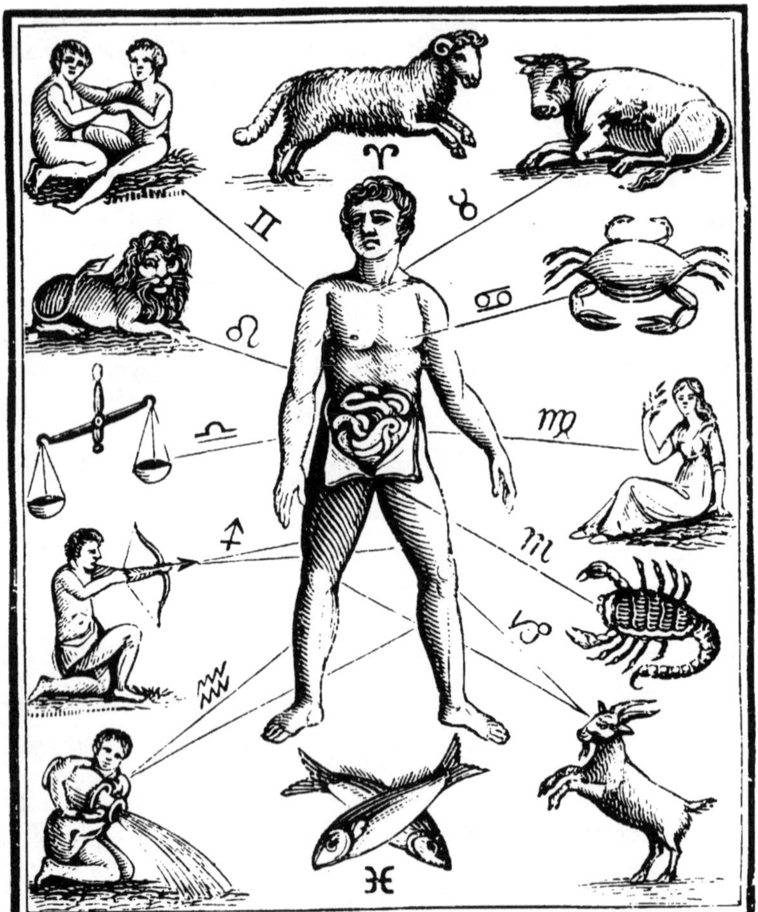

Astrology is an ancient, highly regarded practice in China. A common belief is that humans are just temporary custodians of the world. To maintain peace and equilibrium on earth, one must follow astral advice and signs interpreted by the sages.

The "modern" Chinese system is approximately 1,000 years old. It's based upon a 12-year cycle (rather than a 12-month one), the length of time astrologers long ago determined it took Jupiter to complete an orbit. Each year, or house, was assigned an animal: Dragon, Snake, Horse, Sheep, Monkey, Rooster, Dog, Pig, Rat, Ox, Tiger, and Hare. Each animal represents a house and reflects the personality and temperament of people born in that year.

Astrologers fine-tune an individual's chart by taking into account the actual date, time, and place of birth. Believers say that to a certain extent, everyone's fate and fortune can be predicted by qualified astrologers.

The Dragon (February 17, 1988–February 5, 1989) is extroverted, imaginative, and decisive.

The Snake (February 6, 1989–January 26, 1990) is cultured, subtle, and crafty.

The Horse (January 27, 1990–February 14, 1991) is athletic, eager, and chatty.

The Sheep (February 15, 1991–February 3, 1992) is selfless, affectionate, and artistic.

The Monkey (February 4, 1992–January 22, 1993) is quick-witted, curious, and mischievous.

The Rooster (January 23, 1993–February 9, 1994) is determined, aggressive, and bold.

The Dog (February 10, 1994–January 30, 1995) is honest, steadfast, and entertaining.

The Pig (January 31, 1995–February 18, 1996) is industrious, home-loving, and goal-oriented.

The Rat (February 19, 1996–February 6, 1997) is charming, creative, and adaptable.

The Ox (February 7, 1997–January 27, 1998) is reliable, practical, and loyal.

The Tiger (January 28, 1998–February 15, 1999) is competitive, authoritative, and sincere.

The Hare (February 16, 1999–February 4, 2000) is sociable, perceptive, and truthful.

Christmas Countdown

Can you remember Santa's reindeer? They were named in Clement Moore's 1822 poem, "A Visit from Saint Nicholas." They are Dasher, Dancer, Prancer, Vixen, Comet, Cupid, Donder, and Blitzen. Rudolph is from the song.

The gifts given on the twelve days of Christmas are an annual stumper: a partridge in a pear tree; two turtle doves; three French hens; four calling birds; five golden rings; six geese a-laying; seven swans a-swimming; eight maids a-milking; nine drummers drumming; ten pipers piping; eleven ladies dancing; and twelve lords a-leaping.

Can you name the Magi (the Latin plural of *magus*, or "wise man") and what each brought as a gift? They were Gaspar, "the white one," who brought frankincense as a token of divinity; Melchior, "the king of light," who brought gold to signify royalty; and Balthazar, "the king of treasures," who brought myrrh, a symbol of mortality. Medieval legend refers to them as the Three Kings of Cologne. Ancient Persians honored them as members of the priestly caste who wielded tremendous occult powers.

Crunching NUMBERS

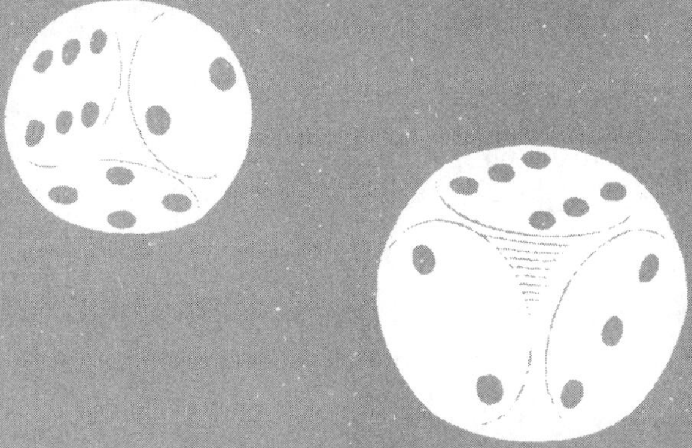

We're Number Fun

- It takes seven shuffles to mix a deck of 52 cards into a random sequence.

- The chances of getting a specific number from the roll of a six-sided die are one in six (the odds are five to one).

- If the sum of all the divisors of a number is the number itself, it is a "perfect" number. An example is 6 (its divisors are 1, 2, and 3). The next perfect number is 28, then 496.

- An American billion is a thousand million. Brits call this a milliard. A British billion is an American trillion, and a British trillion is an American quintillion.

- If the diameter of the sun were equal to the height of an average man, then Jupiter, the largest planet, would be roughly the size of the fellow's head, and the earth would be slightly larger than the iris of his eye.

- The typical spoken sentence in ordinary conversation takes about 2 1.2 seconds to spit out. Most people speak, on average, ten minutes a day. This does not include facial expressions, shrugs, nods, or dramatic pauses.

- The odds for combinations in a family with four children: two boys and two girls = three in eight; three boys and one girl or three girls and one boy = one in four; and four girls or four boys = one in sixteen.

- If a jogger maintained a pace of 6 miles per hour, it would take him or her 173 days to circumnavigate the equator.

- Liberal arts (from the Latin *artes liberales*)—so named because intellectual pursuits were considered the purview of freemen, called *liberi*—take their cue from the Bible's seven pillars of wisdom. Learned folk of the Middle Ages declared there to be seven branches of learning: arithmetic, astronomy, geometry, grammar, logic, music, and rhetoric. (Neither gym, medicine, nor law was in the seven because, they were considered practical matters.)

- Ever wonder about vehicle capacities? The *Mayflower* (no sauna, no manicurist, no spa cuisine) handled 130, while the *QEII* (passengers and crew) accommodates 2,931. A Greyhound bus has room for 43, while a London double-decker carries 72.

➢ Roulette Bets

If you find yourself in Las Vegas, Atlantic City, or sitting across from James Bond, you should know how to gamble. While working the machines is an option, it's not particularly social and doesn't give you the same chance to experience that frisson when you display your sangfroid (as Bond might). If losing a packet of cash quickly doesn't bother you, head for the roulette area.

In case you've never encountered the game, roulette is played with a horizontally positioned wheel. Thirty-six numbers appear on the rim, plus two green pockets, zero, and double zero. Half of the 36 pockets are red, and half are black. The trick is guessing where the little white ball will land when the wheel is spun. The gambler can bet in several ways.

When you bet on:	the payoff is:
Red or black	1 to 1
Odd or even	1 to 1
18 numbers (low or high)	1 to 1
12 numbers (in a sequential dozen or in a column)	2 to 1
6 numbers (on line dividing field from Outside bet)	5 to 1
5 numbers (on line dividing 0/00 from 1, 2, and 3)	6 to 1
4 numbers (on intersection where 4 numbers meet)	8 to 1
3 numbers (on line dividing field from outside bet of the 3 numbers)	11 to 1
2 numbers (any line separating 2 numbers—or 0/00)	17 to 1
1 number (directly on the number)	35 to 1

To be cool, "straight up" means betting on one number, and a "split" is betting on two side-by-side numbers. An "inside bet" means betting within the field of 36 numbers (plus zero and double zero) or betting on 1, 2, 3, 4, 5, or 6 numbers. An "outside bet" is a bet placed outside the field of numbers: even/odd; black/red; any number in the first 12, second 12, third 12, 1 to 18, or 19 to 36.

Weather or Not

• One bolt of lightning can contain enough electricity to service more than 200,000 homes. The voltage of a thunderbolt can reach more than 15 million volts. Lightning is nature's little fertilizing agent. When lightning occurs, it breaks loose nitrogen in the air. Tons of fixed nitrogen, an important fertilizing ingredient, are dropped on the earth when it rains in a thunderstorm.

• Atop Mount Everest (29,000 feet above sea level), water boils at 167°F. as opposed to 212°F. at sea level. That makes for a tepid cup of joe when you need it most.

- How do those weatherpeople calculate the infamous wind chill factor? Multiply the speed of the wind by 1.5 and subtract it from the air temperature. Brrr-illiant.

- The four winds have names. The north wind is known as Boreus or, sometimes, Aquilo. The west wind is Zephyrus or Favonius. The south is Notus or Auster, and the east wind is simply Eurus.

- The Celsius scale, named for Swedish astronomer Anders Celsius, is just another name for the centigrade scale that he devised. In 1741, he first suggested to the Swedish Academy of Science that the Fahrenheit scale (for Gabriel Fahrenheit, a German living in England who perfected a mercury-in-a-bottle method for measuring temperature) be replaced with a more obvious zero to 100 measurement. The scientists agreed. Thus, water freezes at 32° Fahrenheit and 0° Celsius and boils at 212° Fahrenheit and at 100° Celsius.

Weighing In

While many of us have been dragged into the age of metrics and the language of computers, it's comforting to know that many of our weights and measures have arcane and arbitrary roots. The word *inch* derives from the Latin *uncia* meaning "the twelfth part."

On the subject of inches and feet, the barleycorn—an ancient measure equaling about a third of an inch—is the basis upon which we still measure shoe sizes. No ruler handy? Use a buck. The length of a dollar bill is exactly six inches.

Now take yourself by the hand. The average human hand gives us handy common measurements: the nail equals 2¼ inches and is the length from the thumbnail to the joint at the base of the thumb (this was once used for measuring fabric); the palm equals 3 inches and is the breadth of the hand minus the thumb; the hand equals 4 inches and is the whole breadth of the palm (still used to measure the height of horses); the finger equals 3½ inches and is the length of the middle finger (the width of the finger was once used to measure charges of gunpowder and is still popular with bartenders).

Aside from the hand, there are other interesting weights and measures, some still in active use:

bolt—a roll of cloth of approximately 40 yards, depending upon the type of fabric. A skein, while this varies with the type of yarn, usually measures about 120 yards.

pace—a convenient measure that equals the average stride, or about a yard. The military pace "double time" equals a cadence of 3 steps per second, while "quick time" equals 2 steps in a shorter stride of approximately 30 inches.

fathom—an Anglo-Saxon term meaning "embrace." It's the length of rope held between the hands when the arms are outstretched and is most often employed as a nautical term for the depth of water.

furlong—Once this meant the length of a furrow or the distance a team of oxen could plow without having to rest, Now it has been rounded off to 220 yards.

nautical mile—equals 1/60th of the length of a degree of a great circle of the earth. This is not a perfect measure because the earth is not a perfect sphere. A knot is a measure of speed and equals one nautical mile per hour.

league—equals 3 miles on land and 3 nautical miles at sea.

light-year—the distance light travels in one year (about 5.87 trillion miles).

Bushels and barrels were used to transport goods in the old days. The problem was, their size was not standardized. Therefore, if you ordered a barrel of apples in Vermont, expecting it to fill your barrel in your shop on Delancy Street, you might be disappointed and feel cheated. At one time, every state had its own definition of what precisely a bushel and a barrel were.

Now a bushel equals four pecks and a barrel equals 31½ gallons. And a coomb equals 4 bushels; a firkin is a quarter of a barrel; a hogshead equals 2 barrels; a pipe equals 4 barrels; and a tun is a large cask that equals 8 barrels.

Speaking Coincidentally

Coincidences amaze and amuse. Where would romantic fiction be without coincidences? ("You were shanghaied on a banana boat headed for Crete and only just now regained your memory, too, darling?") And what would Great Aunt Yawnie talk about at family reunions if she didn't have her collection of coincidences? Granted, some coincidences are truly remarkable (a woman who drops her wedding ring down a sink in Miami to discover it ten years later in the sand at Atlantic City on her anniversary), but how unusual are they?

Two Harvard statisticians, Dr. Persi Diaconis and Dr. Frederick Mosteller, took a closer look at coincidences, or the laws of very large numbers. They defined coincidence as "a surprising concurrence of events, perceived as meaningfully related, with no apparent causal connection." They found that coincidences are bound to happen with a large enough sample. Even if there is but a mere one-in-a-million chance that something will take place—given enough time and enough participants, it will occur eventually.

What the men term "multiple end point" coincidences are occasions when what might qualify as accidental is not spelled out ahead of time and when many chance events would qualify. For example, is it a coincidence if two people meet on a train and discover they are from the same town? Not really, when you figure that almost anything two strangers have in common would count as a coincidence. The chances of getting a match in any of several categories is bigger than if you look just at one category.

Then there are close-but-not-exact types. Get 23 people together and chances are even that two will have the same birthday. Gather 14 people and chances are even of finding two born within a day of each other. Seven people? A week. So, what are the odds of winning a state lottery two times within four months? One in a trillion? Actually, odds are closer to 1 in 30 that such good fortune would grace someone somewhere in the United States.

Play Nicely Together

What is the makeup of a symphony orchestra, and how many instruments are typically in each section?

strings—12 to 14 violins, 10 to 12 second violins, 8 to 10 violas, 6 to 8 cellos, 4 to 6 double basses

woodwinds—2 flutes, 2 oboes, 2 clarinets, 2 bassoons

brass—2 trumpets, 2 or 4 horns, 2 or 3 trombones, 1 tuba

percussion—2 or 3 kettle drums and various instruments of definite pitch (such as bells or a xylophone) and indefinite pitch (such as cymbals or a triangle)

You earned extra credit if you thought to include a harp.

Playing by the Numbers

Negotiating megadeals is complicated enough without having to worry if your associates mean the same thing you do by "one trillion." For the record, herewith a list of what numbers with scads of zeros are called on both sides of the pond:

# of zero after 1	American	British
6	million	million
9	billion	milliard
12	trillion	billion
15	quadrillion	1,000 billion
18	quintillion	trillion
21	sextillion	1,000 trillion
24	septillion	quadrillion
27	octillion	1,000 quadrillion
30	nonillion	quintillion
33	decillion	1,000 quintillion
100	googol	googol
googol	googolplex	googolplex

FIGURE *It Out*

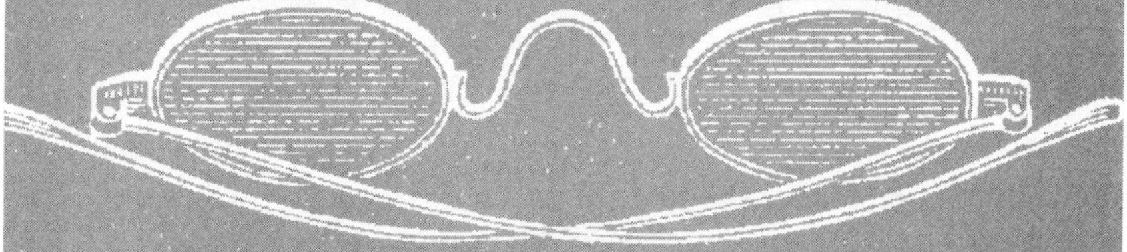

Crowning Achievement

In ancient Greece, Hiero, the tyrant who ruled Syracuse, challenged Archimedes to say whether Hiero's crown was made of pure gold or had been adulterated. Archimedes knew what pure gold weighed, but the crown was irregularly shaped: how could he use this one piece of data to solve the conundrum without melting down the crown itself? The answer came to Archimedes as he was getting into his bath. Noticing the water rise as he lowered himself into the bath, the tale has it, he shouted, "Eureka!" as the solution was revealed: He could determine the volume of the crown by seeing how much water it displaced, then multiply that amount by the weight of pure gold.

Professor Know-It-Almost

Why doesn't electricity leak out of sockets? Junior's science report got you plain stumped, again? Here are some soft lobs so you can be Professor Smarty Pants.

• Why the heck is the sky blue? Start with sunlight. Separate the color of sunlight with a prism. What do you have? A rainbow of red, orange, yellow, green, blue, indigo, and violet. When light travels from the sun to us earthlings, it comes right through the atmosphere. Some is scattered, bouncing off particles of air. It's the blue part of the sunlight that gets scattered the most, ultimately zigzagging to earth. Hence, your eye picks up all the scattered blue light. There's no atmosphere around the moon, so its sky looks black.

• What happens when you swallow gum? Chill. You won't grow a gum tree in your tum. What goes in one end comes out the other eventually—taking about the same amount of time as everything else you eat.

• Why are no two snowflakes ever alike? Truth be told, if you had the time, the magnifying glass, and the snowflakes, you'd probably find matches. Know that not all snow crystals are those picture-perfect six-pointed stars. Some are six-sided cylinders, some are shaped like bullets, some have branches called dendrites, some are hexagonal plates, and some resemble needles.

• What is it like to float on a cloud? You can't sit on one. Like a rock, you'd pass through even the white billowy ones you may see out airplane windows. Actually, if you've been in a fog (literally, not figuratively), it's the same as being inside a cloud. Cool, misty, and damp.

• Why are traffic lights red, green, and yellow? These colors were developed by railroad folk. Red was chosen for stop because it's an eye-catcher and has always been associated with danger. For a while, clear (or white) was used as the all clear–proceed light. However, sometimes conductors and engineers had a hard time telling an ordinary light from an official railroad lamp and accidents occurred. It was then decided to use green for go and yellow for caution. The first such electric lights were set up in Cleveland, Ohio, in 1914. At first, just red and green were used. The need for a yellow caution light became painfully apparent and so was added a few years later.

- Why do earthworms surface after a rain and lie beached on the sidewalk? Those little fellows must breathe. After a rain, their earth homes are waterlogged, so they come up to suck in the air and await low tide.

- If the elevator cable broke and you felt yourself hurtling to the basement, could you jump upward at the last millisecond—at the moment of impact—and save yourself? Very doubtful. Even if you were able to time it just perfectly while watching your life flash before you, you probably couldn't jump up faster than the elevator is dropping. But not to worry. Most elevators have several cables, brakes, and/or giant springs or plungers at the bottom. Still, if you did find yourself zipping southbound at 50 or 60 miles per hour, might as well try something.

- What is quicksand? Simply, it's sand that has mixed with water from underground springs. The top layer, dried by the air and sun, forms a deceptive crust. Below the crust lurks an oozing pool of watery sand. Truth is, it's usually an easy task to wade out of the muck. However, if you do sink to your chest (about as far as an average adult will go), it's more difficult to get out. Though you won't do the fatal "sand glub," the highlight of many Hollywood "B" jungle flicks, you will need help getting out.

Medical Curiosity

It was September 1848. Phineas P. Gage was the foreman of a crew laying railroad track in the rugged Vermont hills. His job was to carve out the landscape for the railway by blasting boulders. He'd drill a hole in a big rock, pour in blasting powder, add a fuse, and cover the hole with sand. After tamping sand with a metal rod 3½ feet long and 1¼ inches in diameter, he'd light the fuse and run like the dickens. Seconds later, there would be an explosion and a rain of gravel.

On this particular day, Gage neglected to lay down the layer of sand and tamped the blasting powder point-blank. In a thundering explosion, the tamping rod was launched upward, entering Gage's head just under his left cheek. It ruined his left eye on its way through his brain—particularly his frontal lobes. The rod landed several yards away after having exited his skull.

His crew watched in amazement as Gage stood up. He talked all the while as his men helped him to a nearby tavern, where he'd stay on for several months recuperating. He recovered, dying some 13 years later of an undetermined illness.

While it is certainly interesting in itself that someone could take a steel rod through the head, the aspect of the case that made it so intriguing to the doctors who examined Gage, and to his family and friends, was that the accident stripped Gage of the ability to make ethical judgments or moral decisions. Choosing right from wrong was something that now eluded him. He could not determine or anticipate the possible consequences of his actions.

He had been a bright young man of 25 at the time of the injury. He was reported to have been well liked, hardworking, and dependable. However, after the accident, he started using profanities, lied to his friends, and was generally untrustworthy. While he still had his memory and intelligence, he seemed to have lost the ability to process

his emotions. A physician who treated him, Dr. John Harlow, wrote that "the equilibrium or balance, so to speak, between his intellectual faculty and animal propensities" had been demolished by the rod. He never again would behave rationally.

Gage was buried with the tamping rod until, at the request of Dr. Harlow, his skull and the rod were recovered. They now reside at the Warren Anatomical Medical Museum at Harvard University, where they continue to intrigue and inform researchers and medical folk.

Plugged In

You think *you've* embarrassed yourself on the computer by deleting files and being incapable of getting out of DOS? Cyberklutzes take heart. Internationally renowned, highly respected, state-of-the-art science writer Isaac Asimov recalled sitting in front of his brand-new word processor (back when word processors were leading edge). He was about to begin work on his 300th-odd book. Confidently, he switched the machine on to begin. Nothing happened. He tinkered as much as he dared and then called his local Radio Shack.

The clerk asked the famous author if he had a service contract, to which Asimov answered no. Asimov explained that, as a spokesperson for Tandy Corporation, he'd been given the machine. The clerk was unimpressed and suggested Asimov come into the shop and buy a service agreement (for a mere $1,402.00). Having little choice, Asimov complied. He then had to wait for the approval on his check from the company's Texas headquarters. Once approved, he had to wait for the repairman. Valuable writing hours ticked by. When the repairman finally arrived, he inspected the machine and then strolled over to the wall switch and flicked it on. The machine hummed warmly, and the repairman took his leave.

Higher Tech

According to *Compaq Compass*, every 18 months, advances in technology virtually double the amount of computing power a single dollar will buy. And in the last 35 years, computer performance increased by a factor of 1,000,000, while the entry-level price of a computer decreased by a factor of 1,000.

To ground these statistics in something more concrete, if automobiles had developed at the same speed, a luxury sedan would be able to cruise at a million miles per hour, get half a million miles per gallon, and sell for just a hair less than $2.40. Now, *that's* progress.

Sticking to It

According to Ralph Waldo Emerson, "In every work of genius we recognize our own rejected thoughts." True, true. Take, for example, two of the most important inventions of the century: Post-it notes and Velcro.

Bursts of bright yellow (and buff, pink, blue, green, and neon colors)—those perky little squares and rectangles flag letters, memos, reports, books, and file folders. They adhere, lift off, and readhere to telephone receivers, doors, refrigerators, mirrors, little sisters, and, yes, even foreheads. Since their introduction, America has come to organize and remind itself with Post-it brand notes—a little convenience we never knew how much we needed until we got them.

Post-it notes are one of the five top-selling office supply products in the country. (The other four are file folders, correction fluid, Scotch tape, and copy paper.) But the history of Post-it notes, a quirky tale of discovery, failure, and success, is really due to one man's stubborn insistence on sticking with a pet project.

Art Fry was a researcher in the product development division of 3M. Of equal importance to this story, he also sang in his church choir on Sundays. He was in the habit of marking his place in the hymnal with scraps of paper. Much to his annoyance, the scraps would often flutter out, leaving him scrambling to find his page. One particular morning his mind began to wander, and he found himself thinking of an adhesive that had been discovered years earlier by another 3M scientist, Dr. Spencer Silver.

Silver's adhesive was a bit peculiar. It was strong enough to hold, but removed easily. He had discovered it accidentally, while trying to develop stronger adhesives, and the initial reaction to this sticky-but-not-too-sticky substance was thumbs down. Silver decided to demonstrate it for some colleagues, however, and one of them was Art Fry. And in church that morning (divine inspiration?), Fry thought that a "temporarily permanent" bookmark might be the ideal use for Silver's adhesive.

Scientists at 3M are allowed to spend up to 15 percent of their time on projects of their own choosing, and Fry took advantage of this policy. He spent a year and a half ironing out technical problems and refining his concept. Along the way, he made the creative leap to use the new adhesive for notepaper and took the new product to the folks at marketing.

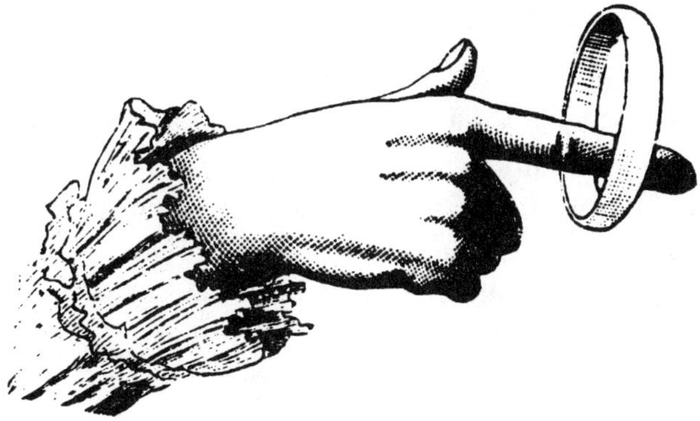

The folks in marketing were unconvinced, but Fry persisted, and in 1977, the product nobody knew they needed was test-marketed in four cities. At first glance, test-marketing results were disappointing. But in taking a closer look at the data, researchers noticed that a few dealers had astonishing sales. It turned out that all those dealers had decided to introduce Post-it notes by handing out free samples. That was all it took. People were hooked, or stuck, or attached to Post-its.

In 1978, 3M descended on Boise, Idaho, to determine once and for all the fate of the Post-it note. Their marketing strategy included heavy consumer sampling, often used to sell products such as toothpaste and detergent, but never before to market office supplies. The Boise Blitz, as it became called, was a huge success, and by mid-1980, Post-it notes were everywhere. How did we ever live without them?

Velcro, which is manufactured in the United States in Manchester, New Hampshire, was invented by Georges de Mestral, who was Swiss, in 1948. After a walk in the woods with his dog, he noted how stubbornly burrs clung to his pant-legs and to the dog's fur. He examined closely how the prickly ends hooked into their target. The sticky burrs were actually the seed heads from burdock plants. He recognized the genius of Mother Nature's design and adapted it.

Fathers of Invention

Benjamin Franklin came up with many things other than bifocal lenses and the kite-and-key trick. For instance, he invented swim fins (and hand fins), the grocer's claw, the rocking chair, and lightning rods. He was also the man behind America's first fire department, insurance company, and circulating library.

We have Thomas Jefferson to thank for figuring out the decimal system for U.S. coins based upon a dollar made of 100 cents. He also helped plan the layout of Washington, D.C. (and was the first president to be inaugurated there), and was one of the founders of the University of Virginia. A gifted architect, Jefferson invented hundreds of devices and time-savers in Monticello, including a kind of horizontal dumbwaiter in the wall separating the kitchen from the dining room so meals would arrive hot. And while he didn't invent them, Jefferson returned from his European travels with French fried potatoes, pasta, anchovies, Parmesan cheese, and olive oil and served them to delighted guests at Monticello.

To Jefferson's chagrin, Alexander Hamilton won approval to create a Bank of the United States (now the Bank of New York). Hamilton also founded the *New York Post.*

Another famous inventor, George Washington Carver, who made a name for himself with peanuts, also developed over 500 dyes in his laboratory. Booker T. Washington "invented" night school.

Listerine? Joseph Lister, the British surgeon, did indeed pioneer medical hygiene. He lectured widely about the necessity of using sanitary conditions in operating rooms. However, the gargle/mouthwash was developed in 1880 by Dr. Joseph Lawrence of St. Louis, Missouri. He named his antibacterial concoction in honor of Lister.

So much for Charles H. Duell, commissioner of the Office of Patents. He urged President William McKinley to abolish his office in 1899, stating "Everything that can be invented has been invented."

You Must Remember This

Mnemonic devices are memory tricks schoolkids learn or invent to remember lists. The neat thing is, they serve you well into adulthood and come in handy if you enjoy quiz shows. To remember a list in proper order, shrink it to the first letters of each item. For example, the colors of the rainbow sound like someone's name, "Roy G. Biv" (red, orange, yellow, green, blue, indigo, violet). British schoolchildren prefer the even more colorful turn of phrase "Richard Of York Gave Battle In Vain." Others include:

- "Do Men Ever Visit Birmingham?" will jog one's recollection of the ranks of peerage, in descending order: duke, marquis, earl, viscount, and baron.

- The order of the nine planets going away from the sun (Mercury, Venus, Earth, Mars, Jupiter, Saturn, Uranus, Neptune, and Pluto) can be recalled with "Mary's violet eyes make Jack sit up nights pining." You're on your own, though, for remembering which *m* applies to Mars and which one to Mercury.

- "HOMES" works for the Great Lakes (Huron, Ontario, Michigan, Erie, and Superior).

- A coded mnemonic device for remembering pi (the ratio between the circumference and diameter of a circle)? If the number of letters in each word counts as a single digit, then "How (3) I (1) want (4) a (1) drink (5), alcoholic (9) of (2) course (6), after (5) the (3) heavy (5) lectures (8) involving (9) quantum (7) mechanics (9)." Or 3.14159265358979.

- From anatomy class, there's "Tully Zucker's Bowels Move Constantly." For premed students, this helps with the branches of the facial nerve: temporal, zygomatic, buccal, mandibular, and cervical.

- From law school, the nine felonies in common law (murder, rape, manslaughter, robbery, sodomy, larceny, arson, mayhem, and burglary) are memorable because of "MR. and MRS. LAMB."

- Geologic time periods are especially tough and, for *Jeopardy!* fans, important to know. "Camels Often Sit Down Carefully. Perhaps Their Joints Creak? Persistent Early Oiling Might Prevent Permanent Rheumatism." Granted it sounds ridiculous, but try committing these to memory (starting with the oldest): Cambrian, Ordovician, Silurian, Devonian, Carboniferous, Permian, Triassic, Jurassic, Cretaceous, Paleocene, Eocene, Oligocene, Miocene, Pliocene, Pleistocene, and Recent.

- Anyone who has ever taken music lessons recalls the notes of the treble-clef line (E, G, B, D, F) with "Every Good Boy Does Fine" and the bass-clef line (G, B, D, F, A) with "Girls Buy Dolls For Amusement." If the "dolls" thing bothers you, substitute dump trucks.

And why mnemonic? The Titaness Mnemosyne, the goddess of memory, knew everything that had ever happened from the beginning of time. She was the mother of the nine Muses conceived by Zeus: Clio (history), Urania (astronomy), Melpomene (tragedy), Thalia (comedy), Terpischore (dance), Calliope (epic poetry), Erato (love poetry), Polyhymnia (songs to the gods), Euterpe (lyric poetry). She told her daughters all of history, and they, in turn, transformed her accounts into stories, astronomical charts, poems, dance, dramas, and song so they'd never be forgotten. Apollo, the god of music, taught them to perform as a choir.

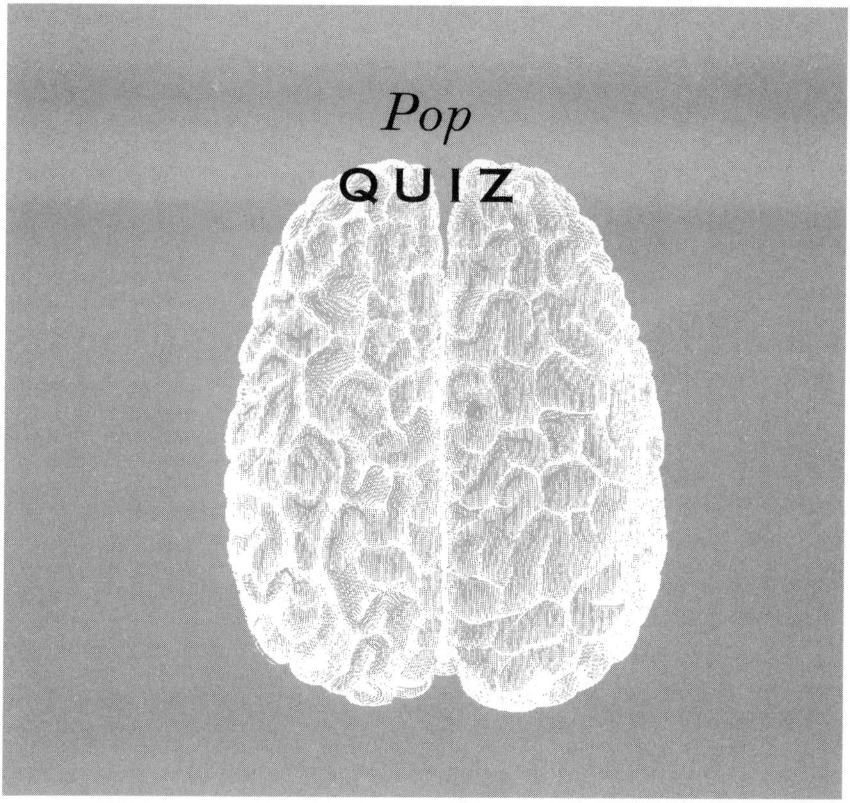

It's All in the Numbers

If you've already filled out the "How Sexy Are Your Eyebrows" quiz in *Cosmo*, done the Sunday crossword, and read every inch of *Sports Illustrated*, try these:

- Can you guess which are the most popular theme and amusement parks in the United States? If it's all the theme to you, according to recent attendance records they are Walt Disney World (which includes the Magic Kingdom, EPCOT, and Disney-MGM Studios) and Disneyland followed by Knott's Berry Farm; Universal Studios, California; Sea World, Florida; Sea World, California; King's Island, Ohio; Six Flags Magic Mountain, California; Cedar Point, Ohio; and Busch Gardens, Florida.

- Can you name the three musketeers of Alexandre Dumas's classic tale? Athos, Porthos, and Aramis. D'Artagnan is the johnny-come-lately who joins the trio. Sorry—no points for Cubby, Karen, or Annette.

• Impress the Little Mermaid socks off a kid: the seven daughters of King Triton in Disney's classic animated film are Andrina, Adella, Attina, Alana, Aquata, Arista, and Ariel—the red-haired heroine.

• Harriet Stone, writing as Margaret Sidney, first published her children's classic *Five Little Peppers and How They Grew* in 1881. Can you name them? Eleven sequels describing the adventures of Ben, Davie, Joel, Phronsie, and Polly followed the original.

• Can you recall the wives of Henry VIII and their fates? Katherine of Aragon (divorced), Anne Boleyn (beheaded), Jane Seymour (died), Anne of Cleves (divorced), Catherine Howard (beheaded), and Catherine Parr (survived).

• Can you name the provinces of Canada? Alberta, British Columbia, Manitoba, New Brunswick, Newfoundland, Nova Scotia, Ontario, Prince Edward Island, Quebec, and Saskatchewan.

• Recall the five oceans of the world? Atlantic, Pacific, Indian, Arctic, and Antarctic.

• If the press is the fourth estate, what are the other three? The Lords Temporal (barons and knights), Lords Spiritual (the clergy), and the Commons. The expression derives from a comment attributed to Edmund Burke by Thomas Carlyle. Carlyle wrote, "Burke said there were Three Estates in Parliament; but, in the Reporters' Gallery yonder, there sat a Fourth Estate more important than them all." However, Carlyle may have miscredited Burke, a British statesman. Lord Macaulay wrote, "The gallery in which the reporters sit has become a fourth estate of the realm."

• Don't confuse the fourth estate, however, with the fifth column, a group of subversives within a country who collaborate with the enemy. The expression comes from the Spanish Civil War. As he watched his army march in four columns, a fascist general happily described his supporters, all Franco sympathizers, as his fifth column.

• The Seven Sisters (no fair if you're an alum) are Barnard, Bryn Mawr, Mount Holyoke, Radcliffe (now merged with Harvard), Smith, Vassar (now co-ed), and Wellesley.

• The Ivy League comprises Brown, Columbia, Cornell, Dartmouth, Harvard, Princeton, University of Pennsylvania, and Yale.

• How about the Big Eleven (formerly the Big Ten)? The University of Chicago was an original member but dropped out of football competition after the 1939 season. They continued with basketball, however, until 1945–46. There were nine teams in the Big Ten until Michigan State joined in 1950. Penn State became the eleventh member in 1994. Add the University of Illinois, Indiana University, University of Iowa, University of Michigan, University of Minnesota, Northwestern University, Ohio State University, Purdue University, and University of Wisconsin.

• Can you name the Big Eight? University of Colorado, Iowa State, University of Kansas, Kansas State University, University of Missouri, University of Nebraska, University of Oklahoma, and Oklahoma State University.

• Do the 10 systems of the human body ring any bells? Circulatory, digestive, excretory, endocrine, integumentary, muscular, nervous, reproductive, respiratory, and skeletal.

• Can you explain the differences between the two sides of the brain? The left hemisphere, in general terms, controls the right side of your body and functions including calculation, speech, and writing. The right hemisphere is in charge of the left side of your body and controls things like spatial perception.

• Can you name the eight juicy ingredients in a V-8? Beets, carrots, celery, lettuce, parsley, tomatoes, spinach, and watercress.

• Aside from Michael Joe, can you name the other brothers who made up the original Jackson Five? Marlon David, Jermaine LaJuane, Toriano Adaryll (Tito), and Sigmund Esco (Jackie). In 1976, Randy replaced Jermaine and the group became the Jacksons.

• What is the only one of the Seven Wonders of the Ancient World still standing? The Great Pyramids of Egypt. The other six Wonders of the Ancient World are the Hanging Gardens of Babylon, the Colossus of Rhodes, the Temple of Artemis, the Statue of Zeus, the Lighthouse of Pharos, and the Mausoleum of Halicarnassus.

• What about the original Four Tops? Levi Stubbs, the lead singer, Renaldo "Obie" Benson, Lawrence Payton, and Abdul "Duke" Fakir.

On the Road

What are the busiest airports in the world? From the most airline passengers to the least:

Chicago O'Hare International
Dallas–Ft. Worth International
Heathrow *(London)*
Los Angeles International
Atlanta International
Tokyo International *(Haneda)*
San Francisco International
Stapleton International *(Denver)*
Frankfurt *(Germany)*
Miami International
John F. Kennedy International *(New York)*
Charles de Gaulle *(Paris)*

When you check your luggage, be sure to note the abbreviation on the tags. And don't worry about bags designated MIA. It's not necessarily a frightening prediction. It means simply they are heading for Miami. To be sure your stuff is heading where you are, commit this list to memory:

ATL *Atlanta International*
BOS *Logan International (Boston)*
BWI *Baltimore–Washington International*
CLT *Charlotte*
DFW *Dallas–Ft. Worth*
DTW *Detroit Metro Wayne County*
HOU *Houston Hobby*
IAD *Dulles International (Washington, D.C.)*
IAH *Houston Inter-Continental*
JFK *John F. Kennedy International (New York)*
LAX *Los Angeles International*
LGA *La Guardia (New York City)*
MCO *Orlando International*
MIA *Miami International*

MSP *Minneapolis-St. Paul International*
MSY *New Orleans International*
ORD *Chicago O'Hare International*
PHL *Philadelphia International*
SEA *Seattle International*
SFO *San Francisco International*

Tripping

"People travel for the same reason as they collect works of art: because the best people do it."
—Aldous Huxley

"Is there anything as horrible as starting on a trip? Once you're off, that's all right, but the last moments are earthquake and convulsion, and the feeling that you are a snail being pulled off a rock."
—Anne Morrow Lindbergh

"Thanks to the interstate highway system, it is now possible to travel from coast to coast without seeing anything."
— Charles Kuralt

"Unusual travel suggestions are dancing lessons from the gods."
—Kurt Vonnegut

"To give you an idea of how fast we traveled: we left Spokane with two rabbits and when we got to Topeka we still had two."
—Bob Hope

"Men travel faster now, but I do not know that they go to better things."
—Willa Cather

"A hundred years ago, it could take you the better part of a year to get from New York to California; whereas today, because of equipment problems at O'Hare, you can't get there at all."
—Dave Barry

"The major advantage of domestic travel is that, with a few exceptions such as Miami, most domestic locations are conveniently situated right here in the United States."
—Dave Barry

"The most common of all antagonisms arises from a man's taking a seat beside you on a train, a seat to which he is completely entitled."
—Robert Benchley

"In America, there are two kinds of travel—first class and with children."

—Robert Benchley

"Except for the Rothschilds and madmen, all first-class passengers travel on expense accounts."

—Russell Baker

"I have found that there ain't no surer way to find out whether you like people or hate them, than to travel with them."

—Mark Twain

Be a SPORT

➤ All in the Name

The names of professional sports teams are familiar to fans the world over (starter jackets and caps are hot tickets everywhere). However, the stories behind how teams acquired their names are little known. Some monikers are fairly obvious, such as the Philadelphia Eagles, Dallas Cowboys, or Pittsburgh Steelers. Here are some other familiar teams and the surprising origins of their names:

• In Green Bay, Wisconsin, an owner of a meat-packing business labeled the team the Packers back in the 1920s. (Fans can be thankful that it was not a funeral home owner who ponied up the money.) Nippon Ham Fighters, a professional baseball team from Japan, is named for the biggest meat-packing company in Japan.

• The Cleveland Rams of the NFL left for California in 1946, to become the Los Angeles Rams. Their place was taken by a new team coached by Paul Brown, who gave his name to the team. (No, not the Pauls, the Browns.) A decade or so later, the star running back was Jim Brown, underscoring the wise choice.

- Los Angeles Lakers: Any "lakes" to be found around the City of Angels are likely to be the pools of the rich and famous. So, how did this name evolve? The NBA team began as the Lakers of Minneapolis, situated in watery Minnesota, land of 10,000 lakes. When the team moved to Los Angeles at the start of the 1961 season, so did the name. This is the same reason that the NBA team in Salt Lake City is called the Jazz; apt when the team played in New Orleans.

- Memphis, in its recent failed bid for an NFL franchise, offered the name the Heartbreakers for the proposed team. The team colors were to be pink and black. Blue suede sneakers for the cheerleaders, perhaps? Sadly, their dreams were not fulfilled.

- During World War II, with so many able-bodied men in the armed services, those left behind to play for the Philadelphia Eagles and Pittsburgh Steelers combined to make up one team. They were nicknamed the Steagles.

➤ Rocking the Boat

In 1994, the Boat Owners Association of the United States issued a list of the ten most popular names for boats. They are:

1. *Odyssey*
2. *Serenity*
3. *Obsession*
4. *Sea Breeze*
5. *Osprey*
6. *Escape*
7. *Wet Dream*
8. *Therapy*
9. *Liquid Asset*
10. *Solitude*

What about *Freudian Sloop*? And in the arena of competition, the America's Cup trophy is not named for the United States but for the first winner of the race, a yacht named *America*.

➤ Who You Gonna Root For?

Indians According to Joann Sloan and Cherryl Watts, authors of *College Nicknames*, the most common athletic team names are

Tigers, Bears, Bulldogs, Wildcats, Eagles, Cougars, Panthers, and, yes, Indians. But lately the Indians have been losing out.

Both Stanford and Dartmouth were originally called the Indians, but with a more sensitive ethnic climate these days than a century ago, the two schools have made a change. Stanford began using the nickname in the 1890s (probably due to the large Native American population nearby) and officially took on the name in 1930. Following protests by native groups, Stanford dropped the name in 1972 and became the Cardinals. Dartmouth discontinued the moniker the same year and became the Big Green. St. John's University discontinued the Red Men as their nickname in the late 1980s, and became the inoffensive Red Storm, while the University of Massachusetts went from Red Men to Minutemen. The Indians did pick up a school in 1971 when Northeast Louisiana University designated Indians as the school nickname.

A few other schools celebrate specific tribes in their nicknames. Florida State University began play in 1947, and the name Seminoles beat out the Statesmen. The school's mascot is Chief Osceola, much better than having a politician marching up and down the field. The Utes of the University of Utah are another team named after a tribe that inhabited the Great Basin.

The Fighting Illini of the University of Illinois have an Indian heritage, named after the loose confederation of Algonquin tribes (Illiniwek) that once inhabited northern Illinois. The war dance of Chief Illiniwek, probably the most colorful and dramatic moment in college mascot performances, dates back to 1926. The University of Illinois continues the proud tradition, a somewhat disputed practice recently upheld by the Illinois Supreme Court. The current Chief Illiniwek uses a costume purchased in 1983 from Sioux Chief Frank Fools Crow.

Notre Dame Fighting Irish This nickname supposedly traces its roots back to 1897, the school's first football season. Notre Dame was battling Northwestern, and with Northwestern losing 5–0 at the start of the second half, their fans started cheering "Kill the Fighting Irish." A better explanation might be that the school was the destination of thousands of sons of Irish immigrants, and the name sounded plucky and manly. But fans can only hope for the season that the Fighting Irish puts on its schedule the likes of the Fighting Scots (Edinboro College; Gordon College), the Fightin' Christians (Elon), the Fighting Saints (Mt. Senario; Carroll College), the Hustlin' Quakers (Earlham), and the Fighting Engineers (Rose Hulman Institute of Technology).

Georgetown Hoyas Nobody recalls that the team was once called the Stonewalls, which would be a tough costume to perform in. But it is suggested that a student applied the Greek and Latin words for the old nickname and came up with "Hoia saxa," meaning "what rocks." Whether this is the derivation or it was an early student cheer of "Hoya" that gave the school the nickname, Georgetown's is unique. The mascot for Georgetown is Jack the bulldog, a little easier to envision than a stone wall.

Ohio State Buckeyes Two species of buckeye trees are found in Ohio, and while the nickname comes from the tree, the name Buckeye predates even the founding of the state. One tale recounts that in the late 18th century Colonel Ebenezer Sproat opened the first court in the Northwest Territory, part of which was present-day Ohio. The Indians referred to Sproat, a large man, as Hetuch, their name for the eye of the buck deer. Sproat was therefore called Buckeye, and the nickname was then used for other prominent Ohioans.

Oklahoma Sooners The school took on the nickname in 1908, a Sooner being anyone who had slipped into what is now Oklahoma before the official opening of the land rush. While thousands waited at the starting line in 1889 to stake out a plot of free land, others would sooner go on ahead and claim the best land for themselves. These folks were aptly named Sooners. Later, in 1906, the remainder of the Indian Territory was opened up.

North Carolina Tarheels While there are several versions of how inhabitants of North Carolina became known as Tarheels, a popular one dates back to a Civil War story. A regiment from the state, having just fought fiercely and successfully in a battle against the Union, passed another column of soldiers that had turned and fled the battle. Some of the Carolinians chided the other group that the next time "Jeff Davis was going to put tar on your heels to make you stick and fight." When General Robert E. Lee heard the story he remarked, "God bless the Tar Heels."

Anteaters and Banana Slugs Two University of California colleges offer the most whimsical of nicknames found on the collegiate scene: the Cal–Irvine Anteaters and the Cal–Santa Cruz Banana Slugs. In 1965, when Cal-Irvine began its search for a nickname, two athletes who were fans of the comic strip "B.C." started a campaign for the lowly anteater. The name was eventually put on the ballot and, on election day, garnered a majority of the votes.

In 1981, UCSC joined the NCAA Division III, and that organization required that a school have a team nickname. The students liked the banana slug, a shell-less mollusk, yellow and slimy, that can be found in the campus's redwood forest, while the chancellor pushed for the more dignified Sea Lions as the mascot. For five years, the Sea Lions reigned as the official moniker, and a sea lion was painted on the floor of the basketball court. But the slug remained number one in the hearts of the students, and in 1986, a straw poll convinced the chancellor to go yellow. A 1992 poll by the *National Directory of College Athletics* ranked the Banana Slug as number one school mascot, beating out Oglethorpe University's Stormy Petrels, Arkansas Tech's Wonderboys, the Anteaters, and the Northern Montana Northern Lights.

Don't Try This at Home

How do those board-breaking karate chops work? Physics, grasshopper. Speed, mass, and a rigid body part, and you've got it made.

speed—A short, sharp chop gives the board no time to recoil. If you remove your hand before it can absorb any vibrations, the board breaks.

mass—While your hand may be capable of making contact faster, for improved mass, the foot is mightier than the hand.

rigidity—The hand or foot must be rigid on impact. The tightness of the body part hitting the wood directs more energy into breaking the board.

A master of karate uses the speed and mass of his or her entire body to drive a hand or foot through the board. Human bones are 60 times more elastic than pine boards that can take up to 200 pounds of force. The rigid hand can take about 2,000 pounds of force. But, as the hand must recoil at 200 mph to make it work, better leave it to Chuck Norris or the Power Rangers.

Just Do It Yourself

A survey of participation sports, games, and physical activities in America conducted by the National Sporting Goods Association in 1993 revealed that walking is the most popular.

Close on its heels is swimming, followed by bike riding, fishing, camping, bowling, exercising with equipment, basketball, and billiards/pool. Aerobic exercise ends the Top 10 list.

Golf, boating, jogging/running, and volleyball are close runners-up to the Top 10, running about neck and neck. Softball beats out baseball, and soccer, while it has become more popular in recent years, still lags behind football.

➤ In Over Your Head

It's July, it's hot, and you've decided to just do it. You're going white-water rafting. Do you need Meryl Streep by your side to negotiate those rapids? Consult the International Scale of Water Difficulty as established by the American Whitewater Affiliation:

Class I	Moving water with a few riffles and small waves. Few or no obstructions.
Class II	Easy rapids. Waves up to 3 feet. Wide, clear channels that are obvious without scouting.
Class III	Rapids with high, irregular waves often capable of swamping an open canoe. Narrow passages that often require complex maneuvering. May require some scouting from shore.
Class IV	Long, difficult rapids with constricted passages that often require precise maneuvering in very turbulent waters. Scouting from shore is necessary, and conditions make rescue difficult. Generally not possible for open canoes. Boaters in covered canoes and kayaks should have the ability to Eskimo roll.
Class V	Extremely difficult, long, and very violent rapids with highly congested routes, which should always be scouted from shore. Rescue conditions are difficult, and there is significant hazard to life in the event of mishap. Ability to Eskimo roll is essential for boaters in kayaks and decked canoes.
Class VI	Difficulties of Class V carried to the extreme of navigability. Nearly impossible and very dangerous. For teams of experts only, after close study has been made and all precautions have been taken.

These grades apply to water above 50°F. If the water is under 50°F or takes you into uncharted wilderness, the river should be considered one class more difficult. Perhaps you should think about spending the afternoon by the pool.

And speaking of pools, if you have ever watched television on a Sunday afternoon, you have undoubtedly seen diving competitions and wondered how the judges arrived at their scores. There are some 2,000 dives an athlete might attempt, and the judges consider the following criteria:

Somersault *(rated by half somersaults)*

Twist *(rated by half twists)*

Flight Position:
Tuck
Pike
Straight
Free
Fly

Position off the Board:
Forward
Backward
Reverse
Inward

Unnatural Entry:
Group 1
- Forward
- Inward
- Armstand reverse (platform)

Group 2
- Back
- Reverse
- Armstand forward (platform)

Approach:
Forward
Back
Reverse (standing forward, diving back)
Inward (standing back, diving in)
Armstand (platform)

The dives are rated according to their degree of difficulty, ranging from a low of 1.2 to a high of 3.5. The easiest dive is a forward dive in a tuck position off the meter board. The toughest is a forward 4½ somersault. Do not attempt these in a backyard pool.

On the Ball

How many types of balls can you name? No, silly…the sporting kind. Here's a list to get things rolling. Bandy, baseball, basketball, billiard, boccie (boule), bowling, cricket, croquet, duckpin bowling, field hockey, flat green bowls, football (American, English, Irish, Australian, Canadian), golf, hackysack, handball, hurling, korfball, lacrosse, marbles, medicine, netball, newcomb, paddle ball, ping-pong (table tennis), polo, roller hockey, rounders, rugby (union and league), shot, soccer, softball, spaldeen, speedball, squash, tennis, ten pin bowls, tether ball, volleyball, water polo, and wiffle.

There are also cannon balls, ball bearings, spitballs, snowballs, and coming out balls but, depending on your point of view, these are much less sporting.

Sporting Thing to Do

- The word *southpaw* comes from baseball. Because a baseball diamond is arranged so the right-handed batter faces east (so he or she won't have to squint into the afternoon sun and perhaps fail to see a wild pitch aimed at the forehead), the pitcher faces west. A pitcher's left hand therefore rests on the south side of the body. *Paw* is a slang word for "hand."

- The famous horse race known simply as the Derby is held every June in Epsom, England. Founded in 1780, it could just as easily have been named the Bunbury. The founders of the race were the 12th Earl of Derby and Sir Charles Bunbury. They tossed a coin to see for whom the race would be named. Guess they'd never heard of Dun & Bradstreet, Gilbert & Sullivan, or Bert & Ernie.

- Hockey's holy grail, the Stanley Cup, is named for Lord Stanley of Preston. He awarded a silver cup (it now has more in common with a mixing bowl) valued at $50 to the winning team in a Canadian amateur hockey game.

- The first rope tow in America was built in 1934 at Gilbert's Hill in Woodstock, Vermont, by David Dodd and Frank Stillwell. An average trip from bottom to top took about two minutes. However, the driver delighted in running the rope at 25 miles per hour, thereby jettisoning skiers into the air at the summit.

• As the host country of the 1904 Olympic Games (held in St. Louis), the United States' committee picked one additional sport to be played in a demonstration event. The choice was croquet or, to be precise, "roque," a variation of croquet played with a one-handed mallet on a court with a shallow wall encircling it. While an Olympic event for just that one year, it made Charles Jacobus, an American, the only croquet gold medal winner in Olympic history. Incidentally, the game figures in Stephen King's novel *The Shining*. A character named Jack Torrence (hauntingly portrayed in the movie by Jack Nicholson) wields a roque mallet in a particularly unsportsmanlike way.

• The official state sport of Maryland is neither crabbing nor terping. It's jousting.

Women's Places

- The only alpine skier to date to have won four Olympic medals is German-born Hanni Wenzel.

- On March 20, 1934, Babe Didrikson (an all-round athlete perhaps best known for her success as a golfer) pitched the first inning for the Philadelphia Athletics in a spring training exhibition game against the Brooklyn Dodgers. She did give up one walk but no hits. She pitched another inning several days later for the St. Louis Cardinals against the Boston Red Sox (giving up four hits and three runs).

- Lizzie Murphy played first base for an American League all-star team in an exhibition game against the Red Sox, which made her, in August 1922, the first woman to play for a major league team. The all-star team won.

- Jackie Mitchell, 17 years old, pitched against the Yankees for the Chattanooga Lookouts in April 1931 in an exhibition game. After striking out Babe Ruth and Lou Gehrig, she walked Tony Lazzeri and then quit for the day.

- Wilma Rudolph, born with a crippling condition that required hours of physical therapy administered by her family, couldn't walk until she was 8 years old. She went on to become a track phenomenon, coming home with three Olympic gold medals when she was just 20.

- Octogenarian Josie Morris captured first place in a rodeo calf-roping competition.

- Janet Guthrie was the first woman to compete in the Indy 500, in 1978. She finished eighth in spite of a broken wrist.

- The only American who snagged a gold medal at the 1968 winter Olympics in Grenoble was figure skater Peggy Fleming.

- The annual cross-country dog sled race from Anchorage to Nome, Alaska, the Iditarod, was won by Libby Riddles in 1985. However, Susan Butcher set a course record the next year with 11 days, 15 hours, and 6 minutes. She also won the 1987, 1988, and 1990 Iditarods.

• In 1974, Irene Horton, joined by two children and three grandchildren, competed in the U. S. Nationals in waterskiing.

Jump to It

What *is* the difference between the pentathlon, heptathlon, biathlon, and decathlon?

The pentathlon, in ancient Greece, consisted of a footrace, long jump, javelin throw, discus throw, and wrestling match. The modern version comprises five track-and-field events. For women it consists of an 800 meter run, 100 meter hurdles, high jump, long jump, and shot put. For men it's a 200 meter run, 1,500 meter run, discus throw, javelin throw, and long jump. The Olympic pentathlon comprises cross-country running, fencing, horseback riding, pistol shooting, and swimming.

The heptathlon, Jackie Joyner-Kersee's main event, has seven parts: a 100 meter run; 800 meter run; 100 meter hurdles; high jump; javelin throw; long jump; and shot put.

The decathlon is part of the Olympics and consists of ten track-and-field events for men: 100 meter, 400 meter, and 1,500 meter runs; 110 meter hurdles; high jump; long jump; javelin throw; pole vault; shot put; and discus throw.

The biathlon, a winter Olympic event, is a combination of rifle shooting and cross-country skiing inspired by the military drills organized by the Norwegian army. On skis, a competitor races with a .22 caliber small-bore rifle slung across his or her back. Targets are placed at distances of 50 meters, and competitors shoot from either a standing or prone position. The target for a standing shoot is 4½ inches; for a prone shoot, 1¾ inches. Having exerted tremendous energy skiing against the clock, competitors must be able to instantly reduce their pulse rates (to about 140 beats per minute) in order to be able to aim and fire with steady hands. Firing a specified number of times, they then surge off to the next target. Missed targets mean a time penalty or racing an extra loop of the course. Men race 10 or 20 kilometers or as a four-man relay team (with each man skiing 7.5

kilometers). Women participate in a 7.5 or 15 kilometer race as individuals or in a three-woman relay team with each woman skiing 7.5 kilometers.

Gridiron Monikers

Most folks know Broadway Joe, L.T., and Mean Joe Greene, but see if you can guess, without peeking, to whom these nicknames belong:

Alabama Antelope—Don Hutson, speedy wide receiver for the Green Bay Packers—the first wide receiver to gain more than 1,000 yards receiving in a season

Too Tall—6′9″ Dallas Cowboy star Ed Jones, who briefly left the team for a career in boxing that lasted six bouts

Bambi—fawn-eyed wide receiver Lance Alworth

The Greatest—Jim Brown, king of the wide receivers

The Tyler Rose—Tyler, Texas's hometown hero Earl Campbell

Mr. Clutch—Otto Graham of the Cleveland Browns, for his cool and steady work on the field

Hog—John Hannah, brilliant offensive guard and resolute on the line

Night Train—rhymes nicely with Dick Lane, defensive back extraordinaire

Sweetness—the NFL's all-time leading rusher, Walter Payton who, with the Bears, set or tied eight major NFL records.

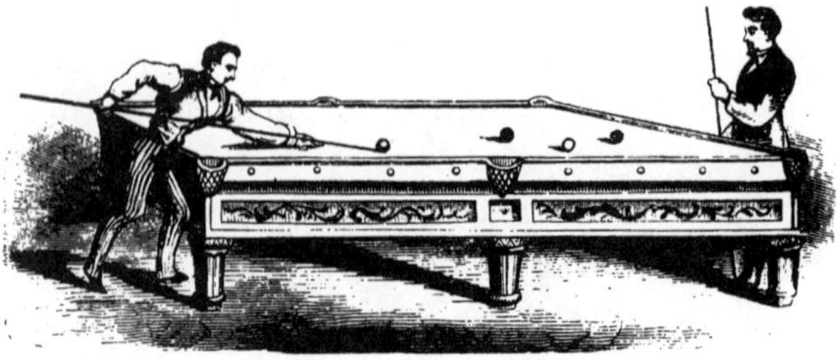

Formerly Football

We've all seen the photographs of Richard Nixon (Whittier College), Gerald Ford (Michigan), and Ronald Reagan (Eureka College) decked out in their football duds. But guess who else interesting had minor careers on the college gridiron?

- Before being appointed as an associate justice on the Supreme Court, Byron "Whizzer" White was an All-American halfback at the University of Colorado in 1937 and an All-Pro running back for the Detroit Lions. Yo, Whizzer!

- Dwight D. Eisenhower was a starting halfback on the 1912 Army team and went up against Jim Thorpe. A knee injury would sideline the future president's career in football forever a week later.

- In the future-actors category, Marion Morrison, a tall, good-looking kid, played for Southern California until the 1926 season when he headed for Hollywood as John Wayne. Buddy Reynolds did well at Florida State but also gave up the game to act—as Burt. Finally, Harvey Lee Yeary played for Eastern Kentucky until a back injury sidelined him. Like Marion and Buddy before him, he packed his bags for Hollywood and changed his name, to Lee Majors.

- And what of hunky actor Ed Marinaro? As a tailback at Cornell, in 27 games he rushed for 4,715 yards, a record average of 174.6 yards per game. That beats O.J., Herschel Walker, and Tony Dorsett. Think about it.

- In 1968, a reserve wide receiver in a University of Houston versus Tulsa game caught a 26-yard pass in the final quarter. Big deal? If you could go to the videotape, you'd note it was Larry Gatlin. Ooee!

Old Sports

The names of sports and games have interesting lineages.

- *Badminton* is for Badminton Hall in Avon, England, where the game developed circa 1870.

- *Billiards* derives from an old French word for a stick with a curved end.

• *Chess* is generally believed to derive from *shah*, a Persian word for a king or ruler.

• There are two schools of thought regarding *croquet*. Some say it's a form of the word *croche*, old French for a shepherd's crook. Others say the game developed in Ireland and got its name from *cluiche* (pronounced "crooky"), a Celtic word for "play."

• *Karate* translates as "empty hand," a Japanese term that refers to having no weapons (but still packing a punch).

• *Lacrosse*, the name French Canadians gave the game they watched Native Americans play and then adapted, gets its name from the stick, which resembled a French bishop's crozier.

• *Rugby* honors the Rugby School in England, where the game was first played.

• *Snooker*, a version of billiards, was created by Neville Chamberlain, who adopted the nickname for first-year cadets at the Royal Military Academy.

• *Squash* is onomatopoetic for the sound and feel of a type of squashy ball favored for the game, which was popular at the Harrow School in England.

➤ Sports Casting

• Ray Ewry of the United States holds the record for winning the most gold medals at the summer Olympic Games. Between 1900 and 1908, he won 10 medals in the long jump, high jump, and triple jump.

• Swimmer Mark Spitz won seven gold medals in the 1972 Games, a standing record for the most won at a single summer Olympics.

• Russian gymnast Larissa Latynina holds the overall top medal winner slot. Between 1956 and 1964, she accumulated nine gold, five silver, and four bronze.

• In the 1992 Olympics in Barcelona, three nations won their first gold medals: Algeria, Indonesia, and Lithuania.

• The smallest arena in use by a National Basketball Association team is Memorial Coliseum, home of the Portland Trail Blazers. Its capacity is 12,888.

• Boasting a capacity of 80,500, the largest stadium presently in use by the National Football League is the Pontiac Silverdome, home of the Detroit Lions. Robert F. Kennedy Stadium, where the Washington Redskins play, is the smallest in the NFL, with a capacity of 55,677.

• The first Indy 500 was won by Ray Harroun driving a Marmon Wasp on May 30, 1911. The Indy 500 Cup is bedecked with miniature reliefs of previous winners.

• The first person known to swim across the English Channel from England to France was Captain Matthew Webb in 1875. He started out on August 24th and finished the next day. It took him 21 hours, 44 minutes, and 55 seconds. Sadly, he'd later drown below Niagara Falls trying to top this feat. Chad Hundeby crossed in 7 hours and 17 minutes in September 1994, toppling Penny Lee Dean's long-standing record of 7 hours and 40 minutes.

• Every year since 1924, the Hart Trophy has been awarded to a player selected by the Professional Hockey Writers' Association as "the most valuable to his team during the season." Wayne Gretzky has the most on his trophy shelf to date. Gordie Howe is second. Nevertheless, the Montreal Canadiens have won the most Stanley Cups.

• The British Open, the U.S. Masters, the U.S. Open, and the U.S. PGA comprise the professional Majors of golfdom. The player to win the most Majors in his career thus far is Jack Nicklaus, with a total of 18.

• Consisting of the Kentucky Derby, the Preakness Stakes, and the Belmont Stakes, the U.S. Triple Crown has had only one jockey win the round twice: Eddie Arcaro. He rode Whirlaway to victory in 1941, and Citation was the dream horse in 1948.

BASEBALL *Yarns*

Name That Team

• Playing in the same stadium as the football team, Cleveland's baseball entry was variously known as the Broncos, the Blues, the Naps, the Spiders, the Molly McGuires, and finally the Indians. Indians became the official choice because of Luis (Lou) Sockalexis, a Penobscot Indian from Maine, who is credited with being the first Native American to play in the majors. Sockalexis, educated at Notre Dame and Holy Cross, was signed by Cleveland in 1897 and was instantly popular with the fans. Because of injuries, he played fewer than 100 games in his three seasons, all with Cleveland, and died of alcoholism in 1913. Several years later, a Cleveland newspaper sponsored a contest to rename the team, and the Indians, in honor of Sockalexis, was the winner.

• Why Pirates? No, there were never buccaneers on the Monongahela River. The Pittsburg (there was no *h* in the 19th-century spelling) team was first called the Alleghenies, then the Innocents, when it joined the National League in 1887. Three years later, they became the Pirates after signing up a second baseman named Lou Bierbauer from Philadepphia. There was much screaming in the Quaker City, and many accusations of "pirating" by Pittsburg. While Bierbauer may be long forgotten, the legacy of his contract negotiations lives on.

• Most baseball fans recall the Dodgers' move from Brooklyn to Los Angeles in 1957. However, the name dates back to the early part of the century when the fans in Brooklyn had to dodge trolley cars to get to the ballpark. The team was briefly known as the Trolley Dodgers, then the Bridegrooms, when, one season, many young players were pledging their troth. After a short stint as the Robins, named after their popular manager Wilbert Robinson, the Dodgers became official.

• The Kansas City Royals, Milwaukee Brewers, Seattle Mariners, Texas Rangers, and Toronto Blue Jays were all named by fans who entered their hit picks in contests.

• The oldest professional baseball team in the country wore red stockings when they ran out on the field in 1869. They were instantly nicknamed the Redstockings and later, during the McCarthy period in the 1950s, were briefly known as the Redlegs. Now they are the plain old Cincinnati Reds.

• The Atlanta Braves may win the Most Names for a Single Team award. Because they resided in Boston until 1953 and Milwaukee until 1966, they've been known as the Bean-eaters, Bees, Caps, Doves, Nationals, and Rustlers.

☛ Heavy Hitters

While Tom Cruise and Paul Newman favor race cars, and Kevin Kline and Dustin Hoffman may wow you with their piano playing, some celebrities are extraordinarily talented on the diamond. Michael Bolton, Kevin Costner, and Charlie Sheen, for example, can really play ball. Other starplayers:

- When Michael Jordan quit baseball to return to the NBA, a number of scouts and coaches agreed that it was his best move. One scout observed, "Jordan never had any pop to his bat. Now Tom Selleck, there's a guy who can hit a baseball." Tom Selleck often plays with the Detroit Tigers during spring training.

- Another actor with links to baseball is Chuck Connors (of *Rifleman* and *Branded* fame). At 6′7″, Kevin "Chuck" Connors wore number 11 on his jersey as a Boston Celtic in 1946. He then tried his hand at baseball, briefly as first baseman for the Brooklyn Dodgers before being traded to Chicago. He played for the Cubs in 1951, then was sent to their farm team in Los Angeles, hitting .321. Connors switched to acting (after being complimented by Ted Williams on his recitation of "Casey at the Bat"), playing a small role in the Hepburn-Tracy classic *Pat and Mike*. When acting took off, his career in baseball was benched.

- Singer Charley Pride played for the Memphis Red Sox in the mid-1950s during the waning era of the Negro Leagues. He had a tryout with the California Angels in 1961 but failed to stick and played for the Mets' farm system until 1964, when he gave up baseball for country music.

- Arguably the most accomplished baseball player among the Hollywood set is Johnny Beradino, who was a child actor in the *Our Gang* series in the 1930s. Berardino (he dropped the second *r* when he took up acting again) played in the majors from 1939 through 1952, taking time out for World War II. He appeared in the 1948 World Series. After baseball, he starred as Dr. Steve Hardy on the ever-popular daytime drama *General Hospital* for 25 years.

Art Imitates Baseball

Art often imitates life. Movies, books, plays, and, well, art frequently contain autobiographic revelations by the creator. Especially in works of fiction, a factual event (a news story or personal experience) may insinuate itself (by design or coincidence) into the plot. It twists around the narrative and blends into the telling of the story. Then again, perhaps it was pure invention and any similarities to persons living or dead, etc., were pure coincidence. Unless we hear the source baring his or her soul to Leno, Letterman, or Kathie Lee, it's impossible to know if the writer was intentionally folding real-life dramas into a work or if every word and subplot sprang from the author's imagination.

An example is Bernard Malamud's *The Natural.* Whether intended by Malamud or not, the story, with its almost mystical overtones and mythic hero, has more than one incident that mirrors actual occurrences in major league baseball.

Roy Hobbs, the protagonist of Malamud's book (published in 1952), is portrayed in the movie by Robert Redford. A dazzling young athlete with obvious promise, Hobbs is shot and his career derailed by a crazed female fan. After years living in oblivion, he reappears, plays in the majors, and leads his team to a hardwon victory with a final, spectacular home run.

The fictional shooting incident is eerily similar to what occurred in June 1949, when Eddie Waitkus, a first baseman for the Philadelphia Phillies, was shot by Ruth Steinhagen in Chicago's Edgewater Beach Hotel. The 19-year-old girl was later placed in a mental hospital. Waitkus battled for his life and miraculously recovered to play the following season.

In 1932, a hotel room in Chicago was the scene of another shooting incident when Cubs shortstop Billy Jurges was shot in the shoulder and hand by a spurned girlfriend named Violet Popovich Valli. Jurges's wounds kept him out of the lineup for two weeks, while Ms. Valli cashed in on the dispute by signing a four-month contract to sing in local nightclubs. Her signature song, incidentally, was "What I Did for Love."

In the film version of *The Natural*, the story climaxes when Hobbs crushes a home run that hits the scoreboard, causing it to explode in a geyser of electric sparks. The scoreboard stops functioning, and the clock is frozen at that moment. Surely a resonating example of poetic license and literary invention, you think, because that would never happen in real life.

But a play that echoes that climactic home run scene actually took place at Brooklyn's Ebbets Field in May 1946. At 4:25 on that May 30, in the nightcap of a doubleheader, the Braves' Bama Rowell lofted a second-inning home run that struck and shattered the Bulova clock high atop the right field scoreboard. As Rowell circled the bases, broken glass rained down on Dodger right fielder Dixie Walker. An hour later the clock stopped.

The Brooklyn-born Malamud has never acknowledged that these dramatic scenes in his classic tale are drawn from old headlines. Readers and viewers have to umpire and make their own call.

Strange Victory

The New York Giants of 1911 were one of the most powerful baseball teams in the National League and, with a little luck, were considered likely contenders for the championship. They got their lucky charm before an early season game in St. Louis.

A tall, gawky man clad in a black suit three sizes too small approached several of the players and asked for manager John McGraw. The man went over and introduced himself. "Mr. McGraw, my name is Charlie 'Victory' Faust. I'm a pitcher. A few weeks ago a fortune-teller told me I was going to join the Giants and, with me, they were going to win the pennant."

McGraw looked Faust over and told him to get on the mound and throw a few pitches. As the players looked on, the skinny Faust windmilled his arms and hurled a pitch that a high school hitter would love to see. He was a funny sight on the mound and just as amusing to the Giants when he picked up a bat and swatted at pitches that McGraw lobbed to him. After hitting one on the ground, Victory took off running. The fielders fumbled the ball and Faust slid, in his suit, into third.

That night, as the train left St. Louis, McGraw came into the club car and, to the astonishment of the team, announced, "Boys, I'd like you to meet the newest Giant, Victory Faust." Faust stayed on, his antics keeping the team loose. They went on a winning streak that swept them to first place with Faust, an entertaining presence in the dugout, yelling at the opposition and encouraging his teammates.

All the while, Faust kept hounding McGraw to put him in. In September, with the pennant assured, McGraw finally let Victory take the mound. Pitching against the Dodgers, he took to the mound in the ninth inning with the Dodgers ahead by three runs. The Dodger batters went along with the gag and swung at Victory's lobs. He got all three batters. Coming to the plate for the first time, Victory was brushed by a slow curve from Brooklyn's Eddie Dent and took his base. Then, with arms flailing, Victory stole second, then third, and finally home in a cloud of dust. The Dodger fielders looked on laughing as hard as the Giants.

Victory Faust turned his talents to vaudeville in 1912, but twice came back to ride the bench and cheer the Giants on to a second pennant. In 1913, McGraw called on Faust when the team was in a slump. True to the fortune-teller's promise, his stays on the bench always helped—the Giants won again in 1913.

At the beginning of the following season, during spring training, Faust vanished. McGraw soon heard that Victory had been committed to an insane asylum in Oregon and would not be with the team. Faust was moved to an asylum in Washington, where he died in June of the following year.

Without Victory, the Giants finished second in 1914. The following year, after receiving news of his death, the team finished in last place.

☛ Short Stop

Eddie Gaedel was a major league baseball player even though he went to bat just once. Another unusual aspect to the Gaedel story is that he was a midget. As Casey Stengel said, "You can look it up."

It was 1951 and Bill Veeck, one of baseball's all-time great promoters, was general manager of the lowly St. Louis Browns (three years away from sprouting Oriole wings and flying off to Baltimore). As usual, the Browns were last in both league standings and attendance. Veeck was looking for anything to generate interest in the team.

In a game on August 19, 1951, Veeck introduced his latest promotional brainstorm: pinch-hitter Eddie Gaedel, who stood just 43 inches tall. Outfitted in a child-sized Browns uniform and carrying a Little League bat, the diminutive batter exited the dugout and headed for the plate. Expecting resistance, Veeck armed his manager, Zack Wilson, with a legitimate major league contract for Gaedel, and, after some spirited discussion with the umpires, the little slugger was allowed to pinch-hit for center fielder Frank Saucier.

The first pitch from Detroit's Bob Cain was, not surprisingly, high, as were the next three. Eddie tossed his bat and took his base (but Jim Delsing went in as a pinch-runner). Gaedel walked back to the dugout and into baseball history.

Major league officials were furious and quickly decreed that all contracts must first go through the league office for approval. But it was not Eddie's final stop on the diamond. Bill Veeck and his promotional genius moved on to the Chicago White Sox. On May 26, 1959, Gaedel made another appearance. This time he brought reinforcements.

Before a Cleveland-White Sox game, a helicopter landed behind second base and, led by Gaedel, four little people dressed as spacemen jumped out. Brandishing ray guns, the four "captured" two Sox infielders, 5′10″ Nellie Fox and 5′9″ Luis Aparicio. Gaedel told the duo, "I don't want to be taken to your leader. I already know him."

Two years later, the 36-year-old Gaedel died of a heart attack following a mugging in Chicago. The only major leaguer to attend his funeral was the man he faced, pitcher Bob Cain.

Foreign Exchange

The only foreigner in the Japanese Baseball Hall of Fame is neither a hurler who mowed down batters at Dodger Stadium nor a slugger who poled home runs into the Yankee Stadium bleachers but, rather, a pitcher who never played organized baseball in America. He is a Russian named Victor Starfin.

Following the Bolshevik Revolution, Konstantin Starfin, his wife, and their young son Victor left Russia and eventually settled in the small city of Asahikawa, on the Japanese island of Hokkaido, in 1925. Young Victor was an exceptional athlete and, by 1934, grew into an outstanding high school pitcher. At 6′4″ he towered over Japanese players, and his fastball smoked. When Yumiuri formed Japan's first professional team, Starfin was recruited to pitch. In 1937, the year that Japan's professional league began, he won 28 games.

Except for a single year (1945), Japanese baseball continued through various military conflicts and World War II, even though most able-bodied men were in the armed forces. Because he was not Japanese, Starfin was exempted from the military.

Starfin's statistics were exceptional by any standards. In 1939, he won 42 games in a 96-game schedule. The following year, he racked up 38 wins. When his career ended in 1955, Starfin had won 303 games and was the first 300-game-winner in Japanese baseball.

Tragically, Starfin was struck and killed by a car while crossing a street in 1957. Today, some 40 years later, he remains the only foreigner in the Japanese Baseball Hall of Fame at Korakuen Stadium in Tokyo.

Baseball purists might quibble that legendary slugger Sadaharu Oh is also not Japanese. Oh is Chinese, but he was born in Tokyo to a Chinese father and retains his citizenship as a matter of pride. He, too, is in the Hall of Fame in Tokyo.

The Diamond and the Oval Office

The first president to throw out the first pitch of the season was none other than William Taft. At Opening Day in April 1910 in the nation's capital, he began a tradition followed by presidents ever since. Benjamin Harrison is believed to be the first president to attend a major league game. He watched Washington lose to the Reds on June 6, 1892. However, the little-known presidential record holder for attending the most major league games while in office is Harry Truman, with 16.

George Bush, captain of his Yale baseball team in 1947, played first base. He is the only president to have played in the College World Series. While a solid hitter with a bat in his youth, Mr. Bush would make headlines in February 1995 by beaning an onlooker with a golf ball while teeing off with Gerald Ford and Bill Clinton.

CHILD'S *Play*

Sticks and Stones

The first time your kid gets into a name-calling match with another kid (and shocks you with a colorful rendition of your pet obscenities) can be horrifying. While bozo, dweeb, putz, klutz, yutz, and doo-doo-head all have a place, it may be time to introduce your urchin to the lost art of descriptive name-calling.

Consider the historical richness of blackguard, blatherskite, buffoon, clinchpoop, codswalloper, costermonger, dotard, galoot, guttersnipe, harridan, hornswoggler, jackanape, jackdaw, knave, milksop, pip-squeak, popinjay, riffraff, rogue, scoundrel, shoat, strumpet, villain, wiseacre, and Xanthippe.

String them all together for a truly stunning effect, you scalawag, you.

Nursery Rhymes

Little Miss Muffet
Sat on a tuffet,
Eating her curds and whey;
Along came a spider
And sat down beside her
And frightened Miss Muffet away.

You probably gave Mother Goose credit for this one, but there is speculation that it was actually written by an eminent 16th-century entomologist named, not surprisingly, Dr. Thomas Muffet. Since Dr. Muffet did author a verse entitled "The Silkworms and Their Flies," it is not a huge leap to surmise that he wrote the above rhyme for his daughter Patience.

Ring a round a rosie
A pocket full of posies
Ashes, ashes
We all fall down.

This rhyme sounds pleasant enough, but you may feel differently about it upon learning of its origins. Many date it to the bubonic plague that struck London in 1665. A rosy rash was a symptom of the disease, posies of herbs were often carried as a preventive, bodies were often burned (in some variations, the third line reads "a-tishoo, a-tishoo"—sneezing was also a symptom), and eventually, of course, everyone fell down dead.

London Bridge is falling down,
Falling down, falling down.
London Bridge is falling down,
My fair lady.
Take the key and lock her up
Lock her up, lock her up,
Take the key and lock her up,
My fair lady.

Build it up with wood and clay
Wood and clay will wash away.
Build it up with bricks and mortar.
Bricks and mortar will not stay.

Build it up with iron and steel.
Iron and steel will bend and bow.
Build it up with silver and gold.
Silver and gold will be stolen away.
Set a man to watch all night.
Suppose the man shoud fall asleep?
Give him a pipe to smoke all night.

As children chant "London Bridge," they are playing out a very real and primal fear—that an often-traveled bridge is in constant danger of collapse. The game was well known in the Middle Ages, and versions have been collected in a number of different languages. Play is similar in every version: Two players form the bridge with arms joined and upraised; the other children form a line and pass underneath one by one, each hurrying through to avoid being caught by the falling arms of the "bridge." The "take the key and lock her up" verse may reflect the grisly ritual of burying people alive within the foundations of bridges to serve as guardian spirits.

Little Jack Horner
Sat in the corner
Eating a Christmas pie;
He put in his thumb,
And pulled out a plum,
And said, What a good boy am I!

A favorite theory regarding this verse says that Jack Horner was steward to Richard Whiting, who was the last abbot of Glastonbury. As the story goes, Whiting sent his steward to London with a Christmas gift for Henry VIII—a pie into which he had baked the deeds to twelve manors. (This may sound odd, but it's not nearly so strange as the four and twenty live blackbirds that were baked into a pie for another king.) On the journey, Horner opened the pie and took the deed to the Manor of Mells for himself. Quite a plum!

Jack be nimble
Jack be quick
Jack jump over
The candlestick.

Believe it or not, candle leaping was practiced in England for many centuries as both a sport and a form of fortune-telling. In one version, a lighted candle was placed on the floor. If the jumper could leap over the candle without extinguishing it, good fortune was supposed to follow in the coming year.

Cafeteria Collectibles

Antique toys and games have become popular collectibles for those who can afford them. And climbing up the ladder of priceyness is vintage kid stuff from the last few decades. Aside from being entertaining, these items play upon our nostalgia. Take lunch boxes. A price list of the some of the most collectible TV-and-movie-related lunch boxes, according to collector-dealer Ralph Persinger, follows. Keep in mind that the prices are for boxes in mint condition with all their bits and bobs.

In the $2,000 category:

Dudley Do-Right *(1962, Okay Industries)*
Underdog *(1974, Okay Industries)*
Superman *(1954, ADCO Liberty)*
Bullwinkle and Rocky *(1962, Okay Industries)*

In the $1,000 bracket:

The Jetsons *(1963, Aladdin)*
Star Trek *(1967, Aladdin)*
Popeye *(1962, Universal)*

In the under $1,000 group:

Lost in Space *(1967, King Sealy Thermos)*
Howdy Doody *(1954, ADCO Liberty)*
Lone Ranger *(1954, ADCO Liberty)*

So fish that Little Mermaid thermos out of the trash and treat that Power Ranger box with a little more respect. You might be able to retire on them someday.

For the Nippers

Does the idea of being introduced to a young child give you the heebie-jeebies? A fear of being in the company of other people's children is right up there on the list of things that scare the pants off of us (along with public speaking, spiders, and IRS audits). Relax. Like dogs, children sense fear. Neither too bubbly nor too laid back an adult be. Take your cues from the child. Herewith some tips:

When addressing babies and toddlers, try using proper names for everything instead of pronouns. Granted, it sounds stilted, but you'll be understood and considered less suspect. Get down on their level, give them space to breathe, and start babbling about how much you like Barney, Elmo, Thomas, and tractors. Start singing "Old MacDonald." When in a jam, go for the broadest possible humor. A pratfall involving a doll or stuffed toy can be hilarious when you're one and a half. Babies really do tend to like higher pitches, but there's no call for sounding like a chipmunk on a double espresso. Chill.

Preschoolers need coaxing. Ask them to name their favorite super heroes or characters. When in doubt, make a paper airplane or boat. For a boat: Take a regular letter-size piece of paper. Fold it in half crosswise. With the fold on top, turn down the top corners at the center and press the crease. You should have a triangle with a flap at the bottom. Now fold the front and back flaps along the bottom upward. You should have a little sailor's hat. Now push the ends toward the center and flatten the paper. Tuck in the bitty corner flaps. Your paper should be diamond shaped. Turn the bottom corners up so you're back to a triangle shape. Again, push the ends together to get that diamond back. Flatten. Now gently pull the top corners open. You will have to shape the gunwales and sides a bit. Place in the sink or tub, enjoy the delighted oohs and aahs from the bystanders or tubee(s), and get to work on a regatta.

Kindergarteners like to talk about what they are interested in. Yup, they start to have interests at this stage. Need a clue? Check to see what emblems appear on their T-shirt, backpack, or sneakers. What sheets do they have? What do they like to collect? Use the words *cool* and *awesome*. Had any quasi-gross or thrilling experiences you can relate? If stuck, go to a simple coin trick by magically finding a quarter behind the kid's ear. Be a real wizard—let the kid keep the quarter.

Super Heroics

Most of us are well aware of Bruce Wayne's and Clark Kent's super-hero identities. How many other alter egos can you name?

Aquaman—Arthur Curry, King of the Seven Seas (1940, D.C. Comics)

Banshee—Sean Cassidy, former Interpol agent (1967, Marvel Comics)

Batwoman—Kathy Kane, one-time circus performer (1956, D.C. Comics)

Beast—Hank McCoy, scientist (1963, Marvel Comics)

Cannonball—Sam Guthrie, former miner (1982, Marvel Comics)

Captain America—Steve Rogers, various careers but began as a delivery boy (1941, Marvel Comics)

Cyclops—Scott "Slim" Summers, X-Man (1963, Marvel Comics)

Doc Savage—Clark Savage Jr., adventurer (1933, Street & Smith Publications)

The Flash—The first Flash was Jay Garrick (1940, D.C. Comics), but in 1956 he was reintroduced as Barry Allen, police scientist.

Green Arrow—Oliver Queen, journalist (1941, D.C. Comics)

Green Hornet—Britt Reid, publisher of the *Daily Sentinel* (WXYZ Radio, Detroit). Reid is related to John Reid, the Lone Ranger.

Green Lantern—The first Green Lantern was Alan Scott, an engineer turned radio announcer turned head of Gotham Broadcasting (1940, D.C. Comics). He was reborn as Hal Jordan, test pilot, in 1959. His oath: "In brightest day, in blackest night, no evil shall escape my sight. Let those who worship evil's might beware my power—Green Lantern's light."

Hawkman—Hawkman was first Carter Hall, millionaire (1940, D.C. Comics) and reintroduced in 1961 as Katar Hol, police officer, when on the planet Thanager and Carter Hall, director of the City Museum, when on earth.

The Hulk—Robert Bruce Banner, physicist (1962, Marvel Comics)

Iceman—Bobby Drake, student and X-Man (1963, Marvel Comics)

Iron Man—Anthony Stark, industrialist (1963, Marvel Comics)

Marvel Girl—Jean Grey, student turned model (1963, Marvel Comics)

Mr. Fantastic—Dr. Reed Richards, scientist and member of Fantastic 4 (1961, Marvel Comics)

Nightcrawler—Kurt Wagner, circus performer (1975, Marvel Comics)

The Phantom—Kit Walker, the ghost who walks (1936, King Features Syndicate). His oath of the skull: "I swear to devote my life to the destruction of piracy, greed, cruelty, and injustice, and my son and their sons shall follow me."

Robin—Dick Grayson, former trapeze artist (1940, D.C. Comics)

Silver Surfer—Norrin Radd (1966, Marvel Comics)

Spiderman—Peter Parker, photojournalist (1962, Marvel Comics)

Storm—Ororo Munroe, female member of X-Men (1975, Marvel Comics)

Sub-Mariner—Namor, prince of Atlantis (1939, Marvel Comics)

Super Chicken—Henry Cabot Henhouse III, playboy (1967, ABC-TV)

Supergirl—Linda Lee Danvers, student (1959, D.C. Comics)

Thing—Benjamin Jacob Grimm, test pilot and member of Fantastic 4 (1964, Marvel Comics)

Wolverine—Logan, Canadian secret agent and X-Man (1973, Marvel Comics)

Wonder Woman—Diana Prince, major in the U.S. Army (1941, D.C. Comics)

For fun, can you name any superpets? Krypto was Superman's superpooch, and Beppo was a stowaway supersimian from Krypton. Streaky was Supergirl's supercat, and Comet was her superhorse.

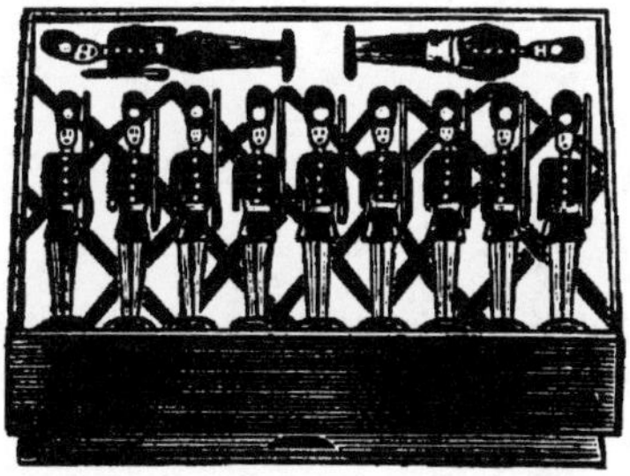

That's an Order

A knight's coat of arms identified not only his family and affiliation but his birth order as well. Called marks of cadency, variations in a basic family design indicated each son's ranking according to how many older brothers he had.

The first-born son used the Label, which looks a bit like a section of Stonehenge in an "M" arrangement. Prince Charles uses it in his coat of arms. Thereafter, second son: Crescent; third son: Mullet (a five-pointed star); fourth son: Martlet (a footless bird, as a fourth son would inherit little or no property upon which to land); fifth son: Annulet (a solid ring); sixth son: Fleur-de-lys; seventh son: Rose; eighth son: Cross moline (a fluted cross); ninth son: Octofoil (an eight-pointed star).

Family Matters

Traditional family names often incorporate prefixes and suffixes to give us a hint about a child's parentage such as *-kin, –son, –sen, –sohn*, and *-datter*. Harrison, say, once meant "Harry's son." Herewith more name prefixes and what they mean:

Ap or **Up**—*Welsh for "son of"*
Bar—*Aramaic for "son of"*
Ben—*Hebrew for "son of"*
Di or **De**—*Italian and French for "of"*
Fitz—*Norman for "son of"*
Mc or **Mac**—*Celtic for "son of"*
O'—*Celtic for "descendant of"*

Name suffixes and what they mean:

-czyk, -wiak, -wicz—*Polish for "son of"*
-escu, -esco, -vici—*Romanian for "like" or "kin to"*
-ez—*Spanish for "son of"*
-ich, -vich—*Russian for "son of"*
-idas, -ides, -poulos—*Greek for "son of"*
-oglu—*Turkish for "son of"*
-ov, -ev, -off, -eff—*Eastern European and Russian for "of the (family) of"*
-sky, -ski—*Eastern European and Russian for "of the nature of"*
-tze—*Chinese for "son of"*
-vna, -ova—*Russian for "daughter of"*

Many other family names are based upon physical characteristics (Small), geography (Field), or profession (Baker).

A Girl's Life

• The YWCA was founded in London in 1855 by Emma Roberts. It was established as a sister organization to the YMCA to serve single women looking for jobs in the city. The Ys offered safe, inexpensive housing, companionship, spiritual guidance, and a general support system.

• Camp Fire Girls was founded in 1910 by Luther Halsey Gulick a pioneer in physical education, and a group of educators for girls 6 to 18 years old. Their idea was to "perpetuate the spiritual ideals of home" as well as "stimulate and aid in the formation of habits making for health and character."

• The Girl Scouts of America, founded in 1912 by Juliette Gordon Low, was modeled after the British Girl Guides (established in 1909 by Agnes Baden-Powell, whose brother had founded the Boy Scouts). While camping has always been an important part of their training, Girl Scouts of the 90s are as likely to pitch tents in malls as in the great outdoors. (Scouts in New York City have been known to "hike" around the Empire State Building and camp out in the enclosed area of the observation deck. Hmm, hand me another one of those precooked wieners, please.)

• The 4-H Club (servicing boys and girls) has been around since the turn of the century. It started up in Minnesota as a produce contest at school fairs. It took off to embrace all types of farmwork and has branches around the world. The four *h*'s stand for head, heart, hands, and health. Members pledge: "My Head to clearer thinking, My Heart to greater loyalty, My Hands to larger service, and My Health to better living, for my club, my community, and my country."

Using Your Bean

"Jack and the Beanstalk" is one of those childhood tales that appears in just about every culture, from Icelandic to the Zulus, in some form or another. The most familiar version (thanks to Walt Disney and collections of nursery tales) has been traced to Teutonic origins from the Eddas (collections of early Scandinavian myths).

It relates the story of a child (representing humanity) who exchanges the family cow for magic beans. Dismayed by his lousy business sense, his mother throws the beans out the window. In the night, Jack discovers that one of the beans has sprouted a stalk through the clouds. He climbs the beanstalk and manages to outfox a giant and steal a magic harp, a hen that lays golden eggs, and the giant's bags full of gold coins.

The three treasures correspond to those of the All-Father (the giant) from the Eddas. They represent wind, rain, and the sun which, when "won" by Man's bravery, wit, and guile, are brought to earth to make everyone "wealthy."

A Happier Birthday

Robert Louis Stevenson (author of *Treasure Island, A Child's Garden of Verses*, and *Kidnapped*) gave his birthday away. The recipient was the young daughter of friends, who lamented the fact she'd been born on December 25. So, in 1891, Stevenson wrote up a formal proclamation that read in part, "In consideration that Miss Annie H. Ide...was born out of all reason upon Christmas Day, and therefore out of all justice denied the consolation and profit of a proper birthday; And considering that I have attained an age when, O, we never mention it, and that I have no further use for a birthday of any description...Have transferred...to the said Annie H. Ide, all and whole my rights and privileges in the thirteenth day of November, formerly my birthday, now hereby, and henceforth the birthday of the said Annie H. Ide to have, hold, exercise and enjoy in the customary manner, by the sporting of fine raiment, eating of rich meats, and receipt of gifts, compliments and copies of verse, according to the manner of our ancestors." Annie H. Ide celebrated her birthday on November 13 until she died at the age of 68.

GAME *Plans*

Board with Games

Perhaps the oldest existing game board, known as Nine Men's Morris (a kind of tic-tac-toe meets checkers), was found carved into the roof of an Egyptian temple which was built in 1400 B.C. Ancient Morris board games have turned up all over the globe, including in Viking ships from the 10th century.

In the 1800s, American children played a board game called Mansions of Happiness (one such set was subtitled "An Instructive Moral and Entertaining Amusement"), a kind of Chutes and Ladders approach to good behavior. Players spun a teetotum to advance around a board. If you had the good fortune of landing on a space marked, say, Honesty or Humility, you could move ahead. However, if you landed on Cruelty or Ingratitude, you could lose a turn or be forced to move backward. A player who arrived at the Summit of Dissipation had to go to Ruin. The winner arrived at the Mansion of Happiness first. (A far cry from *Tank Girl* or *Mortal Kombat.*)

Scratching your head at the word *teetotum*? Wondering what one is? Akin to dreidels and dice, a teetotum can be made with a small cube of six-sided cardboard and a toothpick through the middle. Write a number on each section and spin it.

Monopoly, one of the most successful board games of all time, was introduced by Charles B. Darrow of Germantown, Pennsylvania, in 1935 and patented by him on February 7, 1936. Darrow, an unemployed heating engineer, named the streets of his real estate game for the famous promenades of Atlantic City, where, it is said, he fantasized going but couldn't afford to. He based elements of his game on other games already on the market, but his, after a licensing deal with Parker Brothers, was the one that caught on. Quickly becoming a millionaire, Darrow enjoyed his time traveling and cultivating orchids.

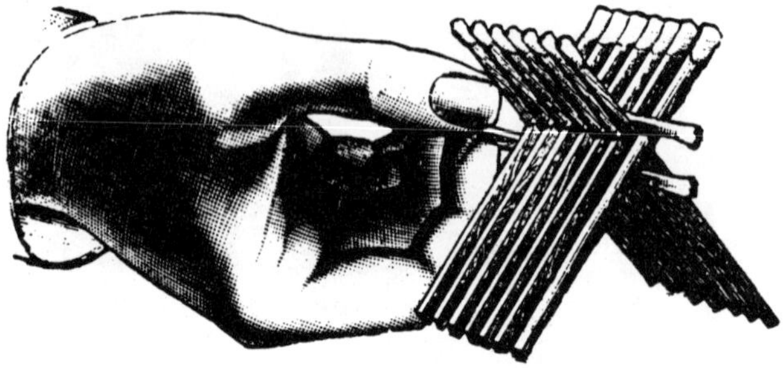

Parker Brothers claims to have sold over 100 million Monopoly sets worldwide since the 1930s, making it the best-selling copyrighted game ever. The game has been translated into 23 languages and marketed in dozens of countries. There are several editions; some of them still use the Atlantic City street names, while others are tailored to other famous cities. The money changes from country to country to mimic local currency. (The first game marketed by Parker Brothers in 1855, incidentally, was called Banking.)

The most-landed-on squares are Illinois Avenue, Go, B&O Railroad, Free Parking, Tennessee Avenue, New York Avenue, Reading Railroad, St. James Place, Water Works, and Pennsylvania Railroad.

Minding P's and Q's

Scrabble, the name of the ever-popular crossword game, means to paw or scratch with one's hands and/or feet. The game's originator, an out-of-work architect named Alfred Butts, first tried to market the game during the Depression as Lexico and then as Criss-Cross. In the 1940s, James Brunot got into the act, and, renamed Scrabble, the game became a success. Over one million games had been sold by 1953. Just about every language has its version and rules to accommodate spelling differences.

The hardest part of winning at Scrabble is learning to take advantage of your high-point tiles. Herewith a handy-dandy list of real words using high scoring *x*'s and *z*'s.

axel	**kazoo**	**toxin**
bazaar	**lexicon**	**tuxedo**
bazooka	**lox**	**vertex**
coxcomb	**lozenge**	**vixen**
cozen	**lynx**	**vizard**
dexter	**maxim**	**vizier**
fez	**nexus**	**waxy**
fizgig	**noxious**	**whiz**
flax	**pixie**	**wizen**
flex	**rex**	**xenon**
foxy	**sextet**	**xylem**
gazette	**texture**	

For those with killer instincts when it comes to lettered tiles, the highest-scoring words in Scrabble (depending upon their placement on the board) are: *quartzy, bezique, cazique, zinkify, quetzal, jazzily, quizzed, zephyrs, zincify*, and *zythums. Zax* (a tool for trimming roof slates) is the highest scoring three-letter word. And when the game is winding down and you still have that pesky *x*, look for an opening for xi (a Greek letter) and xu (Vietnamese money). The Scrabble dictionary gives them the thumbs up.

Such a Doll

Barbie was born in 1959 in southern California. She was created by the founders of Mattel Toys, Elliot and Ruth Handler, and named for their daughter. Jack Ryan, head of Mattel's research-and-development department, worked on some elements of the design of the doll and her accessories. Interestingly, Ryan also designed missiles.

Mattel issues some 20 million garments (give or take an ensemble) per year and introduces some 100 new outfits each year. Worldwide sales, in 1994, topped $1 billion a year, and Mattel estimates that there are 800 million Barbie dolls living among us. That's almost the population of India and doesn't include Skippers and Kens.

An amazing aside, given these numbers, is that Barbies are all hand-painted.

Games Dictionary

- Ouija boards get their name from a combination of the French and German words for "yes"—*oui* and *ja.*

- Mah-jongg is from a Chinese phrase meaning "a sparrow of 100 intelligences."

- The card game canasta is so named for the tray used to hold the cards in the discard pile. The word is Spanish for "basket."

- Baccarat (*baccara* is Italian for "zero") is thought to have originated in Italy in the late 15th century. It became immensely popular among French nobility. Indeed, the French spelling endures. While American gamblers tend to prefer blackjack (or "21"), baccarat found a niche in Havana, Cuba, in the 1950s.

- Roulette is French for "little wheel."

- Tarot cards derive from a medieval Italian word, *tarocchi*, meaning "playing cards."

- Pog, the disc game played by school children, is also known as "milk caps," which they resemble. Kids play for sport or for "keeps" by stacking the thin discs and then trying to knock over the stack with a "slammer," a slightly heftier disc made of cardboard, plastic, or metal. The discs that flip over become the booty of the player who slammed them. The game originated in Hawaii in 1992 and got its name from the abbreviation on the caps of a popular island juice containing passion fruit, orange, and guava.

Animated SHORTS

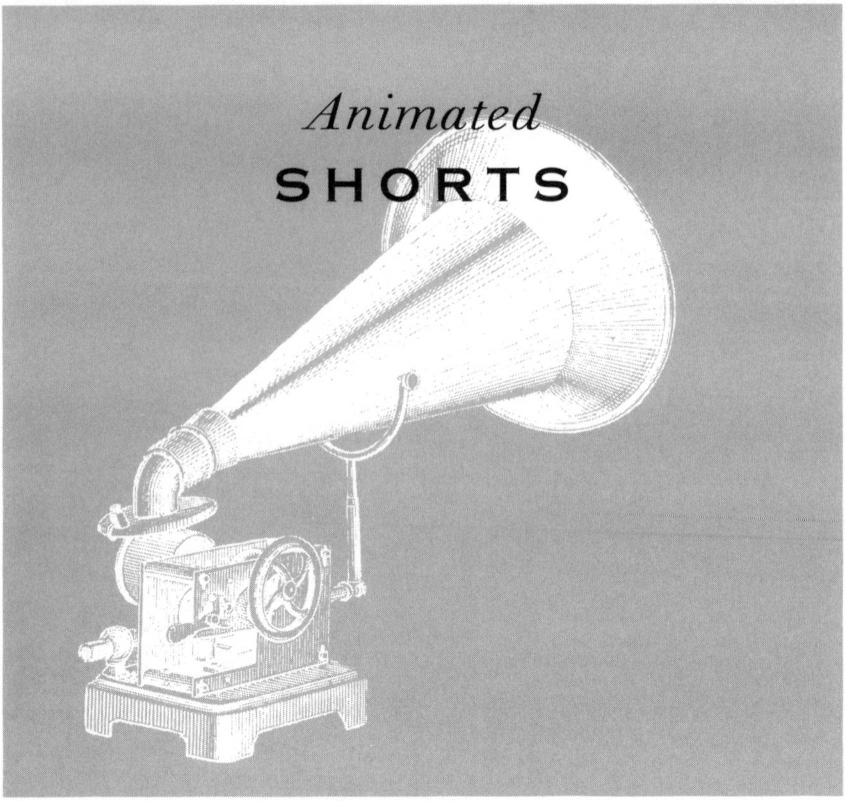

Disney's World

While most of us know that Robin Williams lent his voice to the fast-talking genie of Disney's *Aladdin*, how many are aware that Mike Douglas is the singing voice of Prince Charming in *Cinderella*? Disney's movies have featured many intriguing celebrities, some of whom were tapped for their mannerisms and features as well as their voices.

For example, the growly voice of Bagheera, the panther, in Disney's animated telling of *The Jungle Book* is Sebastian Cabot (who also narrated *The Sword in the Stone* and *Winnie the Pooh*). Phil Harris is the voice of Baloo, and Sterling Holloway, a Disney favorite, is Kaa. Louis Prima provided the voice for King Louie, the monkey king.

Basil Rathbone narrated *The Wind in the Willows*. In *Alice in Wonderland*, Ed Wynn is the voice of the Mad Hatter and Jerry Colonna does the March Hare. Maurice Chevalier, then in semiretirement, agreed to sing the title song for *The Aristocats* because, he said, he respected Walt Disney. Roger Miller is the singing narrator, based on Allan-a-Dale, in the animated version of *Robin Hood*, which also featured the whimsical deliveries of Peter Ustinov and Terry-Thomas.

In *Winnie the Pooh*, Paul Winchell is the bouncy Tigger, and Sterling Holloway is Pooh. Bob Newhart and Eva Gabor are the heroic mice Bernard and Bianca in *The Rescuers.* George C. Scott is the poacher McLeach in *The Rescuers Down Under*, and John Candy's voice is that of Wilbur the Albatross. Robby Benson is the grizzly-voiced Beast and Angela Lansbury singsongs Mrs. Potts in *Beauty and the Beast.*

Kurt Russell, a popular Disney actor in his youth, performs in *The Fox and the Hound* along with Pearl Bailey as the watchful owl. Buddy Hackett's unmistakable voice is Scuttle, the seagull, in *The Little Mermaid.* Matthew Broderick is the older Simba, Whoopi Goldberg is a snarling hyena, and Jeremy Irons a conniving lion named Scar to James Earl Jones's thundering Mufasa in *The Lion King.* Mel Gibson is the voice of John Smith in *Pocahantas.*

Leopold Stokowski conducted the Philadelphia Orchestra in *Fantasia*, and Deems Taylor, a radio personality associated with the Metropolitan Opera, narrated the animated classic.

And what of the flying elephant, Dumbo? Can you name the voice behind the pint-sized pachyderm? Gotcha! Dumbo never speaks.

Hearing Voices

In Steven Spielberg and Don Bluth's *An American Tail*, Dom DeLuise voices Tiger. Listen also for Madeline Kahn as an activist mouse. James Stewart's voice enters the character of Wylie Burp and John Cleese and Jon Lovit play, respectively, a villainous cat and spider in the sequel, *An American Tail: Fievel Goes West.* Phil Harris's voice can also be heard in Don Bluth's *Rock-a-Doodle*, along with Glen Campbell as Chanticleer. *Rock-a-Doodle* also taps the talents of Christopher Plummer, Sandy Duncan, Charles Nelson Reilly, and Ellen Greene.

Aside from his brilliantly daffy genie, Robin Williams is also the voice of Batty the bat in FAI Films' *FernGully*. In Hanna-Barbera's *Charlotte's Web*, Paul Lynde, Agnes Moorehead, and Henry Gibson's voices animate, respectively, Templeton, the Goose, and Wilbur. Debbie Reynolds plays Charlotte.

➳ Voice Lessons

Most fans of animation know that Don Adams of *Get Smart* fame provided the voice for Tennessee Tuxedo (and, more recently, Inspector Gadget) and that Jim Backus was the short-sighted Mr. Magoo. But there are some surprises lurking when you listen carefully to classic cartoons.

Garry Owens was Roger Ramjet and Jayce in *Space Ghost.*

Scatman Crothers was Hong Kong Phooey.

Aldo Ray was Musclemutt, and **Arte Johnson** was Rhubarb, in *The Houndcats.*

Harvey Korman was the Great Gazoo in *The Flintstones.*

Mickey Dolenz was Skip in *The Funky Phantom.*

Jodie Foster was Pugsley in *The Addams Family.*

Sally Struthers was teenage Pebbles in the *The Pebbles and Bamm-Bamm Show* and **Jay North** the teenage Bamm-Bamm.

Tim Matthieson was Samson in *Young Samson and Goliath* and was also Johnny Quest.

Carl Reiner played various characters in *Linus the Lion-hearted.*

Herschel Bernardi played assorted characters in *The Mighty Mouse Show.*

Agnes Moorehead was the Black Widow in *The Lone Ranger.*

Edward Everett Horton was the narrator of the "Fractured Fairy Tales" segment in *Rocky and His Friends,* and **William Conrad** was the narrator of the "Rocky and Bullwinkle" segments.

Wally Cox was Underdog.

Mark Hamill was Cory in the *I Dream of Jeannie* spin-off called *Jeannie.*

Casey Kasem, of Top 40 Countdown fame, played assorted characters in *Josie and the Pussycats, Josie and the Pussycats in Outer Space, The New Scooby Doo,* and *Hot Wheels.*

Classic Comments

Daws Butler, who was a well-known radio personality, was a Hanna-Barbera favorite. He was the voice of Jinks the Cat and Dixie the Mouse, Snagglepuss, Wally Gator, Peter Potamus, Uncle Waldo, Lippy the Lion, Yogi Bear (a voice he modeled after Art Carney's Ed Norton in *The Honeymooners*), Huckleberry Hound (the blue dog created to showcase Daws's great southern drawl), Augie Doggie, Elroy Jetson, Quick Draw McGraw, Baba Looey, and Snuffles (the orgiastic dog).

Daws Butler also voiced Reddy in the first major animated show for television, *Ruff-n-Reddy*, which premiered in 1957. Each show had a budget of $3,000, which inspired limited animation—less detail and repeated backdrops.

Don Messick was Ruff (and, later, Astro on *The Jetsons*). Like Butler, Messick was a seasoned pro from radio days.

Of his cartoon voices, Butler once said, "You don't think of them as voices, you think of them as characters. You do it physically—nothing changes. You're an actor, except that all they are getting is the voice." Butler died in 1988.

Perhaps one of the best-known voices in cartoondom belongs to Mel Blanc. His voice was used for every major Warner Brothers character except one. Can you name which? Blanc was not wascally wabbit hunter Elmer Fudd.

Mirror Images

Fans of more recent animated shows such as *The Simpsons* and *Animaniacs* are used to seeing names of celebrities roll by in the credits. While voice cameos satisfy the stars these days, there were entire cartoon shows developed around real folks like Bill Cosby and Muhammad Ali.

- The stand-up routines of Bill Cosby were brought to cartoon life in a show called *Fat Albert and the Cosby Kids*. Cosby lent his voice to many of the characters.

- *I'm the Greatest—The Adventures of Muhammad Ali* featured the voice of the champ.

- Bud Abbott played himself in a cartoon series called, cleverly, *Abbott and Costello.*

- While Jerry Lewis helped create the show and helped develop scripts based upon his comedic personae, he didn't do voice-overs for *Will the Real Jerry Lewis Please Stand Up?*

- Most of the cast of *Gilligan's Island* gathered in the studio to give authenticity to their animated selves in *The New Adventures of Gilligan.*

- There have been cartoon series based upon the Partridge Family (in A.D. 2200), *The Dukes of Hazzard*, Gary Coleman, the Beatles, the Osmonds, the Jackson Five, *Star Trek*, *Happy Days* (with Ron Howard and Henry Winkler doing voices), and the Harlem Globetrotters.

Little Town of Bedrock

The Flintstones, which premiered in 1960, is based on *The Honeymooners.* The creators thought about making the characters Pilgrims, then Native Americans, and finally Romans in togas before settling on prehistorians.

The original sponsors were Winston cigarettes and Miles Laboratories One-a-Day Vitamins. Hence, Flintstone vitamins. (There was no Betty vitamin supposedly because she was too hard to tell apart from Wilma—Dino took her place.)

Other Flintstone trivia:

- Pebbles was born in Rockapedic Hospital in February 1963. Fred was so excited, he took Dino to the hospital instead of Wilma.
- Wilma's maiden name was Slaghoople.
- The paper boy's name was Arnold.
- The piano was a Stoneway.
- They vacationed at Rockapulco.
- Ann-Margret gave her voice in a cameo role as Ann-Margrock, and Tony Curtis played Hollywood star Stony Curtis.
- Birds appear in many guises, from phonograph needles ("Watch it buster, I'm a precision instrument") to clothespins.

FILM *Clips*

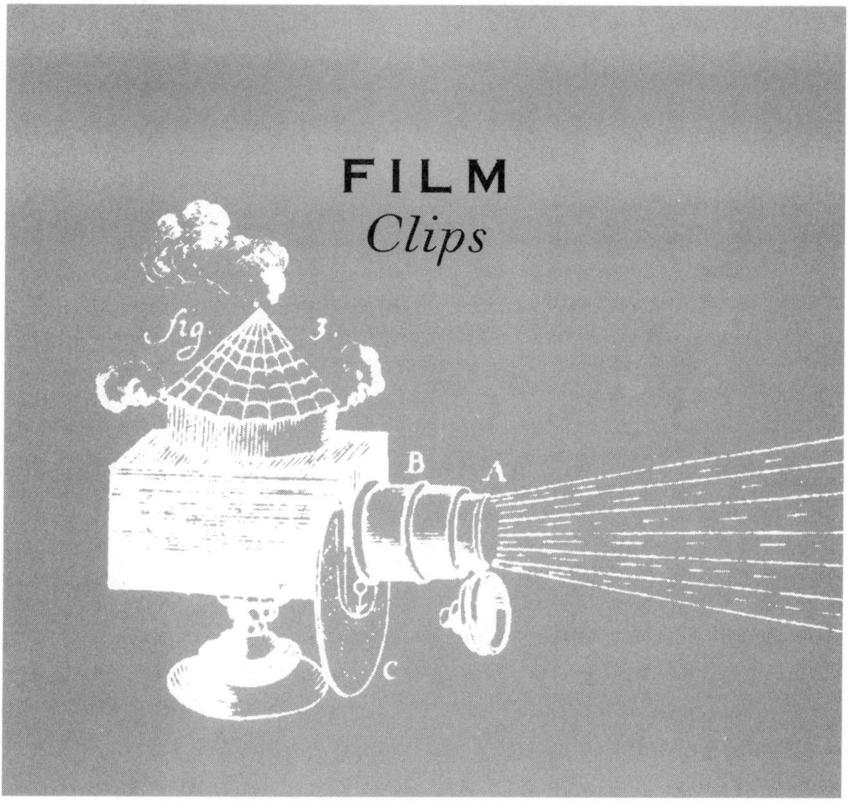

Picture This

The first time the principles of motion and still photography were blended was to settle a $25,000 bet. In 1872, California governor Leland Stanford enlisted Edward Muybridge to prove his theory that, when a horse is galloping, all four of its hooves are in the air at some point.

Muybridge set up 12 separate cameras alongside a track with strings set to trigger the shutters. A horse was galloped by, its hooves springing the shutters. The sequence captured the proof Stanford needed to win his bet.

The big winner, though, was Muybridge. He took his 12 shots of the horse and installed them inside a revolving wheel. Then, with the help of a light source in the form of a bright lantern, he could project the images and make the horse "gallop." His gizmo fascinated people, and he displayed his invention for years to come.

Quick Takes

- The first motion picture studio opened its doors on February 1, 1893, in the West Orange, New Jersey, laboratories of Thomas Edison. Filmstrips were seen through a Kinetoscope, a contraption devised by William Dickson, who worked for Edison.

- The first actual movie theater offered entertainment in the form of "peep shows." The brainchild of Edison opened in 1894 on Broadway in New York City. Customers paid five cents to watch a filmstrip of a weightlifter/gymnast or of Buffalo Bill Cody.

- In April 1896 at a music hall at Broadway and 34th Street (Herald Square), "Via the Vitascope" was the first film projected in the United States to paying customers. The first half showed the Leigh Sisters doing their famous umbrella dance and the second was simply waves crashing on a shore. Some audience members drew away from the film of the sea, afraid they'd get wet.

- "The Great Train Robbery," created by Edwin S. Porter (in charge of Edison Company Studios), was released in 1903. The first film made in America to incorporate a full plot, it also was the first to make dramatic use of close-ups. It ran 12 minutes.

- By 1915, over half of all American-made movies were being made in Hollywood. Aside from the weather and topography, the shift to California was, in part, to enable independent filmmakers to explore the new medium without being socked with a suit by Edison's lawyers. Edison held control of many filmmaking patents and didn't like competition.

Casting Around

Have you ever watched a movie and thought that a certain actor or actress was miscast in the role? Why Dustin Hoffman would have been much better, or Sean Connery! Or maybe you've read a best-seller and cast the parts in your mind, only to find out a year later that the star-making machinery in California has taken a completely different tack. Why and how particular actors or actresses get cast has always been a mysterious process, one that is peculiar to that "land of fruits and nuts."

Humphrey Bogart's films are usually considered, well, Humphrey Bogart's. Therefore, it's difficult to imagine that Ronald Reagan was under consideration to play Rick in *Casablanca.* (Ann Sheridan and Hedy Lamarr were at various stages slated to play Ilsa, eventually portrayed by Ingrid Bergman.) George Raft was first offered the part. Raft, immensely popular in the 30s, also turned down the role of Sam Spade in John Ford's *The Maltese Falcon.* Just a contract player

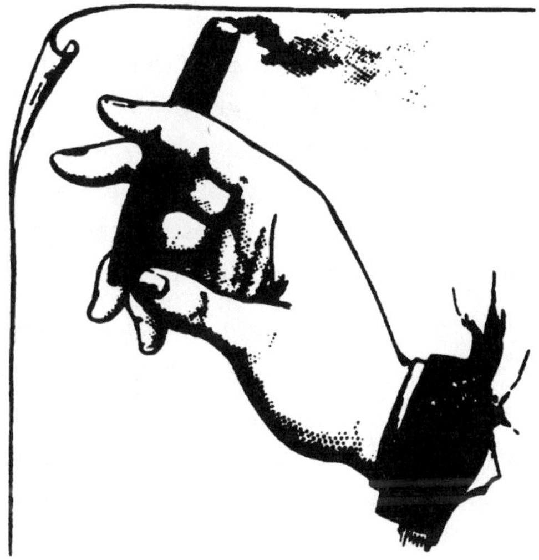

at the time, Bogart got the part. Bogart quickly picked up another Raft fumble, the choice role in *High Sierra.*

Now if that isn't scary enough, try to superimpose David Niven's face on Bogie's as the crusty captain of the *African Queen.* Bette Davis was to have played the role Kate Hepburn eventually won.

But Bogie didn't always get the big part. While Sean Connery and Michael Caine won critical acclaim in *The Man Who Would Be King,* John Huston had originally planned to have Bogart and Clark Gable play the wayward English soldiers in the 1950s. After Bogart's death,

Gable pulled out. There was a rumble that Robert Redford and Paul Newman would star, but neither liked the script. Huston had to wait until the early 1970s before he was able to get the financial backing and the appropriate actors to make his movie.

Ill health forced Bogart to decline the role of Colonel Bogie in *The Bridge over the River Kwai*, which went eventually to Alec Guinness. He also declined the Gary Cooper role in *The Fountainhead.*

Shirley MacLaine was set to star in the movie version of *Cabaret*, made from a Christopher Isherwood story and directed by Bob Fosse. But when the Fosse-directed *Sweet Charity*, starring MacLaine, bombed, Shirley dropped out of Fosse's next venture and the director went to his second choice, Liza Minnelli. Minnelli was a smash in the movie and won the 1972 Academy Award for Best Actress.

Reversal of Fortune, the Allan Dershowitz best-seller about his defense of Claus Von Bulow, was originally to star Woody Allen as the frizzy-haired Harvard law professor. When Allen was unavailable, the edgy Ron Silver inherited the role. Dershowitz, a player in the O. J. Simpson saga, crossed paths, and swords, with Woody Allen again when he represented Mia Farrow in the rancorous child custody battle.

From Here to Eternity, the 800-page opus about army life before Pearl Harbor, was a monumental best-seller for author James Jones. The 1953 movie, directed by Fred Zinnemann, who had just directed *High Noon*, and produced by Harry Cohn, seemed like a box office guarantee. Stars begged for roles, and the cast included Burt Lancaster, Deborah Kerr, Ernest Borgnine, Montgomery Clift, and Donna Reed. For the juicy role of Maggio, Zinnemann wanted Eli Wallach, and Cohn was all for using the actor then starring in *The Rose Tattoo* on Broadway.

At the same time, Cohn was being bombarded with telegrams and phone calls from Frank Sinatra, who was in Africa with his wife Ava Gardner, who was filming *Mogambo*. The crooner's career had taken a nosedive in the early 1950s. His records weren't selling; there were no Hollywood offers; his marriage seemed rocky. Suddenly, Wallach's agent upped his price and started making demands about when Wallach would shoot. It was then that Cohn called Sinatra and told Frank that if he paid his way to Hollywood and passed the screen test, the part was his. For $8,000. The movie was a tremendous success, garnering thirteen Oscar nominations and winning Sinatra an award for Best Supporting Actor.

Taking Up a Collection

Some of us collect rubber bands, and some of us, like Elizabeth Taylor, collect jewelry (from the 33-carat Krupp Diamond to historic pieces once belonging to the Duchess of Windsor). What else are the celebs drawn to?

- Stephen Sondheim collects antique games and puzzles.

- Publisher Robert Gottleib collects vintage plastic purses and published a book about his sideline.

- Truman Capote was exceedingly fond of paperweights, which he collected on his travels and from his friends.

- Upon his untimely death, Andy Warhol left many stunning collections, including a set of unusual cookie jars.

- Malcolm Forbes may have been the only person in the world, outside royalty, to be able to fancy and own Fabergé eggs.

- Sylvester Stallone, Madonna, Richard Gere, Jack Nicholson, and Steve Martin curate extraordinary collections of artwork.

- John Travolta maintains a hangar-full of planes, including a World War II Vampire fighter jet, which he pilots. (His son, incidentally, is named Jett.)

- Brad Pitt has admitted to a hankering for stained glass with a special interest in Tiffany windows.

- Motorcycles and cars old and new are the true love of Jay Leno.

- Rose Kennedy maintained a vast doll collection, a passion of Demi Moore's as well.

- Charlie Sheen has been known to bid small fortunes on developing his collection of baseball memorabilia.

• Madison Avenue has tapped Jerry Seinfeld's legendary affection for Porsches—to date, he owns eight. Arnold Schwarzenegger prefers Hummers and Hum-Vees (massive all-terrain vehicles).

• Betty Talmadge, a former first lady of Georgia, collects mementoes associated with *Gone with the Wind*, including the papier-mâché Tara used in the epic movie. Local historians believe the house in which she now resides, the Lovejoy Plantation, was the inspiration for Twelve Oaks, the Wilkes residence. Talmadge also owns Margaret Mitchell's maternal grandmama's home—a model for the original Tara. Fiddle-dee-dee!

Counting the Stars

Sure you can rattle off the seven dwarfs in Disney's animated classic *Snow White*? Betcha missed one! Sneezy, Dopey, Bashful, Grumpy, Sleepy, Doc, and Happy.

Can you name George Lucas's blockbuster trilogy (it's the middle three of a nine-part epic still in the works) and the years each movie was released? *Star Wars* (1977), *The Empire Strikes Back* (1980), and *Return of the Jedi* (1983).

Can you name the actors who appeared in the 1960 classic as the magnificent seven? Yul Brynner (Chris), Steve McQueen (Vin), Horst Buchholz (Chico), Charles Bronson (O'Reilly), Robert Vaughn (Lee), James Coburn (Britt), and Brad Dexter (Harry). Not to be confused with the 1967 epic *The Dirty Dozen*, which starred Charles Bronson, Jim Brown, Ben Carruthers, John Cassavetes, Stuart Cooper, Richard Jaeckel, Trini Lopez, Colin Maitland, Lee Marvin, Robert Phillips, Donald Sutherland, and Clint Walker.

Switching over to the smaller screen, can you name the kids from *Eight is Enough*? David, Elizabeth, Joannie, Mary, Nancy, Nicholas, Susan, and Tommy.

Can you name the children who made up *The Brady Bunch*? Craig, Marcia, Peter, Jan, Bobby, and Cindy.

How about the Douglas boys on *My Three Sons*? Mike (Tim Considine), Robbie (Don Grady), and Chip (Stanley Livingston). Ernie, played by Barry Livingston, was adopted by Steve Douglas and moved in after Mike married and moved on to greener faraway pastures.

Hollywood Babble On

"Hollywood: They only know one word of more than one syllable there, and that is *fillum*."
—Louis Sherwin

"What I like about Hollywood is that one can get along by knowing two words of English—*swell* and *lousy*."
—Vicki Baum

"There'll always be an England, even if it's in Hollywood."
—Bob Hope

"In Hollywood, brides keep the bouquet and throw away the groom."
—Groucho Marx

"Hollywood's a place where they'll pay you a thousand dollars for a kiss and fifty cents for your soul."
—Marilyn Monroe

"Hollywood is like Picasso's bathroom."
—Candice Bergen

"Hollywood is a carnival where there are no concessions."
—Wilson Mizner

"Over in Hollywood they almost made a great picture, but they caught it in time."
—Wilson Mizner

"Hollywood is loneliness beside the swimming pool."
—Liv Ullman

"Hollywood is full of genius. And all it lacks is talent."
—Henri Bernstein

"The only 'ism' Hollywood believes in is plagiarism."
—Dorothy Parker

"The only way to be a success here is to be as obnoxious as the next guy."
—Sylvester Stallone

"Hollywood is an extraordinary kind of temporary place."
—John Schlesinger

"Hollywood grew to be the most flourishing factory of popular mythology since the Greeks."
—Alistair Cooke

"No one has a closest friend in Hollywood."
—Sheila Graham

"Strip away the phony tinsel of Hollywood and you'll find the real tinsel underneath."
—Oscar Levant

"In Hollywood, the women are all peaches. It makes one long for an apple occasionally."
—Somerset Maugham

"It was one of history's great love stories, the mutually profitable romance which Hollywood and bohunk America conducted almost in the dark, a tapping of fervent messages through the wall of the San Gabriel Range."

—John Updike

"Hollywood was born schizophrenic. For 75 years, it has been both a town and a state of mind, an industry and an art form."

—Richard Corliss

"All Hollywood corrupts; and absolute Hollywood corrupts absolutely."

—Edmund Wilson

"Hollywood is a dreary industrial town controlled by hoodlums of enormous wealth, the ethical sense of a pack of jackals, and taste so degraded that it befouled everything it touched."

—S. J. Perelman

"Hollywood is a place where they place you under contract instead of under observation."

—Walter Winchell

"The Hollywood tradition I like best is called 'sucking up to the stars.'"

—Johnny Carson

"'Hello,' he lied."

—Don Carpenter quoting a Hollywood producer

"An associate producer is the only guy in Hollywood who will associate with a producer."

—Fred Allen

"You can take all the sincerity in Hollywood, place it in the navel of a fruit fly, and still have room enough for three caraway seeds and a producer's heart."

—Fred Allen

"I believe that God felt sorry for actors so he created Hollywood to give them a place in the sun and a swimming pool. The price they had to pay was to surrender their talent."

—Cedric Hardwicke

"In Hollywood a marriage is a success if it outlasts milk."

—Rita Rudner

"You can't find any true closeness in Hollywood because everybody does the fake closeness so well."

—Carrie Fisher

"The people are unreal. The flowers are unreal, they don't smell. The fruit is unreal, it doesn't taste of anything. The whole place is a glaring, gaudy, nightmarish set, built up in the desert."

—Ethel Barrymore

FOOD *for* THOUGHT

➤ Love Food

The ancients believed that twigs of rue and rosemary held under one's nose would ward off the plague. Optimists, in a way, it's not surprising they also empowered certain foods with the ability to rejuvenate flagging sexual powers. Some treats were, and still are, believed to out-and-out seduce.

On the list of aphrodisiacs: oysters, snails, ginseng, truffles, sweetbreads, strawberries, bull testicles, rhino horns, eels, chocolate, and wild boar. Of course, for some, it's a bag of corn chips and a cold beer. "Chacun à son goût."

➤ Popcorn, Peanuts, and a Prize

Cracker Jack, that crunchy combination of caramelized popcorn, peanuts, and a prize, is over 100 years old. It was introduced at the

1893 World's Columbian Exposition in Chicago. It got its name from a popular expression for something really spiffy.

The trademark toy surprises didn't always come in the box. Before 1912, toy prizes were only featured occasionally. In 1910, the company printed coupons on the back of the box that could be collected and redeemed through special catalogues.

More than 17 billion toys have been given away since 1912. Some prizes have become collectible and a few quite valuable. A 1915 Joe Jackson baseball card, for example, is estimated to be worth over $7,000.

A favorite was the lenticulars, little pictures that are one image when held one way and another image when tilted.

➤ World's Fair Fare

Although ice cream can be traced back centuries to China, the cone is generally considered to be a 20th-century invention. The story goes (although some of the particulars will be disputed forever) that at the 1904 World's Fair (a.k.a. the St. Louis Louisiana Purchase Exposition), two vendors worked side by side. One was selling ice cream in dishes, and one was pushing Persian waffles called zalabias. When the ice-cream vendor ran out of cups (it was unseasonably hot), he rolled one of his neighbor's waffles into a cone. Voilà. It was called the World's Fair Cornucopia and was an instant success. The term *ice-cream cone* didn't enter the language until 1909, however.

A footnote to history is that a New Yorker, Italo Marchiony, with a pushcart in Little Italy sold ices in paper cups and pastry cones. This cool-headed entrepreneur actually secured a patent for his creation just before the World's Fair opened but, alas, never marketed his invention of the pastry cone.

World's Fairs also account for the introduction or invention of such tasty treats as iced tea (thank you, Richard Blechynden) and Welch's grape juice (developed by Dr. Thomas Bremwell Welch as an unfermented "wine" for churches), which made its debut at the 1893 Chicago World's Fair. The bun for the Coney Island "dachshund sausage" was introduced at the 1904 St. Louis World's Fair also.

Some Gum Fun

When Mexico's General Antonio López de Santa Anna, after his defeat at the hands of Sam Houston's army, went into exile in the United States, he introduced his habit of chewing chicle (dried sap from the sapodillo tree first enjoyed by ancient Aztecs) to Staten Islander Thomas Adams.

Adams, a photographer and inventor by trade, created "Adams's New York Gum—Snapping and Stretching" and first sold it in a drugstore in Hoboken, New Jersey. One of his sons, acting as his traveling salesman, sold it on the road.

Adams added licorice flavoring and created Black Jack, the oldest living gum in America. Wrigley soon followed suit with his own flavors: Wrigley's Spearmint and Juicy Fruit (these two recently celebrated their 100th anniversaries).

Use Your Noodle

The Inuits do indeed have hundreds of words for snow and ice, but Italians boast just as many words to describe variations of noodles.

Consider the poetry of pasta with capelli d'angelo ("angel hair"), cappelletti ("little hat"), conchiglie ("conch shell"), farfalle ("butterflies"), fusilli ("fuses"), gemelli ("twins"), linguine ("little tongues"), mostaccioli ("mustaches"), rotelle ("wheels"), spaghetti ("strings"), strozzapreti ("strangled priests"), and vermicelli ("little worms").

Okay, some are a bit more appetizing than others but they are all colorful.

That's a Spicy Meatball

Wilbur Scoville was a pharmacologist with Parke-Davis in 1912 when he began studying the properties of capsaicin, the active ingredient in chile pepper. Capsaicin was being used in a muscle salve called HEET, and Scoville was looking for a way to more accurately assess the amount of heat generated by different types of peppers.

Scoville developed what became called the Scoville-oranoleptic test. An exact measurement of pepper was placed in a solution of alcohol, diluted with sugar water. This concoction was then sampled by five human testers. Heat was measured in multiples of 100 Scoville units, and three testers had to agree on just how fiery the particular solution was. This largely subjective test has today been replaced by a more sophisticated high-tech version, but Scoville units are still official measures of chile heat. Now that salsa has replaced ketchup as the most popular condiment in the U.S., the following scale may be useful to those with and without asbestos tongues:

Rating	**Approximate Scoville Units**	**Type of Chile**
0	0	Mild Bells, Sweet Banana, Pimento
1	100–500	Mexi-Bells, Cherry
2	500–1,000	New Mexico, Anaheim, Big Jim
3	1,000–1,500	Ancho, Pasilla, Espanola
4	1,500–2,500	Sandia, Cascabel
5	2,500–5,000	Jalapeño, Mirasol
6	5,000–15,000	Yellow Wax, Serrano
7	15,000–30,000	Chile de Arbol
8	30,000–50,000	Aji, Cayenne, Tabasco, Piquin, Rocoto
9	50,000–100,000	Santaka, Chiltepin, Thai
10	100,000–300,000	Habenero, Scotch Bonnet

If you happen to dip into salsa that registers too high in Scoville units, remember this tip from House of Fire, a spicy little retail shop in Boulder, Colorado. Milk is superior to beer or any other foodstuff in restoring your mouth to something approximating its normal conditions.

➤ Getting Sauced

Don't be a sauce wimp! ("Okay, I'll try it, but could you please put it on the side?") Go ahead and get sauced!

béarnaise—a creamy sauce of egg yolks, butter, shallots, vinegar, wine, and tarragon

béchamel—a mild-tasting white sauce (named for its inventor, Louis de Béchamel, a steward of Louis XIV)

bordelaise—a rich sauce of wine, brown stock, bone marrow, shallots, and parsley

choron—béarnaise with tomato purée added, giving it a pinkish color (named for the chef who first served it)

colbert—another member of Louis XIV's court, Colbert, came up with this blend of meat drippings, butter, shallots, wine, lemon juice, and tarragon

cumberland—a blend of red currant jelly, port, citrus rind, mustard, and seasoning

figaro—hollandaise mixed with tomato purée and parsley

hollandaise—a rich, velvety mix of butter, egg yolk, and lemon juice

mornay—béchamel with cheese mixed in along with, on occasion, egg yolk or cream

mousseline—any basic white sauce with whipped cream added

périgueux—named for the city in France famed for its truffles, this brown sauce includes Madeira and truffles

rémoulade—mayonnaise with mustard, anchovies, capers, and seasonings as well as the occasional minced gherkin

velouté—a basic white sauce made with chicken or veal stock, with many variations

Little Bites

- There are no fewer than four varieties of sauerkraut juice on the market in the United States.

- Catsup was originally a patent medicine.

- Seltzer is named for the natural springs of Seltzer, Germany.

- Life Savers were invented by the poet Hart Crane's father, Clarence.

- The first paper straw, rolled from manila paper coated with paraffin, was patented in 1888 by Marvin Chester Stone of Washington, D.C. Straws were hand-rolled until Stone invented a successful straw-making machine in 1905.

- Need to ripen some fruit in a hurry? Stick a moldy lemon in a paper bag with the unripe fruit. The green mold on a lemon gives off ethylene, a gas that speeds up the process.

- Other than cows, people around the world collect and consume milk from buffalo, camels, ewes, goats, mares, reindeer, yaks, and zebras.

- Military downsizing can have unexpected benefits. Consider the age-old problem of keeping pizza warm. Pizza Hut uses heat-retaining mesh in a plate that keeps pizza toasty for more than 90 minutes. The mesh was originally designed as a defense against laser attacks as part of the "star wars" program.

- Hormel, the company that, uh, manufactures Spam, recently issued a Spamwear catalogue featuring items such as boxer shorts emblazoned with Spam (the word, not the, uh, product).

- An ancient Tibetan tradition is to sculpt offerings (called "Chupas") to Buddha during festivals that take place every January. The works are made of colored butter.

• Somerset Maugham is credited with bringing avocados to France. A great fan, he brought several to his home in Cap Ferrat by hiding them from customs in his golf bag. He had seven avocado trees in the gardens around his villa. Avocados, incidentally, get their name from the Nahuatl (an Aztec language) word for "testicle."

• We have Alexander the Great to thank for bringing apricots back to Greece from Asia, where they still grow wild. The Romans, in turn, planted pits in Italy. Henry VIII imported Italian apricot trees to England so his royal gardens would have every kind of fruit tree known across Europe.

• The ten best-selling grocery store items in the United States, according to a recent study, are: Marlboro cigarettes, Coke Classic, Pepsi, Kraft cheese products, Diet Coke, Tide, Campbell's soups, Folger's coffee, Winston cigarettes, and Tropicana juice. And some say Americans aren't concerned about nutrition. Ha!

Cream of the Crop

Like society, the world of food lends itself to hierarchical rankings. Ever wonder, for example, why the labels on cans and bottles of olives use such monstrous-sounding descriptions with regard to size? What

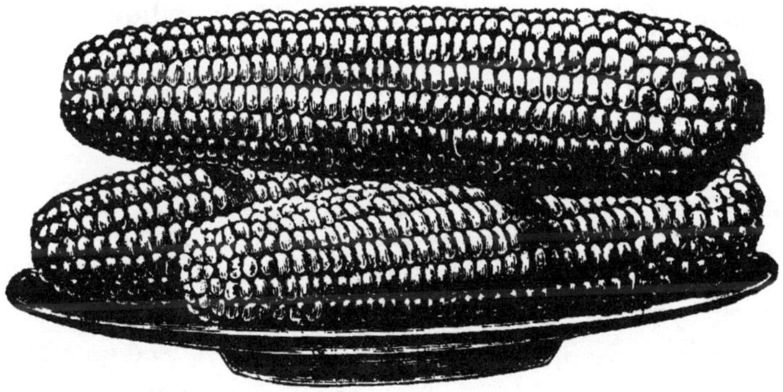

happens to wee, petite, or even average-sized ones? According to the California Olive Growers guidelines, olives are rated:

Small = *128–140 per pound*

Medium = *106–121 per pound*

Large = *91–105 per pound*

Extra Large = *65–88 per pound*

Jumbo = *51–60 per pound*

Colossal = *41–50 per pound*

Super Colossal = *26–40 per pound*

If you ever find a one-pound olive, call the *National Enquirer* Agricultural Oddities Editor.

The U.S. Department of Agriculture rates meat according to quality, value, cut, and grade. Most cuts of meat are stamped with their USDA ranking. From the highest to the lowest, they are graded USDA Prime, USDA Choice, USDA Good, USDA Standard, USDA Commercial, and USDA Utility.

Eggs graded and sized as Medium (one dozen must weigh 21 ounces), Large (24 ounces), and Extra Large (27 ounces) can be found in supermarkets. Grade AA means the eggs are designated "general purpose." Such eggs have thick whites and firm yolks and are virtually free of defects. Grade A may have a defect or two, while Grade B eggs, usually not sold retail, are fine for cooking, baking, lawn games, and political rallies.

➤ All-American Name Game

• *Barbecue* is an adaptation of the American-Spanish word *barbacoa* borrowed, in turn, from the Bahamas. Washington Irving used the word in 1809 to mean an open-air picnic with foods cooked on a grill. When you cross the Mason-Dixon line, you also cross a barbecue line. It's an art form in the South, and BBQ fans travel great distances for the best-tasting beef or pork, chopped or pulled, ribs or sandwich, mild or spicy.

- The Dagwood, a heaping sandwich, is named for Blondie's husband in the ever-popular comic strip.

- A Shirley Temple is a child-safe "cocktail," in honor of the child star.

- Hush puppies, according to southern lore, were invented by a cook who would drop spoonfuls of cornbread batter into hot fat, and then toss the fried tidbits to quiet the family dogs. It's tough to bark with your mouth full. Hush, you puppies, hear?

- Chess pie, a southern custardy classic, is said to have been created by another enterprising cook. When it came time to prepare dessert, the only ingredients she had on hand were sugar, eggs, butter, and lemon juice. Undaunted, she whipped them together and baked the mixture in a pie shell. When her pie was admired by family and friends, they wanted to know what kind of pie it was. "I don't know," she replied. "It's jes' pie."

- The ubiquitous Caesar salad was not named for Julius, but after an Italian-American restaurateur named Caesar Cardini. He created the salad in 1924 for his restaurant in Tijuana. His original version called for romaine lettuce, garlic, olive oil, Parmesan cheese, croutons, Worcestershire sauce, and a coddled egg. Anchovies snuck in there after the fact.

- Of chicken à la king, two separate restaurants claim to have created this dish to honor Mr. J. R. Keene, whose horse won the 1881 Grand Prix. Claridge's of London credits their chef, while Delmonico's of New York insists it was their legendary chef, George Ranhofer, who invented it. Whether fit for a Keene or a King, the dish of chicken, sherry, and cream is a banquet classic.

- There are also two stories about the beginnings of Sally Lunn, a traditional American sweet bread, and neither originates on these shores. Sally Lunn, according to one version, was an 18th-century Englishwoman who sold the sweet buns from her basket. The French claim the bread was sold in Paris by vendors who called it *sol et lune* ("sun and moon"), a reference to the golden top of the bun (the sun) and the lighter, almost white bottom (the moon). Brought to this country by French immigrants, it was Americanized to Sally Lunn.

International Cuisine

- Medieval cooks in Hamburg, Germany, prepared a dish of highly seasoned raw meat and named it for the Tartars, known for their ferocity in battle and preference for uncooked meat. (Eventually another Hamburg chef had the bright idea of shaping the mixture into patties and actually cooking it, thus creating the first hamburger.) Tartar sauce is a mayonnaise mixed with diced pickles, onions, capers, herbs, and lemon juice—ingredients often used to season steak tartare.

- Schillerlocken is a dish of smoked fish arranged in curls in honor of the curly head of hair belonging to Johann von Schiller (1759–1805). Schiller, one of the great names of modern German letters, wrote the "Ode to Joy" used by Beethoven in his Ninth Symphony.

- Legend has it that the sandwich owes its existence to a lecherous 18th-century Englishman, John Montagu, the fourth Earl of Sandwich. Reluctant to leave the gaming table for a meal, he ordered his servant to bring him roast beef layered between two slices of bread. Did he have a winning hand that day? Perhaps not his cards, but his handheld sandwich certainly was.

- Yes, there really was an Earl Grey. He was a 19th-century English statesman who had tea specially blended for him by the George Charlton tea shop. In 1836, he gave permission for the tea to be sold to the public. Robert Jackson & Company eventually bought the rights to the secret formula.

- *Duxelle* is not a French word for a kind of mushroom. It is, in fact, a sauce made from puréed mushrooms and onions, and was created by the incomparable 17th-century French chef François Pierre de la Varenne. His original name for the dish was *champignons à l'Olivier*, but it was eventually renamed to honor his employer, the Marquis d'Uxelles.

- According to pretzel lore, the shape of a pretzel was developed by monks in Italy and France in roughly the eighth century. The ends of dough left over from making bread were rolled and folded into the shape of arms in prayer. Pretzels were awarded to the diligent children who remembered their prayers.

• Melba toast and peach Melba were named for the 19th-century Australian opera star Helen Porter Mitchell, who adapted her stage name, Nellie Melba, from her hometown of Melbourne. When battling a chronic weight-gain problem, she limited herself to thin slices of dry toast. When not dieting, she enjoyed a dessert of peaches, ice cream, and raspberry sauce created in her honor by Escoffier.

• You may be unaware of how many Japanese culinary terms you already know. For example: bata, beikon, bifuteki, chiizu, hamu, pikunikku, remon, sarada. Can you venture a guess? That's right: butter, bacon, beef steak, cheese, ham, picnic, lemon, and salad. Now, if you find yourself in Japan without a single dictionary or English speaker around, you won't starve.

Tasty Morsels

"The food here is so tasteless you could eat a meal of it and belch and it wouldn't remind you of anything."

—Redd Foxx

"As for butter versus margarine, I trust cows more than chemists."

—Joan Gussow

"I did not say this meat was tough. I just said I didn't see the horse that usually stands outside."

—W. C. Fields

"I have known many meat eaters to be far more non-violent than vegetarians."

—Mohandas Gandhi

"I simply cannot imagine why anyone would eat something slimy served in an ashtray."

—Henry Beard

"Be content to remember that those who can make omelettes properly can do nothing else."

—Hilaire Belloc

"Cucumber should be well-sliced, and dressed with pepper and vinegar, and then thrown out, as good for nothing."
—Samuel Johnson

"Artichokes...are just plain annoying. After all the trouble you go to, you get about as much actual 'food' out of eating an artichoke as you

would from licking thirty or forty postage stamps. Have the shrimp cocktail instead."
—Miss Piggy

"Cheese—milk's leap toward immortality."
—Clifton Fadiman

"Most vegetarians I ever see looked enough like their food to be classed as cannibals."
—Finley Peter Dunne

"I believe that if I ever had to practice cannibalism, I might be able to manage it if there were enough tarragon around."
—James Beard

"If I can't have too many truffles, I'll do without truffles."

—Colette

"Seeing is deceiving. It's eating that's believing."

—James Thurber

"Canapés—a sandwich cut into twenty-four pieces."

—Billy Rose

"Licorice is the liver of candy."

—Michael O'Donoghue

"The truth is that any dish that tastes good with capers in it tastes even better with capers not in it."

—Nora Ephron

"Peanut butter [is] the pâté of childhood."

—Florence Fabricant

"As life's pleasures go, food is second only to sex. Except for salami and eggs. Now that's better than sex, but only if the salami is thickly sliced."

—Alan King

"The most remarkable thing about my mother is that for thirty years she served the family nothing but leftovers. The original meal has never been found."

—Calvin Trillin

"Working solely from the evidence of what's presented to someone who orders Surf 'n' Turf in an American restaurant—a slab of red meat and a shellfish claw—I deduced that a surfnturf might be a tiny aquatic Hereford."

—Calvin Trillin

"No man is lonely while eating spaghetti."

—Robert Morley

"To eat is human. To digest divine."

—Mark Twain

"Never eat more than you can lift."

—Miss Piggy

Do You MENU?

Taco, bagel, wonton, and croissant have entered the gastronomic mainstream. They even appear on Plexiglas menus at the local fast-food drive-through. But who hasn't been stumped by unfamiliar phrases? As long as you're sitting here, commit some of these to memory so you'll never again order blood sausage in grapefruit purée with pink peppercorns à la mode.

Dining French

Most of us picked up the French we know from Pepe LePew. The problem is, no matter how accomplished your imitation of Inspector Clouseau, you still need to memorize some French so you won't end up having Parisian waiters fall over laughing when you order "une hamberguerre et une mewlkshayk" or, worse, lamb's teeth with duct tape.

agneau—lamb (gigot is leg of lamb)

apéritif—a beverage, usually alcoholic, enjoyed before a meal to engage one's appetite

baguette—a long loaf of bread with a crispy crust and chewy middle

beurre—butter

canard—duck

champignon—mushroom

coq au vin—chicken and wine stew

coquilles—shells or scallops

croque monsieur—a ham-and-cheese sandwich dipped in egg batter and grilled in butter (add a fried egg for croque madame)

epinard—spinach

fraise—strawberry

fromage—cheese

fruits de mer—a combination of seafood

gâteau—cake

haricots verts—string beans

jambon—ham

lardons—bits of cooked bacon

niçoise—in the style of Nice, prepared with olives, tomatoes, anchovies, and garlic

oeuf—egg

pâte—paste or pasta (pâté is the seasoned ground meat)

petit pois—little green peas

poisson—fish

pomme—apple

pomme de terre—potato

poulet—young chicken (poussin is very young chicken)

ris—sweetbreads

vol-au-vent—"flying in the wind," a puff pastry laid atop a filling of cream sauce and some kind of meat and vegetables

Dining Italian

A bowl of spaghetti certainly has a place, but it may be time to branch out, take a chance, and *mangia bene.*

al dente—"to the tooth," a method of cooking pasta so it offers a little resistance when bitten

antipasto—"before the pasta," a plate of hors d'oeuvres typically including sliced meats, cheeses, and olives (it may be served cold or hot)

cacciatore—prepared "hunter" style with tomatoes, onions, and mushrooms

calamari—squid

calzone—a kind of stuffed pizza that looks like a turnover

cannoli—a dessert of a tube-shaped crunchy pastry shell filled with creamy, sweet ricotta cheese

fagiolo—any bean, but usually refers to white kidney beans

focaccia—round, flat bread flavored with olive oil and spices and occasionally tomatoes, olives, rosemary, and onion

formaggio—cheese

gelato—ice cream

insalata—salad

mascarpone—buttery, rich, creamy cheese

mortadella—smoked sausage akin to bologna

pancetta—cured, unsmoked Italian bacon

parmigiana—with Parmesan cheese

pesto—a green sauce made from fresh basil, olive oil, garlic, pine nuts, and grated Parmesan cheese

polenta—cornmeal mush served a variety of ways

primavera—"spring style," with fresh vegetables

risotto—a flavorful creamy rice dish

scungilli—whelk or large sea snail

zabaglione—a custardlike dessert made from egg yolks, wine, and sugar ("sabayon" in France)

zuppa—soup

Dining Kosher

Pastrami on rye and the ubiquitous bagel have become all-American staples. But why not sample slightly more exotic fare the next time you find yourself at a deli or dairy restaurant?

bialy—a cousin to the bagel, a roll flavored with minced bits of sautéed onions

blintz—a thin pancake with a filling of fruit and/or ricotta cheese, sautéed and served with sour cream

challah—traditional yeast bread made with lots of eggs

hamantaschen—triangular-shaped cookies with poppy seed, apricot, or prune filling traditionally served at Purim

knaidel—akin to a matzoh ball, a dumpling made of matzoh meal, eggs, and seasoning

knish—a yeast crust with either a mashed potato, sweet potato, ground meat, and groats or cheese filling

kosher—food that conforms to strict Jewish laws, from the Hebrew word for "proper" or "pure"

kreplach—noodle dumplings filled with ground meat or cheese

kugel—a noodle or potato pudding

latke—a fried potato pancake associated with Hanukkah

matzoh—thin, unleavened bread of water and flour resembling a cracker served during Passover. (A matzoh ball, traditionally served in chicken broth, is made from matzoh meal, water, eggs, and shortening.)

tzimmes—a sweet casserole traditionally served on Rosh Hashana, made from some combination of prunes, apricots, sweet potatoes, carrots, and apples

Dining Southern

Cajun, Creole, Soul, and plain old home-style have become very chic. Herewith a road map as you embark on your gastronomic travels south.

andouille—spicy, smoked pork sausage

beignet—dough fritter sprinkled with confectioners' sugar

blackened—preparing meat or fish by dredging a fillet with crushed peppercorns and searing it quickly over intensely high heat

burgoo—thick stew of several types of meat and vegetables

cayenne—orange-red spicy powder made from chili peppers

chitterlings (chitlins)—small intestine of pigs (or other animal) simmered until tender (sometimes batter-dipped) and fried

collards—vitamin-rich greens with a taste similar to cabbage mixed with kale

crawdads—variety of crayfish or crawfish, they look like mini-lobsters (langoustine)

cush—cornmeal pancake that may be fried, or a cornmeal soup

dirty rice—Cajun dish of rice mixed with ground chicken livers and bacon drippings, onions, stock, garlic, and minced bell peppers

grillade—Creole dish of bits of fried beef mixed into a stew with tomatoes and vegetables

grits—usually a bland-tasting cooked mush of hominy (similar to groats and kasha)

hoppin' John—stew of black-eyed peas cooked with salt pork and seasonings, usually served on rice

hush puppies—deep-fried cornmeal dumplings with seasonings

jambalaya—Creole dish of cooked rice and a combination of ingredients including tomatoes, onions, bell peppers, meat, poultry, sausage, or shellfish

muffaletta—variation on a sub, grinder, or hoagie

potliquor (potlicker)—vitamin-rich broth left in the pot after cooking vegetables or meat, served alone or over cornbread

redeye gravy—thick gravy made from ham drippings and, occasionally, flavored with hot coffee

tasso—slow-cooked cured pork used to flavor other Cajun dishes

☛ Dining Mexican or Spanish

We're not talking Taco Bell here. The regional cuisines of Spain and Mexico offer a tantalizing variety of dishes, many of which do *not* come on a combo platter.

albóndiga—spicy Mexican meatballs

arroz—rice

bunuelo—crisp pastry dusted with cinnamon sugar

burrito—flour tortilla wrapped around a filling of some combination of stewed meat, refried beans, shredded cheese, sour cream, and guacamole

chalupa—"small boat," a boat-shaped fried tortilla with a filling

chiles rellenos—batter-dipped, deep-fried cheese-stuffed peppers

chimichanga—deep-fried burrito

chorizo—savory pork sausage

empanada—a turnover with a pastry crust and a seasoned meat and vegetable filling

enchilada—soft corn tortilla with a filling of meat, cheese, or vegetables usually served with a topping of salsa and cheese

fajita—marinated and grilled strips of meat in a tortilla

flauta—"flute," a deep-fried corn tortilla with a filling

frijoles (refritos)—beans

guacamole—dip made from mashed avocados, garlic, lemon juice, and minced tomatoes or salsa

jalapeño—a hot green chili pepper, named for Jalapa, Mexico

jicama—root vegetable similar to a potato

quesadilla—kind of tortilla "pizza"

paella—Spanish dish of saffron rice and a savory stew made from a mixture of vegetables, tomatoes, garlic, shellfish, meats, and sausage

picadillo—dish or filling of ground meat (pork and beef, usually), tomatoes, onions, and garlic

pollo—chicken

queso—cheese

taco—crispy corn tortilla filled with some combination of ground meat, shredded lettuce and cheese, tomatoes, salsa, and guacamole

tamale—meat and vegetable filling rolled in dough and cooked in a corn husk (also filled with fruit as a dessert)

tapas—variety of savory appetizers

tortilla—unleavened "bread" patted flat like a pancake (In Spain, *tortilla* usually refers to a type of omelette.)

tostada—flat, crisp tortilla with various toppings

Dining Indian

Dipping tandoori-baked bread hot from the oven into spicy aromatic curries and condiments is a rare treat. Don't limit yourselves to single dishes—go with a group and share.

chapati—unleavened bread made of flour and water

chutney—spicy condiment of fruits, vinegar, spices, and sugar

curry—generic term for a spicy, savory East Indian dish incorporating curry powder (a powdery blend of many spices)

dal—spicy dish of lentils or mung beans, tomatoes, onions, and seasonings

ghee—clarified butter

korma—spicy meat curry and, occasionally, vegetables

mulligatawny—rich soup of meats and vegetables and, occasionally, other ingredients such as shredded coconut

naan—puffy bread with a slight smoky flavor

paratha—flaky bread fried on a griddle

pilaf—butter-flavored rice dish with, occasionally, chopped vegetables or meat

poppadam—crunchy, thin bread made with lentil flour

puri,* or *poori—round, flat, deep-fried bread

sambal,* or *bajak—condiment traditionally made with chili peppers, spices, and lime juice—but includes many variations

samosa—snack of fried triangular-shaped pastries with a meat and/or vegetable filling

tandoori—traditional dome-shaped oven made of brick or clay in which breads and meats are cooked for a distinctive flavor

Dining Chinese

Chop suey, chow mein, and egg foo yung are Chinese-American dishes tending toward the bland side. If you think this is authentic Chinese fare, you are missing out. Cantonese dishes tend to be much milder than the tangy variations found on Szechuan or Hunan menus. Branch out!

bean curd—tofu

bok choy—mild-tasting cabbage-like vegetable

dim sum—Cantonese for "heart's delight," a variety of savory snacks made from various ingredients in a wide range of shapes

ginseng—anise-flavored root used as a restorative, for its medicinal powers, and as a flavoring in tea and soups

hoisin—thick, tangy brown sauce made from soybeans and spices

litchi,* or *leechee—a fruit with white, sweet flesh

loquat,* or *Japanese plum—similar to an apricot

moo shu—dish of shredded meats, Chinese vegetables, and seasonings mixed with scrambled egg and rolled in paper-thin pancakes

oyster sauce—brown sauce made from soy sauce and oysters

spring roll—a type of egg roll with a thinner crust

wonton—meat and vegetable-filled dumpling either boiled, steamed, or fried

Dining Japanese

The formality of Japanese dining can be as pleasurable as the food. Leave your shoes at the door and enliven your palate by sampling the delicate flavors and artful presentations. Finish off your meal with red bean or green tea ice cream.

adzuki—sweet-flavored bean used whole or ground into a fine powder for sweet treats

daikon—a sweet, white radish

dashi—fish stock made with tuna flakes and kelp

hand roll—any of a variety of rice, vegetables, raw or smoked fish, and seasonings artfully wrapped in nori

Kobe beef—special type of very tender, flavorful beef that, because of the attention given the cattle it comes from, is extremely expensive and highly regarded

maki—hand rolls cut into slices

miso—bean paste

mochi—sticky, sweet rice

nori—paper-thin sheets of dried seaweed

ramen—soup of broth, noodles, and bits of meat and/or vegetables

sake—flavorful rice wine usually served warm

sashimi—sliced raw fish served decoratively with condiments

shoyu—soy sauce

soba—noodles made with buckwheat flour

sukiyaki—stir-fried mélange of meats and vegetables

sushi—any variety of rice, raw fish, nori, chopped vegetables, pickles, and sesame seeds dabbed with wasabi

tempura—pieces of vegetable or fish batter-dipped and deep-fried

teriyaki—meat marinated in soy sauce, sake, sugar, and ginger and then either grilled, broiled, or fried

wasabi—potent, green paste made from a kind of horseradish

yakitori—small pieces of meat, usually chicken, marinated and grilled on a skewer

Dining German

It's the wursts! Try a variety along with a sampling of rich, dark beers and you've got a most satisfying meal. Besides, it's fun just listening to people as they order.

bauerwurst—smoked, flavorful sausage with a coarse texture

bierwurst—red sausage flavored with garlic

bockwurst—sausage of ground veal, chopped parsley, and chives served with bock beer

bratwurst—spiced pork and veal sausage

braunschweiger—spreadable liverwurst-type smoked liver sausage

fasnacht—deep-fried potato pastry

hasenpfeffer—thick stew of rabbit meat seasoned with pepper

lebkuchen—thick cookie flavored with honey, spices, and citron

sauerbraten—"sour roast," slow-cooked beef stew

sauerkraut—"sour cabbage," spicy, fermented shredded cabbage

schlag—whipped cream

schnitzel—"cutlet," cutlet dipped in egg, rolled in bread crumbs, and fried (wiener schnitzel is with veal)

spaetzle—"little sparrow," little noodles or dumplings

stollen—sweet yeast bread filled with dried fruits and topped with icing and candied fruit, traditionally served at Christmas

streusel—"sprinkle," sweet crumb topping

strudel—"whirlpool," crisp, phyllo-like pastry with a fruit filling

weisswurst—"white sausage," mild veal, cream, and egg sausage

wurst—generic sausage

☛ Dining Middle Eastern

It's hard not to have your palate seduced by the intriguing combinations found in Middle Eastern cooking.

baba ganoush—dip or spread made from puréed eggplant, tahini, olive oil, garlic, and lemon juice

baklava—sweet pastry of phyllo, honey, and chopped nuts

falafel—deep-fried balls made from spiced, ground chickpeas—usually found inside a pita pocket with tahini and slices of onion and tomato

fava—similar to a lima bean

gyro—slices of meat, typically lamb, roasted on a spit—usually served wrapped in pita with grilled vegetables and sauce made from cucumber and yogurt

halvah—fudge-like sweet made from ground sesame seeds and honey and, occasionally, pistachio nuts

hummus—dip of mashed chickpeas, oil, lemon juice, and garlic

pita—round flat bread that can be split to form a sandwich pocket

tabbouleh—cold dish made from bulgur wheat and minced parsley, mint, tomatoes, onion, lemon juice, and olive oil

tahini—thick sauce or dip made from ground sesame seeds

☛ Dining English

While not revered for their gourmet contributions by the chefs of the world, the British do come up with interesting names for what amounts to solid comfort food.

bangers and mash—mild pork sausage and mashed potatoes

bubble and squeak—dish of mashed potatoes and boiled cabbage mixed together and fried until brown

spotted dog—a steamed bread pudding with currants or raisins

toad in the hole—the same batter used for Yorkshire pudding cooked with bits of sausage

Yorkshire pudding—a batter of eggs, flour, and milk baked in meat drippings until puffy and browned, traditionally served with roast beef

On the Bottle

For centuries the symbol *x* has been branded on kegs by distilleries to show how many times a liquor had been distilled. The strongest and purest liquors were designated *XXXX*. Later, the number of *X*'s came to mean that the brew was of a certain strength. While not in common use nowadays, cartoonists still resort to putting *X*'s on liquor bottles or kegs.

Cognac makers have their own system for grading the quality and age of their liquor. V.S. stands for "very special or superior." V.S.O.P. is for "very special old pale," while "very very special old pale" is, you guessed it, V.V.S.O.P. Stars on the label denote the number of years the cognac has been aged in Limousin oak. One star means the cognac has aged at least three years; two stars means at least four years; and three stars means the potent potable has been lolling around in oak for at least five years.

Drink Up

According to the trade magazine *Nation's Restaurant News*, these are the most popular mixed drinks served up at America's bars:

fuzzy navel—peach schnapps and orange juice

Long Island iced tea—vodka, gin, tequila, rum, Triple Sec, lemon juice, cola, and a lemon slice

white Russian—coffee liqueur, vodka, and cream

black Russian—coffee liqueur and vodka

strawberry daiquiri—rum, strawberry schnapps, and strawberries (sometimes sugar syrup is added)

sea breeze—vodka, cranberry juice, and grapefruit juice

piña colada—rum, cream of coconut, and pineapple juice

kamikaze—vodka, Triple Sec, and lemon juice

tequila sunrise—tequila, grenadine, and orange juice

sex on the beach—vodka, peach schnapps, and orange juice

What'll You Have?

While fuzzy navels can be quite tasty, what to order when in Rome, or Athens, or Oslo? If you find yourself on the road and are game to sample local concoctions, try ordering:

absinthe—potent (68 percent alcohol), licorice-flavored, green-colored liqueur distilled from wormwood and infused with herbs. When mixed with water, it turns milky white. Considered addictive and a health hazard, it's prohibited in many countries including the United States.

amaretto—almond-flavored, amber-colored liqueur usually made from apricot pits

amontillado—sherry from Spain made from palomino grapes

anisette—clear, sweet, licorice-flavored liqueur made from anise seeds

aquavit—transparent, potent liquor from Scandinavia distilled from either grains or potatoes and lightly flavored with caraway, served icy cold

arak—generic Asian and Middle Eastern liquor sometimes flavored with anise seed or dates. It packs a kick.

bitters—generic name for a distillation of herbs, barks, roots, and plants, used for flavoring, as an apéritif, in cooking, and as a digestive aid. Angostura, Campari, and Fernet-Branca are popular brands.

calvados—apple brandy, often 100 proof, from Normandy

cassis—black currant used to make a liqueur called creme de cassis as well as a nonalcoholic syrup for flavoring

claret—British term for red Bordeaux

curaçao—liqueur with a distinctive citrus flavor, made from the bitter-tasting peel of oranges grown on the island of Curaçao

fino—very light, dry Spanish sherry

glögg—spicy punch from Sweden

grappa—clear brandy from Italy distilled from grape skins and pulp left over in the wine press

grenadine—scarlet syrup derived from pomegranates and named for Grenada (like cassis, may or may not be alcoholic)

kefir—Russian yogurty drinks made from fermented milk, slightly alcoholic (kumiss is a Mongolian version)

kirsch—German for "cherry," sweet, clear brandy made from cherry pits and pulp

kümmel—clear herbal liqueur infused with the flavors of caraway, cumin, and fennel

manzanilla—very light, very dry Spanish sherry

mead—ancient drink made from fermented honey and yeast and flavored with herbs, spices, and sometimes flowers

mescal—Mexican beverage akin to tequila made from the agave plant

mirin and sake—rice wines from Japan. Mirin is sweeter, and sake is traditionally served warm in tiny porcelain cups.

okolehao (oke)—made from the Hawaiian ti plant

olorosa—another name for cream or golden sherry

ouzo—liqueur from Greece that features a distinctive anise flavor. Like its cousins, pastis and pernod, it is typically mixed with water, which turns it from clear to milky.

port—fortified wine. Types of port include tawny, vintage, and ruby, and vary in color, flavor, and potency.

retsina—from Greece, wine treated with pine tree resin to give it a unique flavor not unlike turpentine

sambuca—often served with a few coffee beans afloat in it, another anise-flavored liqueur from Italy

sangria—blend of red wine, fruit juice, seltzer, and sliced fruit

schnapps—comes in a variety of flavors, the most popular being peppermint

slivovitz—from the Balkans, a dry brandy made from plums

sloe gin—liqueur made from mixing sloe (a wild plum that grows on blackthorns) and gin

wassail—from the Norse "be in good health," spiced blend of ale or wine sweetened with sugar and slices of apple

High Spirits

- In ancient Greece, cups were fashioned from amethyst because it was commonly held that drinking from a vessel of blue quartz prevented intoxication. The name translates as "not to be drunk."

- "Going on the wagon" (to describe someone who abstains from alcohol) and "falling off the wagon" (to describe someone who partakes) are credited to W. A. McIntire, the Salvation Army commish in 1909. Around the turn of the century, every Thanksgiving Day, the water wagons of New York City traditionally went around collecting the seriously inebriated.

- The color of wine is not attributable solely to the color of the grapes used to make it. Rather, the color comes from the length of time the skins are allowed to remain in the juice. With white wine, skins are removed after a brief bath. For rosés, the skins of darker grapes sit in the juices for a few extra days. For reds, the skins remain for the longest periods.

- A proper cocktail relies heavily on accurate measurement. When experimenting with mixology, keep in mind: 1 dash = 6 drops; 3 teaspoons = ½ ounce; 1 pony = 1 ounce; 1 jigger = 1½ ounces; 1 large jigger = 2 ounces; a standard whiskey glass = 2 ounces; 1 pint = 16 fluid ounces; 1 fifth = 25.6 fluid ounces; and 1 quart = 32 fluid ounces.

- Cutty Sark, a popular brand name, is Scottish not for "magnificent schooner on the label" but, rather, for "short shirt." A cutty is also a light-hearted term for a "hussy." Robbie Burns gave the name to a mocking witch in his poem "Tam O'Shanter."

Whiskey Down

A lad or lass from Scotland is a Scot or Scottish. Scotch is the drink—a blend of several whiskeys. Some blends incorporate as many as 50 different malts.

A single malt is never called scotch. It's called a single malt and originates from a single distillery. (There are also single-grain whiskeys, but that's something to sample after a wee hike on the moors.)

Whiskey, from old Gaelic meaning "water of life," is made from barley, malt, and yeast mixed with water. It must be aged in solid oak casks for at least three years to be legally sold as Scotch whiskey. Many age far longer than that and reflect distinctive tastes, depending upon the maker and the region. Skilled aficionados can recognize the region and age of a whiskey by its bouquet.

And if you do find yourself taking a taste test as you sightsee in Scotland, read the labels. Only the words *deluxe* and *reserve* mean anything. Both may be applied to aged, premium brands.

Scotch whiskey is the world's leading alcoholic beverage and accounts for more than $2 billion worth of Scotland's annual exports. Most Americans prefer blended whiskeys to single malts.

A Rob Roy (named for Robert Macgregor, a kind of Robin Hood of the Highlands and the hero of a novel by Sir Walter Scott) is a Manhattan (equal parts sweet vermouth and bourbon with a dash of bitters) wherein scotch replaces the bourbon. If you incorporate a dash of Drambuie in this libation, you've got a Robbie Burns (in honor of Scotland's poet).

A Bit of Bubbly

Champagne is usually fermented only in half bottles, bottles, and magnums. For all the other sizes (amusingly named from smallest to largest below), the wine is fermented and riddled (a process of collecting and removing the sediment created by the second fermentation) in regular-sized bottles, then transferred to the splits and special larger sizes. A select group of producers—Pommery, for example—state that all their wines (except the splits) are fermented in the bottles in which they are sold.

Split = *187 ml. (6.3 oz) 1/4 bottle*
Half bottle = *375 ml. (12.7 oz) 1/2 bottle*
Bottle = *750 ml. (25.4 oz) 1 bottle*
Magnum = *1.5 liters (50.7 oz) 2 bottles*
Jeroboam = *3 l. (101.4 oz) 4 bottles*
Rehoboam = *4.5 l. (152.4 oz) was 6 bottles; no longer a legal size*
Methuselah = *6 l. (202.9 oz) 8 bottles*
Salmanazar = *9 l. (304.3 oz) 12 bottles*
Balthazar = *12 l. (405.8 oz) 16 bottles*
Nebuchadnezzar = *15 l. (507.2 oz) 20 bottles*

Remember, though, that an American "champagne" can be any sparkling wine (red or white) as long as it's bottle-fermented and labeled with its place of origin (typically although not exclusively New York or California). French champagne evolves via time-consuming and labor-intensive processes and must come from the Champagne region of France. The sweetness of champagne comes from the addition of sugar. The driest is brut, then extra dry, then dry or "sec."

Wine Tasting

To oenophiles, wine is an art form, worthy of reverence. A subtle shift in the weather, chemistry of the soil, or the mood of the grower can make or break a vintage. Matters of sweetness, body, bouquet, clarity, and nose come into play.

To the rest of us, selecting wine is a question of red or white. Once that's settled, there are still many choices to be made. Take Beaujolais, a popular red wine named for the region of France where it's produced. In one simple wine, there are many variations—twelve Beaujolais, to be exact.

Beaujolais-Villages (produced in some 39 separate villages) represent 25 percent of the total Beaujolais production. Cherry-colored, their bouquet hints of strawberries and black currants.

There are ten crus (or growths): Brouilly is named for Mount Brouilly and is usually dark ruby and on the robust side; Chénas is garnet-colored with a more floral bouquet; Chiroubles has a floral nose; Côte de Brouilly is almost violet-colored and improves with a bit more time on the shelf; Fleurie is velvety smooth with a complex aroma of fruits and flowers; Juliénas has a heady bouquet of peaches and berries; Morgon also develops well with aging and is deep garnet; Moilin-a-Vent is named for an ancient windmill and is considered one of the best French reds; Régnié, a recent addition, is cherry-colored with a suggestion of red currants and blackberries; and Saint-Amour has a bouquet of spices and cherries.

Beaujolais Nouveau is the one introduced each year on the third Thursday of November. Two thirds comes from vineyards in the

Beaujolais region and one third from the Beaujolais-Villages area. Bright cherry red in color, the bouquet tends toward floral, and the flavor is fruity. These are best enjoyed chilled and soon after purchase.

Hops to It

There's a lot more to beer brewing these days than malt and hops. For those who enjoy ales and lagers, there are many varieties to be found in the world of microbreweries. Micros have slowly been establishing themselves in the 90s, growing steadily. Under the watchful eyes of the Big Four (Anheuser-Busch, Miller, Adolph Coors, and Stroh, which account for 80 percent of the beer industry in the United States), local brewers are enjoying great success with micros, also known as baby, craft, or specialty beers.

While pricier than the big boys, micros are infused with deeper flavorings with hints of, for example, apricots, honey, and wheat. They are limited editions, with an average of several thousand barrels brewed a year to be sold where it's made, sometimes just in their own microbrew-pubs.

But the major brewers, not to be outdone, have tried to get into the act of specialty beers, nicknamed "macros." Anheuser-Busch has introduced various labels including Red Wolf and Elk Mountain. Miller's Red Dog and Ice House were kicked off in the early 90s, along with Coors's George Killian and Stroh's feature, Red River Valley. While far from being limited editions, they do have unusual tastes, and some may be sold regionally. Only time will tell which brews will keep their heads.

PROFESSIONALLY *Speaking*

Jet Jargon

How many times have you heard, "Well, I'm no rocket scientist, but..." Have some fun. Impress total strangers (preferably folks you'll never see again) and tell them, "Why, yes, actually I *am* a rocket scientist." Practice an intelligent look and memorize this short list of terms. If you can toss around expressions such as "femtosecond" (a millionth of a billionth of a second) and "cold dark matter" (no, it's not frozen beef liver), you might pull it off.

- An Endostat is an experimental aircraft designed by Endostat, Inc. Powered by microwaves and unmanned, it is able to fly at higher altitudes and across greater distances than present-day crewed aircraft. It's being tested by the military for atmospheric research not covered by satellites or regular aircraft. Its "sister" ship is the *Condor*, developed by Boeing. The *Condor* is capable of soaring at very high altitudes for covering distances of up to 20,000 miles. It can go for several days (sometimes weeks) without touching down for refueling.

• ERIS is an acronym for Exoatmospheric Re-entry Vehicle Interceptor System. Huh? It's an antiballistic defense system designed to separate the booster rocket of a two-stage antimissile device while it's approaching a target so that the main part will slam into the target at optimum speed. Ah, give me a Patriot missile.

• On a smaller scale, a Stinger is a rocket capable of shooting helicopters and other low-flying aircraft out of the sky. It's launched from the shoulder.

• COBE is an acronym for Cosmic Background Explorer, a NASA satellite that's out looking for the origins of the universe. It's checking out teeny bits of background radiation in space.

• What *is* cold dark matter? Hypothetical stuff, it's matter made up of subatomic particles that, if you believe some theories of how the cosmos formed, came into being around the beginning of time and comprise up to 90 percent of all matter within the universe.

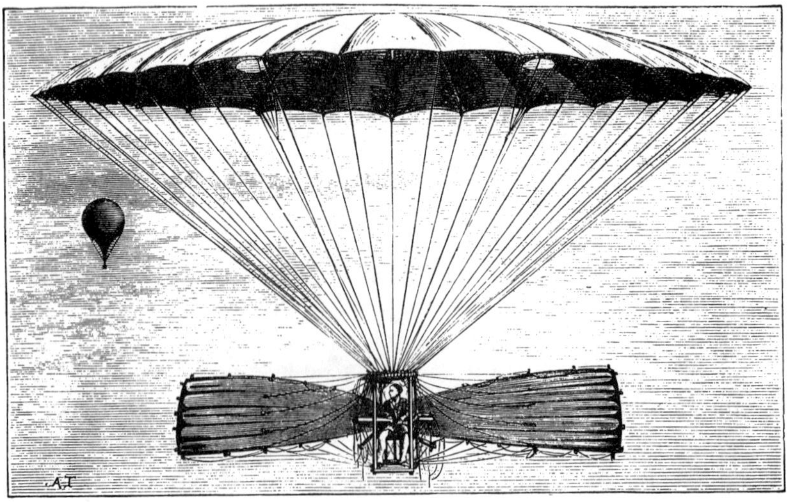

➢ Getting Antiquated

Herewith a primer for the next time you decide to forego Ikea and check out antiques. It's important to toss around some of these phrases so the dealer will think you know what you're admiring.

antique china—Of the great British china, Royal Crown Derby is a brand fancied by Queen Victoria and many subsequent royals. Royal Doulton (which also produces Minton china) is renowned for figurines. Royal Worcester has had the royal warrant for centuries and now makes Spode (for Josiah Spode). The Wedgwood name and ever-popular sky blue and bas-relief white figures are known throughout the world. Earthenware is a generic name for pottery that has been fired at a relatively low temperature, and stoneware has been fired at a higher temperature.

blue and white—Either blue-and-white porcelain exported from China or blue-and-white "transferware." Transfer printing is a complex technique thought to have been developed in the late 18th century by Josiah Spode. You've probably seen his name around. The blue pattern (scenic landscapes or botanicals) is made from cobalt paste printed or transferred onto white china. A popular traditional pattern is called willow.

Chippendale—Thomas Chippendale the Elder (1718–1779) was a British furniture designer. He was widely known because he published his designs. Chippendale usually means a piece of mahogany furniture made in the 1750s or 1760s in a rococo style with suggestions of Chinese and Gothic-inspired elements. Pricey stuff.

collectible,* or *collectable—Anything you want to collect or is deemed by others worthy of collecting, whether it's Pez dispensers, old thimbles, or antique barns.

Hepplewhite—This furniture, designed by George Hepplewhite in the late 1700s, has neoclassical lines.

Jacobean—A kind of furniture and symmetrical architectural style popular in the 1600s. Jacobean furniture is usually massive oak stuff with ornate carvings.

pewter—An alloy of tin and copper and occasionally lead, pewter has been made since medieval days and was considered a middle-class silver. Whereas American colonists used wooden trenchers for eating, British immigrants introduced pewter smithing.

Queen Anne—Queen Anne applies to 18th-century furniture with a walnut veneer, curved legs, and elegant simplicity. Historically, it covers Queen Anne's reign as well as William and Mary's.

It's Magic

So what if your only "trick" is dazzling your three-year-old nephew by pulling a quarter from behind his ear. You may never have the pizzazz of David Copperfield or the theatricality of Harry Houdini, but at least you can sound like a master magician.

- Illusions are "impossible" feats such as making large things seem to disappear or sawing someone in half.

- Escapology is the art of wriggling out of stocks, bonds, ropes, shackles, straightjackets, locks, and such.

- Mentalism is seeming to read someone's thoughts or bring about an event, like bending a metal fork, by concentrating on it.

- Close-up magic is done before a small audience with a deck of cards or little odds and ends excavated from a pocket or purse.

- Silent magic is done by magicians who say nothing and typically work to music. Miming, dramatic facial expressions, and gestures are used to communicate.

- Cabaret magic is what is usually performed for a television or club audience. It traditionally involves humor, patter, and a variety of tricks.

Now, just say the magic words: Abracadabra, Presto, Open Sesame, Hocus Pocus, Sim Sala Bim, Shimbaree Shimabara...

Laying Down the Law

Lawyers, district attorneys, and judges have long been staple characters in television dramas, from classics like *Perry Mason* and *Dragnet* to more recent shows such as *NYPD Blue* and *Law and Order*. Aside from the running meter bolted to the briefcase, criminal lawyers on television are conspicuous because of their command of legalese—an impenetrable lexicon of nifty phrases that sets them apart. And with televised court cases further piquing our interest in the language of law, what better time to take a quick course in TV Law Talk 101?

- *Corpus delicti* is Latin for "body of the crime." It is the objective proof that a crime was committed. While not necessarily the actual dead body at a crime scene, a corpus delicti shows that an alleged victim died by someone's criminality (as opposed to, say, an accidental death).

- *Habeas corpus,* Latin for "you have the body" (gee, thanks), refers to a variety of criminal and civil situations. Known as the Great Writ, a writ of habeas corpus is a procedure for getting a judicial decision on the legality of an individual's custody. In other words, "If you say my client here behind these bars did the crime, it's up to you to produce the victim."

- *Mirandizing,* also known as the Miranda Rule, is reading someone his or her rights, a legal requirement. Upon being taken into police custody, a person must be warned against self-incrimination (in other words, remain silent) and is entitled to the presence and advice of a lawyer before any kind of interrogation by law enforcement authorities can take place. Now, book 'em, Dan-o.

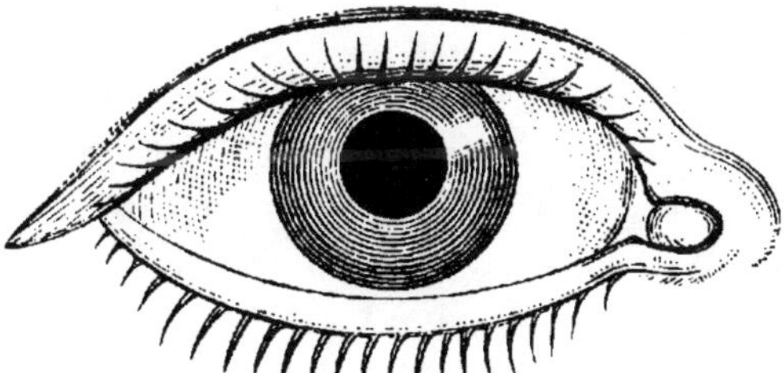

• What's the big deal with getting a *search warrant* before knocking a door down? A warrant is a written order (or writ) from a proper authority permitting a certain action, and a search warrant allows authorities to enter premises or examine property looking for evidence in a trial. No warrant? Then whatever is uncovered may not be admissible as evidence in a case.

• *Intent* is one of those words that emerges frequently in a trial. "It goes to intent, your honor." A person who knows and wants the consequences of his or her act is acting with intent. For purposes of criminal liability, such intent must exist at the same time as when the crime or offense was committed. "I'll allow it as it goes to state of mind."

• A *homicide* is complicated by the fact that there are different classifications of murder and, so, different terms of punishment. Murder means unlawfully killing someone with malice aforethought (intent to kill accompanied by an element of hatred). Murder in the first degree is the most serious. It entails killing willfully, deliberately, and with premeditation. A felony murder, which applies to a defendant who accidentally kills someone while in the process of committing a felony, is considered first degree murder. Hurting someone badly enough to cause eventual death is also tried as first degree. Second degree incorporates malice aforethought but no deliberation or premeditation. For example, someone who shoots into a crowd and kills someone may be tried for second degree murder.

• *Manslaughter* is murder without malice aforethought and is usually broken down into voluntary (heat-of-passion kind of thing) and involuntary manslaughter (criminal negligence).

• *Taking the Fifth* refers to the Fifth Amendment to the Constitution, part of the Bill of Rights. It protects citizens from the government, specifically entitling you not to have to testify against yourself. It also addresses issues of double jeopardy, due process, and other rights of the accused.

• An *indictment* is a formal written accusation submitted by the public prosecuting attorney to a grand jury that charges someone with a crime.

• *"Due process of law"* comes from the Fifth Amendment and is repeated in the Fourteenth. The Constitution provides that no one shall be "deprived of life, liberty, or property, without due process of law." While not pinpoint precise in its application or interpretation, it basically means, "Hey guys, play fair."

When the perp gets iced, now you can guess what kind of plea the shooter will cop.

Medical Report

"Code Blue! Stat!" Yeah, yeah, hold onto your scrubs. To get the most out of a medical drama you need to know what the doctors are talking about. And ever since *Saint Elsewhere* haven't you wondered what Ringer's is?

• *Flatlining* is not good. It means the response of someone hooked up to an EKG machine is showing a flat line—no life. Little blips on the screen reflect a steady heartbeat. If a patient flatlines, the doctor might ask if the patient was "Danforthed." This refers to a 1991 law (named for the cosponsor, Senator John Danforth) making it mandatory that, at the time of admission to a hospital, a patient must be advised of his or her right to refuse life-sustaining treatments or measures should the need arise. DNR is the code for Do Not Resuscitate.

• *Cardiomyoplasty* is a good one. It's a surgical procedure in which tissue from the muscle in a patient's back is used to replace damaged heart tissue.

• *Monoclonal imaging* is a sophisticated diagnostic technique. Antibodies, manufactured in a lab, are introduced into a patient to determine the location of, say, a tumor or some other site under attack by disease. The processes, nature, and causes of the disease (known as the pathology) can be studied by tracking the antibodies.

• A *patch* is a small adhesive strip treated with medication. Over time, it releases the medication into the wearer's skin (transdermally). For example, patches may be infused with nicotine to help wean cigarette smokers off tobacco or with an anti-motion-sickness drug to help sailors fend off the queasies.

• Finally, *Ringer's* is a colorless solution that mimics some of the properties of blood serum. It's sometimes used to maintain organs or live tissue outside the body for brief periods. Intravenous sterile Ringer's solution is used to treat dehydration.

All in Your Mind

Freud and Jung had a grand time writing up their theories of everything from slips of the tongue to dream therapy. The following are recent syndromes on record.

• In psychiatry, *Stendahl's syndrome* is a condition in which a person imagines him or herself a renowned literary figure. The person may actually begin behaving like that figure.

• *Erotomonomania* is a psychological condition in which a man is convinced (without the benefit of cause) that women are desperate to have sexual relations with him and are out to bed him no matter what the cost.

• *Jerusalem syndrome* is named for the phenomenon some may experience while visiting the shrines of Israel. Some tourists find themselves overwhelmed by the spiritual and profound religious significance of the place. They may find themselves identifying with or behaving as if they were someone from the Bible, such as Moses.

• *Munchausen syndrome* is another intriguing mental disorder in which someone goes to great lengths to fake an illness and be admitted to a hospital. Sufferers of this malady may be able to describe symptoms in precise detail. Some may actually go as far as self-inflicted wounds to gain sympathy and/or to authenticate their claims.

LEGALLY *Bound*

On the Books

- The Pilgrims fired a minister for growing tomatoes, considered poisonous, in his garden. Although George Washington grew them for decorative purposes, it wasn't until the early 19th century that Colonel Robert G. Johnson of Salem, New Jersey, ate several of them in public, proving they were edible.

- It was against the law to celebrate Christmas (by enjoying a special meal or not going to work) from 1659 until 1681 in the colony of Massachusetts.

- For playing tennis on a Sunday, Upton Sinclair was sent to jail in Wilmington, Delaware.

- In New York in 1968, nudity was illegal onstage if the actor moved. Hence, the nude performers stood stock still in the smash production of *Hair*.

- It's against the law in Topeka, Kansas, for a waiter to serve wine in a teacup.

- The sundae was invented in the Midwest in the 1880s when it was against the law to use carbonated water on Sundays (thereby scotching the production of ice-cream sodas).

- America's first smoking ban was passed in Massachusetts in 1638. It prohibited the smoking of tobacco outdoors to help prevent fires.

- Lawyers were outlawed in the colonies of Massachusetts and Virginia in the 1640s. An interesting sidebar: In 1700, a total of seven lawyers practiced in New York City.

- In Sweden, it's against the law to cut or bob a dog's tail simply for cosmetic reasons. Astrid Lindgren, author of the Pippi Longstocking children's stories, campaigned for the regulation, which became effective in 1988. The law is known informally as *Lex Astrid* or Astrid's Law.

- During the reign of Henry II, there were laws on the books regulating prostitution. Brothels were licensed and enforced such rules as "No single woman to take money to lye with any man, except she lye all night, till the morn."

- A diet, from the same Latin root that gave us *day*, used to be a day in Scotland set aside for a particular meeting and, more specifically, the day on which someone so ordered was to appear in court. *Diet* came to mean the court session itself (especially if the session was to last a day or less). To diet, meaning monitoring one's caloric intake, comes from the Greek word meaning "way of life."

That Old Gang

We may think of gang warfare and weapons in schools as relatively modern phenomena, but a fierce adolescent feud, lasting three decades, was ignited at the Walsh School in Chicago in 1881.

Members of rival gangs fought with guns, knives, clubs, and brickbats both inside and outside the school walls. Over the years, they were responsible for killing several boys and injuring more than 20 others.

The gangs were known as the Bohemians and the Irish. The names, however, were misleading. They had nothing to do with ethnicity or a propensity for black turtlenecks and Beat poets. Rather, one's neighborhood was the touchstone of gang allegiance. Boys who lived east of Johnson Street were the Irish, and those living west of Johnson Street were the Bohemians.

After a gun battle in December 1905, daily weapons searches were instituted and were continued for several years until the intensity of the rivalry diluted and the level of violence dropped off.

Call Me Madam

People who read *People* may be familiar with Heidi Fleiss, the Hollywood madam. Many recall Sydney Biddle Barrows, the Mayflower madam who operated in New York City. But long before these two women found themselves in national headlines, Manhattan had Polly Adler, considered one of the last great madams.

Polly ran her operation in the 1930s and 40s out of swank apartments on Manhattan's posh East Side. Her clients included members of the Social Register, politicians, police, literary lights, and a few famous gangsters.

Before she retired from the business, she had become a celebrity in her own right. The press loved to interview her, and her comings and goings were dutifully recorded in the gossip columns. Even glowing descriptions of her homes appeared in magazines and newspapers.

Despite the publicity, Polly always used her clients' real names with her "girls," and the clients never objected. They were secure in knowing that their names would never make the papers and that Polly would never give up a name. In fact, when gangster Dutch Schultz was a very wanted man, he continued to visit Polly's establishments several times a week and was never betrayed.

After her retirement in 1944, Polly was encouraged by friends to begin a new career as a writer, which she did and at which she had some success until her death in 1962. Her autobiography, *A House Is Not a Home*, was a best-seller in 1953 and eventually sold nearly 3 million copies.

Throwing the Book

Until January 1, 1994, these laws were on the books in the golden state of California.

"Wanted: Dead or Alive" posters could only be hung in an approved spot. (Catchy name for a TV show, though.)

The spouse of the loser in a duel had to be compensated by the winner.

Mares, stallions, and bulls were to be prevented from running wild (you know, procreating in plain sight) within 400 yards of a city, town, or village.

You Say Tomato, I Say Vegie

On the books is the case of *Nix et al. v. Hedden, Collector of the Port of New York* (May 10, 1893), regarding the definition of tomatoes as either vegetables or fruits. At issue was that while vegetables were subject to duty, fruits were duty-free. Nix, an importer of tomatoes from the West Indies, went to court to argue that tomatoes should be classified as fruit and the duties he'd paid under protest returned.

Mr. Justice Gray delivered the opinion of the court as follows.

> "The single question in this case is whether tomatoes, considered as provisions, are to be classed as 'vegetables' or as 'fruit,' within the meaning of the tariff act of 1883. The only witnesses called at the trial testified that neither 'vegetables' nor 'fruit' had any special meaning in trade or commerce different from that given in the

dictionaries, and that they had the same meaning in trade today that they had in March 1883.

The passages cited from the dictionaries define the word 'fruit' as the seed of plants, or that part of plants which contains the seed, and especially the juicy, pulpy products of certain plants, covering and containing the seed. These definitions have no tendency to show that tomatoes are 'fruit,' as distinguished from 'vegetables,' in common speech, or within the meaning of the tariff act.

There being no evidence that the words 'fruit' and 'vegetables' have acquired any special meaning in trade or commerce, they must receive their ordinary meaning. Of that meaning the court is bound to take judicial notice, as it does in regard to all words in our own tongue; and upon such a question dictionaries are admitted, not as evidence, but only as aids to the memory and understanding of the court.

Botanically speaking, tomatoes are the fruit of the vine, just as are cucumbers, squashes, beans, and peas. But in the common language of the people, whether sellers or consumers of provisions, all these are vegetables which are grown in kitchen gardens, and which, whether eaten cooked or raw, are, like potatoes, carrots, parsnips, turnips, beets, cauliflower, cabbage, celery, and lettuce, usually served at dinner in, with, or after the soup, fish, or meats which constitute the principal part of the repast, and not, like fruits generally, as dessert.

The attempt to class tomatoes as fruit is not unlike a recent attempt to class beans as seeds, of which Mr. Justice Bradley, speaking for this court, said: 'We do not see why they should be classified as seeds, any more than walnuts should be so classified. Both are seeds, in the language of botany or natural history, but not in commerce or common parlance. On the other hand in speaking generally of provisions, beans may well be included under the term 'vegetables.' As an article of food on our tables, whether baked or boiled, or forming the basis of soup, they are used as a vegetable, as well when ripe as when green. This is the principal use to which they are put. Beyond the common knowledge which we have on this subject, very little evidence is necessary, or can be produced.'

Judgment affirmed."

Reigning Supreme

Among the most significant and oft-quoted Supreme Court cases are:

Dred Scott v. Sanford (1857). Did a slaveholder still own his "property" when in a free state? The Missouri Compromise was declared unconstitutional because, without due process of law, a slaveholder was deprived of his property. This infamous decision went on to state that slaves were not citizens.

Schenk v. the United States (1919). The Supreme Court upheld the Espionage Act of World War I regarding free speech. Justice Oliver Wendell Holmes said that someone who encourages draft resistance in a time of war is "a clear and present danger."

Brown v. the Board of Education of Topeka (1954). Overturning *Plessy v. Ferguson* (1896), which allowed for "separate but equal" segregation, this decision called for the immediate desegregation of schools.

Roth v. the United States (1957). This decision helped define obscene materials as those which lack any "redeeming social importance."

Miranda v. Arizona (1966). This decision is where "mirandize" comes from. Before questioning them, police must inform suspects of their rights.

Roe v. Wade (1973). Frequently quoted, this decision relied upon the Fourteenth Amendment to allow for a woman's freedom regarding her reproductive decisions (with some exceptions). The *Webster v. Reproductive Health Services* (1989), however, upheld a Missouri state law restricting access to abortions.

Walls a Prison Make

Sitting behind bars with the time and the writing material has allowed some prisoners' poetic skills to take flight. To wit:

Stone walls do not a prison make
Nor iron bars a cage;
Minds innocent and quiet take
That for an hermitage;
If I have freedom in my love
And in my soul am free,
Angels alone, that soar above,
Enjoy such liberty.

These lines are from "To Althea, from Prison," written in Westminster's Gatehouse prison in 1642 by Richard Lovelace. It seems the poet was sentenced by the crown to serve seven weeks for some less than flattering remarks he made in Parliament.

Sir Walter Raleigh spent a dozen years in the Tower of London writing his *History of the World.* The first volume was published in 1614. His publisher, Walter Burre, would visit him in his cell. Upon hearing of the dismal sales of the first volume that had all but destroyed Burre's business, Raleigh destroyed the second volume. After Raleigh's death, the first volume sold thousands of copies, making Burre a wealthy man.

Miguel de Cervantes, who was both a prisoner of war and convicted of causing shortages while serving as a navy quartermaster, started *Don Quixote* behind bars. He had been taken prisoner by Barbary corsairs and sold into slavery in Algiers. Happily, he was ransomed by priests of the Order of Mercy in 1580 and returned home to finish the story he had begun in prison.

Voltaire wrote from the Bastille and Thomas Paine wrote a section of *The Age of Reason* in a prison in Paris. The *I-Ching* was written by Won-Wang, who was imprisoned by the emperor Chou-sin. The author's son eventually overthrew Chou-sin and established a new dynasty. John Bunyan, put away for his religious beliefs, wrote *Pilgrim's Progress* in a jail cell. Oscar Wilde was imprisoned for his unabashed homosexuality and took the opportunity to write. John Cleland wrote *Fanny Hill* while serving time for debt. Sir Thomas Malory was a twice-convicted rapist, burglar, and extortionist who wrote the chivalric epic poem *Le Morte d'Arthur* before dying in prison.

William Sydney Porter worked as a bank cashier until he was charged with embezzling. He tried to make a run for the border, heading for South America, but eventually turned himself in. He spent five years (1898 to 1903) in an Ohio penitentiary. As the night watchman of the prison infirmary, he passed the time writing short stories.

Borrowing the name O. Henry from a prison guard, Porter began submitting his work to magazines. By the time he was released, he had a wide and dedicated following. A dilemma, however, raised its ugly head. A former acquaintance starting blackmailing Porter, threatening to tell his fans about his time behind bars. For years to come, Porter made a nuisance of himself by stopping by his publishers asking for advances on his advances.

Some authors have chronicled their prison experiences in works such as *The Gulag Archipelago*, *Soul on Ice*, and scandal-du-jour confessionals. Other inspired imprisoned writers include Marco Polo, Diderot, Adolph Hitler, and Ezra Pound.

Patently So

Patents (and copyrights) are described in the Constitution as being under the purview of Congress. "Congress shall have power...to promote the progress of science and useful arts, by securing for limited times to authors and inventors the exclusive rights to their respective writings and discoveries."

The discovery may consist of "any new and useful process, machine, manufacture, or composition of matter, or any new and useful improvements thereof." Patents have been granted for many things including new forms of vegetation. Is a genetically engineered mouse now as likely to hold a patent as the better mousetrap?

Before a patent is considered, the entity must be deemed original. This requires thorough research in the patent library's Search Room to confirm that the entity is unique.

If you think you might have a widget worth patenting, contact the Patent and Trademark Office in Washington, D.C., for more information. But be patient. They receive about 100,000 applications every year. Since 1790, over 4.5 million patents have been granted.

Patents cost between $300 and $600 (depending upon the size of the invention) and are good for 17 years. Patented things must be marked "patent" and include the patent number. While some inventors bandy about "patent pending" or "patent applied for," these terms have little legal meaning.

The first U.S. patent grant went to Samuel Hopkins of Philadelphia in 1790. The patent was for Mr. Hopkins's improved technique for making potash and pearl ash and was signed by Attorney General Edmond Randolph, George Washington, and Thomas Jefferson.

Not surprisingly, the most prolific patent winner in the United States was Thomas Alva Edison with over 1,000. Alfred Nobel, of Nobel Prize fame, was also a chemist and inventor who held 355 patents. He made a fortune on one particularly explosive invention: dynamite.

A MATTER *of* FACT

Return Tickets

What happened when Christopher Columbus (Cristóbal Colón) returned to Barcelona from San Salvador in May 1493?

The Genoan sea captain returned to Spain (sadly without the *Santa Maria*, which went down off the coast of the West Indies) a hero. He was received with unrivaled pomp and unprecedented displays of extravagance at the court of King Ferdinand II (who was recovering from an assassination attempt) and Queen Isabella (who was overseeing the royal edict calling for the expulsion of all Jews from Spain). Cheering crowds lined the streets to see the parade of wondrous things he brought back from the New World.

He made a gift to the crown of parrots, golden masks, pearls, tropical fruits, and several live natives (most had perished on the trip to the Old World). The king and queen conferred upon him the title he craved,

"Don Cristóbal, our Admiral of the Ocean Sea and Viceroy and Governor of all the Islands which have been Discovered in the Indies."

Columbus was thrilled with the attention and immediately set about organizing his second voyage. Incidentally, it was common knowledge that the world was round in 1492. Ultimately Columbus died a sad and embittered man, holding steadfastly to the belief he had discovered the sea route to the West Indies.

Heroes and Heels

As for some of the lesser-known adventures from the lives and times of those famous guys we studied and whose stats we memorized:

- Balboa, who liked to sic his dogs on natives he encountered, was hanged in 1517 in land-grabbing disagreements in Central America.

- La Salle was killed on the Gulf Coast in 1687 by what was left of his crew. He had started off in 1684 with 400. A fed-up crew of 20 was all that was left.

- Henry Hudson is thought to have been set adrift in Hudson Bay by a mutinous crew in June 1611. He was never heard from again.

- Paul Revere charged for his services. So much for patriotic fervor.

The Other Tea Party

While the extravaganza in Boston Harbor on December 13, 1773, got most of the press, there was another tea party in the historic town of Chestertown, Maryland.

To set the stage: Chestertown was described by a traveling Princeton graduate, Philip Fithian Vickers, in his journal on April 24, 1774. "Rode from Rock Hall over a delightful part of the country to Chestertown 13 miles—this is a beautiful small Town on a River out of the Bay navigable for ships." His travel journal expounded at some length on how the British had proposed to punish those Bostonian "Indians" who had dumped the tea in Boston harbor. (Vickers would lose his life serving as a chaplain with the Continental Army.)

The Tea Act of 1773 had pushed the colonists to challenge what amounted to a British monopoly on the prosperous tea trade. Bostonians, still deeply wounded by the Boston Massacre of March 1770, wanted a newly arrived shipment of tea to be returned to England. Vaguely dressed as Native Americans, a few men boarded the ships at night and tossed the tea overboard.

Vickers's notes were, in a way, prophetic. Like Boston, Chestertown was a bustling port—supporting four silversmiths (a helpful index for measuring the relative wealth of a community). When the British closed the port city of Boston as retribution for their tea party, Chestertowners feared it could happen anywhere. Trade had ground to a halt with Boston, and the aftershocks were felt up and down the Atlantic and Chesapeake.

The residents of Chestertown voted to act. They wrote up a set of "resolves" and pledged not to drink tea. And when the *Geddes* docked on May 24 with a hold full of tea, the townsfolk tossed it into the sea. It was no idle copycat affair. They risked their businesses, their homes, their freedom, and their lives.

The Chestertown Tea Party is dutifully reenacted every year with locals dressed in appropriate garb spouting rhetoric around the commons. However, aside from tea tossing, everyone also partakes of local delicacies such as crab cones and enjoys a colonial parade.

Civil War Peculiarities

Welshman Henry Stanley fought for the South's Sixth Arkansas until taken prisoner. He then fought for the North. Later, after searching Africa for Dr. David Livingstone, a Scottish missionary and explorer, Stanley discovered Livingstone had lost an 18-year-old son at Gettysburg.

Other folk, known for other reasons, who served in the Civil War? Frank and Jesse James (outlaws), Abner Doubleday (official founder of baseball), George Armstrong Custer (Little Big Horn casualty), Nathan Bedford Forrest (founder of the KKK), Arthur MacArthur (General Douglas MacArthur's dad), Oliver Wendell Holmes Jr., and the following future presidents: Hayes, McKinley, Grant, Arthur, Garfield, and Harrison.

The first and only woman (thus far) to receive the Congressional Medal of Honor was Dr. Mary Edwards Walker, who served in battle as a doctor during the Civil War. Because of her penchant for wearing men's clothes (and hats) and her feminist politics, the government tried to reclaim the medal. But she held tight and saw to it she was buried with her award.

During the war with Mexico, Ulysses Grant, two years out of West Point, served as a lieutenant. He would later call that war "one of the most unjust ever waged by a stronger against a weaker nation." Jefferson Davis, a colonel with the Mississippi Rifles, was a hero in the Battle of Buena Vista. He made major by 1847. Stonewall Jackson entered as an artilleryman fresh out of West Point and was a major by 1847. Also serving in Mexico were soldiers by the names of Robert E. Lee, George B. McClellan, and P. G. T. Beauregard.

Brother did fight brother. Major H. B. McClellan, who served with Jeb Stuart, was the cousin of George B. McClellan, a Union general. Of Henry Clay's seven grandsons, three fought for the Union and four for the Confederacy, and four of Abraham Lincoln's brothers-in-law were Confederate soldiers.

Ironic, Isn't It?

• In a report home from a Spanish minister to the Court of Saint James's in 1611: "Their principal reason for colonizing these parts [Virginia] is to give an outlet to so many idle, wretched people as they have in England and thus prevent the dangers that might be feared from them."

• No doubt suffering from hunger, John Smith noted in his Jamestown diary, "Though there be fish in the sea, fowls in the air, and beasts in the woods, their bounds are so large, they so wild, and we so weak and ignorant, we cannot much trouble them." The entire colony almost starved because few of the early settlers knew how to

fire a gun (they were coopers, village postmasters, weavers, brewers, and shoemakers).

- In 1848, Henry Highland Garnet decreed, "It is too late to make a successful attempt to separate the black and white people in the New World. This Western world is destined to be filled with a mixed race."

- On February 14, 1892, Representative Lucas Wilson of Wisconsin proposed changing the name of the nation to "the United States of Earth." He explained, "It is possible for this republic to grow through the admission of new states...until every nation on earth has become a part of it."

- On October 9, 1905, President Teddy Roosevelt contemplated abolishing a brutal sport by executive decree. Men were being hurt, maimed, paralyzed, and killed at an alarming rate. Bare-knuckled boxing? Knifethrowing? Actually, it was football.

- While serving as secretary of commerce, Herbert Hoover steadfastly claimed, "American people will never stand for advertising on the air." He was talking about the radio, and after his statement, commercials on the radio began.

Money Magic

The main medium of exchange during the Middle Ages was silver. Silver was used to pay for the exotic treats (such as spices) merchants brought back to Europe from Asia. Large coins were preferred by traders to multiple small coins. A mint was established in 1486 in a town called Joachimsthal in Bohemia to manufacture the coins that were called Joachimsthalers. (Say that ten times fast.) A nickname developed, as nicknames do, and the coins became thalers or dalers. When the coins became internationally recognized, they became known in the trade circle as dollars.

Around the same time, the Spanish were busying themselves in Mexico, where they discovered mother lodes of silver and began minting the coins as pieces of eight or Spanish dollars.

In the 18th century, one of the symbols that appeared on these dollars was the Spanish coat of arms. On a shield were two pillars (representing the Pillars of Hercules at Gibraltar). An S-shaped ribbon wrapped around the pillars. Voilà! An explanation for the dollar sign. (The belief that it is an *S* superimposed on a *U* for the U.S. is doubtful.)

This Spanish dollar was the currency commonly used throughout colonial America. After the Revolution, the fledgling American government of the United States gave its new currency a familiar name. The dollar was born. (*Buck* probably comes from a buckskin container used to hold the pot in games of chance.)

Amid the portraits, architecture, and Freemason symbols, there are two phrases on every dollar bill borrowed from Virgil's *Aeneid: Annuit Coeptis*, "He [God] has smiled on our undertaking" or "God has been favorable to these things begun"; and *Novus Ordo Seclorum*, "A new order of the ages."

"In God We Trust" first appeared on a bronze two-cent piece issued April 22, 1864, probably inspired by the horror of the Civil War raging. Theodore Roosevelt lobbied to have the phrase removed from all American currency. *E Pluribus Unum* ("from many, one") was suggested as a motto for the country by John Adams, Benjamin

Franklin, and Thomas Jefferson in 1776. It first appeared on an American coin in 1786.

Now, without looking in your wallet, do you know whose picture is on the $100,000 bill? Give up? Okay, go ahead and look. Do you believe it? Woodie Wilson! For the record, here's a list of denominations and their corresponding portraiture.

Coins *(minted after 1972)*

penny—*Abraham Lincoln*
nickel—*Thomas Jefferson*
dime—*Franklin D. Roosevelt*
quarter—*George Washington*
half dollar—*John F. Kennedy*
dollar—*Dwight D. Eisenhower (or) Susan B. Anthony*

Bills

$1—*George Washington*
5—*Abraham Lincoln*
10—*Alexander Hamilton*
20—*Andrew Jackson*
50—*Ulysses S. Grant*
100—*Benjamin Franklin*
500—*William McKinley*
1,000—*Grover Cleveland*
5,000—*James Madison*
10,000—*Salmon Chase (he was appointed secretary of the treasury and then chief justice of the Supreme Court by Lincoln; we knew you'd want to know)*

Money Talks

"Money is better than poverty, if only for financial reasons."
—Woody Allen

"I have enough money to last me the rest of my life unless I buy something."
—Jackie Mason

"My problem lies in reconciling my gross habits with my net income."

—Errol Flynn

"The chief value of money lies in the fact that one lives in a world in which it is overestimated."

—H. L. Mencken

"The two most beautiful words in the English language are *check enclosed.*"

—Dorothy Parker

"Saving is a very fine thing. Especially when your parents have done it for you."

—Winston Churchill

"If you can count your money, you don't have a billion dollars."

—J. Paul Getty

"To turn $100 into $110 is work. To turn $100 million into $110 million is inevitable."

—Edgar Bronfman

"I'd like to be rich enough to throw the soap away after the letters are worn off."

—Andy Rooney

"Sudden money is going from zero to $200 a week. The rest doesn't count."

—Neil Simon

"I don't want to make money. I just want to be wonderful."

—Marilyn Monroe

"There was a time when a fool and his money were soon parted, but now it happens to everybody."

—Adlai E. Stevenson

"I'd like to live like a poor man—only with lots of money."

—Pablo Picasso

"I'd like to have money. And I'd like to be a good writer. These two can come together, and I hope they will, but if that's too adorable, I'd rather have money."

—Dorothy Parker

"Money it turned out was exactly like sex: you thought of nothing else if you didn't have it and thought of other things if you did."

—James Baldwin

"Money doesn't change men, it merely unmasks them. If a man is naturally selfish or arrogant or greedy, the money brings that out, that's all."

—Henry Ford

"Actually I have no regard for money. Aside from its purchasing power, it's completely useless as far as I'm concerned."

—Alfred Hitchcock

"If only God would give me some clear sign! Like making a deposit in my name in a Swiss bank account."

—Woody Allen

"The only people who claim that money is not important are people who have enough money so that they are relieved of the ugly burden of thinking about it."

—Joyce Carol Oates

"Being very rich, as far as I am concerned, is having a margin. The margin is being able to give."

—May Sarton

"The safest way to double your money is to fold it over once and put it in your pocket."

—Kim Hubbard

"Money is the poor people's credit card."
—Marshall McLuhan

"I have tried to become conservative. In 1958 I resolved to be simply a piano player. That was the year I lost $800,000."
—Liberace

"Where large sums of money are concerned, it is advisable to trust nobody."
—Agatha Christie

"No one would remember the good Samaritan if he'd only had good intentions. He had money as well."
—Margaret Thatcher

Body Parts

- The largest glandular organ in the human body is neither the brain nor the lungs. It is the liver, weighing in at 48 to 55 ounces.

- Among the most common foods to cause allergic reactions are nuts, shellfish, and various seafoods, milk, wheat, and eggs. Environmentally, the dreaded house dust mite, grass and tree pollens, and cats and dogs are the major culprits.

- The most common blood group shared by Americans is O positive.

- There are many phobias (a morbid fear disproportionate to the object of that fear) on the books. Common ones with which you may be familiar are arachnophobia (spiders) and agoraphobia (open spaces). Phobias with less familiar prefixes include trypanophobia (fear of injections) and ophiophobia (snakes).

- Want to live longer? If you're a man, consider moving to Japan, Iceland, Macau, or Hong Kong, where the male life expectancy, over 75 years, rates the highest in the world. Women who stand a good chance at celebrating 80 years live in Japan, France, Andorra, Switzerland, Iceland, Hong Kong, Macau, Sweden, the Netherlands, or Norway.

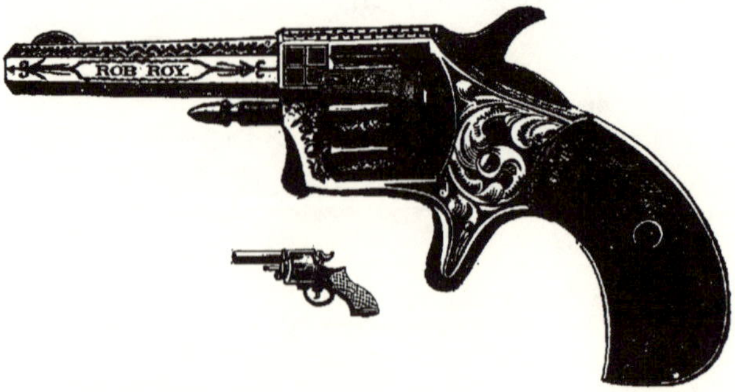

Guns Control

The right to bear arms. Maybe it was a misprint and the authors of the Constitution meant the right to bare arms, as in to wear sleeveless ensembles? Okay. Maybe not. But let's take a look at the original intent of the controversial line: "A well regulated Militia, being necessary to the security of a free State, the rights of the people to keep and bear Arms, shall not be infringed."

Colonists had had their fill of the soldiers who made up "standing armies." These men tended to be the dregs of society—mercenaries who could in turn be brutally treated by their commanding officers. They could swipe your livestock, feed themselves from your stores, and help themselves to your hearth and home.

The colonists never again wanted a government (American or foreign) to have that much control over the common people. The framers of the Constitution wanted to rely on citizen soldiers who would have nobler motivations than mercenaries. Alexander Hamilton reminded people in *The Federalist* that the sextupling of the king's army to 30,000 troops was one of the abuses that led to the British Revolution of 1688. In the British Bill of Rights (1689), there was an express prohibition against "raising or keeping a standing army within the kingdom in time of peace, unless with the consent of Parliament." The idea was to limit the power of the British monarch to send the army against the people (who may well have had legitimate grievances).

The American militia was organized (with the right to bear arms) to insure that the government (yes, the American government) didn't follow an inclination to assert and wield undue force in an effort to limit the personal freedom of the common folk. As Thomas Jefferson was fond of saying, a little rebellion now and then is a good thing.

War with Words

Many words and phrases have interesting historical roots, some evolving during wartime and remaining in common usage long after the signing of the peace treaty. *Bailing out* (as from a plane), shouting *Geronimo* (a ritual among some Native American paratroopers in World War II), *trooper* (a member of the cavalry), *KP* (kitchen police), *rookie* (from "recruit"), *shell shock*, *black market*, and *Dear John letter* are examples of words with military roots. Others include:

AWOL—an acronym for "absent without leave" that dates back to the Civil War

banzai—Japanese for "[may you live] 10,000 years," shouted when one goes on the attack or when one embarks on a suicide mission, from a Japanese war cry

barrage—evolved from the French *tir de barrage* ("barrier fire") in World War I

blimp—from B-limp, the name of the design of a British dirigible (zeppelins are named for their German creator, Count Ferdinand von Zeppelin)

blitz—from the German word for "lightning" or "flash," a full and aggressive attack. *Blitz* is used regularly by sports commentators and in strategy meetings at ad agencies. *Blitzkrieg* means, literally, "lightning war."

blockbuster—a method of saturation bombing that could level an entire city block

camouflage—based on a French slang word, *camoufler*, meaning "to disguise." Both British and American soldiers used it in World War I.

civvies—civilian clothes, as opposed to military uniforms

D-Day—the day on which a planned military action is due to begin. The actual D-Day was June 6, 1944. British, American, Canadian,

French, and Polish soldiers landed on the beaches in Normandy, France, to begin the Allied invasion of Europe against Hitler.

dreadnought—a kind of battleship, after the British vessel *Dreadnought.* "Dread naught," of course, means "fear nothing."

dud—a bullet, bomb, or shell that failed to explode

khakis—Hindi for "dusty," from the camouflage-colored uniforms first worn by the British Corps of Guides in India in the 1840s

flak—acronym from a type of German antiaircraft gun (Flieger, Abwehr, Kanonen). By the end of World War II, American soldiers used it to mean a barrage of criticism, and it eventually came to also embrace someone who does public relations.

fubar—acronym for "F—ed Up Beyond All Recognition"

gizmo—navy slang for a little gadgety doohickey

gung ho—adapted from a Chinese war cry meaning "with more fire," refers to zeal or intense devotion

R and R—"rest and rotation"

sack—nickname for bed, from military bed sacks

shrapnel—for its inventor, Colonel Shrapnel, who devised the new secret weapon in the early 1800s and originally named it "spherical case shot"

snafu—acronym for "Situation Normal: All F—ed Up"

snorkel—from the German *Schnorchel*, a ventilator developed in World War II to be used aboard submarines

whizzbang—sound-alike name given to a type of shell that whizzed through the air before exploding

zero—as a verb, derives from the fighter planes of Japanese pilots in World War II. The planes, light and maneuverable, had deadly aim.

zero hour—British military slang for the moment when an attack or operation was to go into effect

The PRESIDENTIAL *Beat*

➤ We Salute You

The president of the United States, ex-presidents, and a president-elect may receive a 21-gun salute upon his or her arrival and departure. And why does the president get a 21-gun salute? It is the sum of the digits in 1776; the year the country was founded adds up to 21.

After the final volley, there are four ruffles (on drums) and flourishes (on trumpets), followed immediately, depending upon the circumstances, by "Hail to the Chief" or the national anthem.

This noisy tribute may also be given to a visiting sovereign, chief of state of a foreign country, or member of a reigning royal family. The one difference is that the national anthem of the visiting dignitary is played.

The vice president, speaker of the house, American or foreign ambassadors, and premiers or prime ministers must settle for a 19-gun salute, but only upon arrival. The veep enjoys "Hail Columbia" after his or her ruffles and flourishes.

White House Factoids

- George Washington held the first cabinet meeting in 1793 with an attorney general, postmaster general, and secretaries of war, state, and treasury. Washington also has the dubious honor of being the first president to have a disagreement with the White House chef. He fired Sam Fraunces for spending too much to procure the first of the season's shad. However, Fraunces defended himself, saying that it was the responsibility of the chef to see that the nation's leader ate well. Fraunces was rehired.

- And since Washington was first in many regards, herewith another "first." What to call the great man. When the First Federal Congress convened, no one knew how to address G.W. One of the many little ironies of the new democracy was the ferocity of the debate surrounding this issue. Vice President Adams wanted pomp and ceremony. He favored royal titles. William Maclay, a senator from Pennsylvania, did not believe that an elected official should hold an honorific title. He pointed out that the Constitution specifically rejected titles. The merits of Your Highness, Your Elective Highness, and the Honorable were debated. Finally, the debate over an allowance for a standing army became a more important issue.

- As his predecessors bowed to their visitors, Thomas Jefferson was probably the first president to develop the presidential handshake. Jefferson was also the first to plant a kitchen garden on the White House lawn.

- Abraham Lincoln was the first to wear a beard.

- Grover Cleveland, in the 1880s, was the first to enjoy a telephone in the White House. He'd answer the line himself.

- Teddy Roosevelt was the first president to ride in an automobile, fly in an airplane, and go underwater in a submarine.

- Via radio, Warren G. Harding was the first president to have his inauguration broadcast to the masses. He installed the first radio in the White House in 1922.

- Franklin Roosevelt was the first president to make use of a White House pool. He and Eleanor were also probably the first to serve hot dogs to visiting dignitaries such as the king and queen of England.

- William H. Taft was the first to consume eight-course breakfasts as a daily ritual. A man of his times, Taft believed that a good and fit constitution came from eating amply.

- Warren Harding was the first "health nut." He ventured to John Harvey Kellogg's famous sanitorium in Battle Creek, Michigan, many times for meals of whole grain cereals and toxin-ridding enemas.

- Dwight D. Eisenhower was probably the first president to order up TV dinners from the White House kitchen, topped off by Mamie's fudge.

- John F. Kennedy was the first president to be born in the 20th century (1917).

- Jimmy Carter was the first president born in a hospital.

- Abe Lincoln was related to Paul Revere. Revere had two sons-in-law, Amos and Jedediah Lincoln, and their cousin, Thomas, was the father of Abe.

- John F. Kennedy was the first president who had been a Boy Scout.

- Richard Nixon was the first president to visit all 50 states.

- Herbert Hoover was the first president born west of the Mississippi River. He was born in West Branch, Iowa.

- Andrew Johnson was the only president who never attended a day of school. As a youngster, Johnson was an indentured servant, and rather than serve, he ran away. His owner then put advertisements in the paper to get him back.

- James Buchanan was the first and only bachelor in the White House. Two presidents were widowers, however.

- James Garfield was the only ambidextrous president, and he could write simultaneously with both hands.

- James Polk is the only president to adjourn a cabinet meeting so that he could meet a dwarf, the famous Tom Thumb.

- The longest-serving president was Franklin D. Roosevelt, who spent 12 years and 39 days in office. William Harrison had the misfortune of having the briefest term, 32 days.

- Ronald Reagan was a few weeks shy of his 70th birthday when he was inaugurated, the oldest president to date. While many believe John F. Kennedy was the youngest (he was 43), Theodore Roosevelt was 42 years old on the day of his inauguration. Bill Clinton (46) beats out Ulysses S. Grant by several months for the third youngest.

- The tallest president was Abraham Lincoln, who was 6′4″. The shortest was James Madison, who stood a foot shorter than Lincoln.

Our First Ladies

Martha Dandridge Custis Washington

Abigail Smith Adams

Martha Wayles Skelton Jefferson

Dorothea "Dolley" Payne Todd Madison

Elizabeth Kortright Monroe

Louisa Catherine Johnson Adams

Rachel Donelson Robards Jackson

Hannah Hoes Van Buren

Anna Symmes Harrison

Leticia Christian Tyler

Julia Gardiner Tyler

Sarah Childress Polk

Margaret Smith Taylor

Abigail Powers Fillmore

Caroline Carmichael McIntosh Fillmore

Jane Means Appleton Pierce

Mary Todd Lincoln
Eliza McCardle Johnson
Julia Dent Grant
Lucy Ware Webb Hayes
Lucretia Rudolph Garfield
Ellen Lewis Herndon Arthur
Frances Folsom Cleveland
Caroline Lavinia Scott Harrison
Mary Scott Lord Dimmick Harrison
Ida Saxton McKinley
Alice Hathaway Lee Roosevelt
Edith Kermit Carow Roosevelt
Helen Herron Taft
Ellen Louise Axson Wilson
Edith Bolling Galt Wilson
Florence Kling De Wolfe Harding
Grace Anna Goodhue Coolidge
Lou Henry Hoover
Anna Eleanor Roosevelt
Bess Wallace Truman
Mamie Geneva Doud Eisenhower
Jacqueline Lee Bouvier Kennedy
Claudia "Lady Bird" Alta Taylor Johnson
Thelma Catherine Patricia "Pat" Ryan Nixon
Elizabeth "Betty" Bloomer Warren Ford
Rosalynn Smith Carter
Anne Frances "Nancy" Robbins Davis Reagan
Barbara Pierce Bush
Hillary Rodham Clinton

First Lady Facts

- The first president's wife to be called "First Lady" was Mrs. Rutherford B. Hayes in an article written by Mary Clemmer Ames on March 5, 1877.

- Harriet Lane, niece of James Buchanan, served as the official White House hostess, and was the most celebrated first lady since Abigail Adams. The popular song "Listen to the Mockingbird" was dedicated to her.

- The only first lady born outside the United States was John Quincy Adams's wife, Louisa. She was born in London, of an American father and a British mother.

- Dolley Madison was an official hostess even before her husband James was elected president. When Madison was secretary of state, both President Jefferson and his vice president, Aaron Burr, were widowers, and called on Dolley to act as the official hostess at presidential functions.

- The youngest first lady was Francis Folsom Cleveland, a White House bride at the tender age of 21. Cleveland's sister served as the official hostess for the first 15 months of his term.

- Edith Wilson, wife of Woodrow, claimed to be a descendant of Pocahontas. When Woodrow Wilson had a stroke in October 1919, his illness was kept very quiet. For the 17 months he was recuperating, many of the decisions of state were made by Edith.

- Mary Todd Lincoln annoyed her frugal husband with her profligate spending. She bought an $80 handkerchief and once purchased a $4,000 bolt of fabric. Over one four-month period, she bought 300 pairs of gloves. Shades of Imelda Marcos! Ten years after Lincoln was assassinated, his son Robert had his mother committed to a mental institution in Chicago. She was soon released and died in 1882.

- Mrs. Theodore Roosevelt abhorred shaking hands with people. If she had to greet White House guests in a receiving line, she would hold a bouquet of flowers in each hand and bow instead of shaking hands.

- The only child born in the White House was to President and Mrs. Cleveland in 1893. They had a daughter, Esther.

- Calvin Coolidge's wife, Grace, was called "the number one Boston Red Sox fan."

First Exits

William Henry Harrison holds the record for the longest inaugural speech, some two hours in length, and he did it in cold, raw weather without wearing a hat or overcoat. During the ceremonies following the speech, Harrison twice had to be revived after he fainted, and that night he went to bed with a cold. The cold turned worse, and Harrison died a month later.

July 4, 1850, was a hot and humid day in Washington, and President Zachary Taylor ordered cold drinks, ice cream, and sherbet to be served at the day's festivities. Taylor helped himself to the ice cream and then collapsed at ceremonies at the Washington Monument. He suffered severe indigestion and then caught pneumonia and died.

As President John Adams was leaving office, one of his last official acts was to recall his son, John Quincy Adams, from his post as ambassador to Prussia. Adams did this to deprive his successor and rival Thomas Jefferson the pleasure of firing the younger Adams. John Quincy came back, made a successful run for the Senate, and, to the dismay of his father and the Boston Brahmins, became an avid supporter of Jefferson. John Quincy Adams then became president.

At the funeral ceremony following the death of Andrew Jackson, his parrot had to be removed from the proceedings because of the bird's profanity.

When ex-president John Tyler died there was no mention of his passing. The reason was that at the time of his death in 1862, he was a Confederate congressman, and it was in the middle of the Civil War. Not until 50 years after his demise did Congress finally authorize money for a statue to Tyler.

The U.S. government doesn't always pay its bills, at least in the case of the funeral for President Garfield after he was assassinated. The undertaker, a Mr. Spear, submitted a bill for $1,890.50, but it was never paid.

One first lady was even suspected of poisoning her husband. When Warren G. Harding died suddenly in San Francisco in 1923, some thought that he had been done in by his wife. The last to see him alive were his wife and his nurse.

Action Jackson and Honest Abe

While there are many myths with a choke hold on the real Andrew Jackson (he was far from the rowdy, uncouth, mannerless rube his political opponents made him out to be—although his enthusiastic supporters, called "hurrah boys," were notoriously obnoxious) and Honest Abe (the Gettysburg Address went through many thoughtful drafts and was not jotted down on the back of an envelope), the following stories about these two presidents are generally believed to be accurate:

- In South Carolina, 9-year-old future president Andrew Jackson was asked to read the just-arrived Declaration of Independence to a gathering of townsfolk.

- Jackson fought in the Revolutionary War at 13 and received a saber cut when, as a prisoner, he refused to clean the boots of a British soldier.

- Jackson was the first president to be the target of an assassination attempt. On January 30, 1835, Richard Laurence tried to shoot him not once but twice. Both pistols misfired. Jackson smacked his would-be assassin about with his cane.

• The nickname "Old Hickory" was bestowed by Jackson's troops because he disobeyed a direct order from John Armstrong, the secretary of war, in order to remain with his men. They declared him as tough as hickory.

• While serving as a defense lawyer, Lincoln once proved that a key prosecution witness was lying. The witness claimed to have seen the murder take place by the light of the moon. Lincoln pulled out an almanac to prove that there was a new moon that night.

• Often depicted as dour and remote, Lincoln was an avid joke-teller as well as a loving father who doted on his rambunctious sons.

• A man of many habits and superstitions, Abe liked keeping important notes and documents close by—under his stovepipe hat.

By Executive Order

Not one president between the administration of John Adams and that of Woodrow Wilson ever personally addressed Congress. The habit started with President Thomas Jefferson, who preferred sending written messages to Congress. Long made the butt of jokes because of his awkwardness as a speaker, he didn't want to risk appearing foolish if he didn't have to.

Although accused of hypocrisy and fathering children out of wedlock, Warren G. Harding was one of the hardest-working presidents in history. His routine was to be at his desk by 8:00 A.M. and knock off close to midnight.

Although every U.S. president has worn glasses, few deigned to wear them in public.

Franklin Roosevelt's famous line "The only thing we have to fear [beat] is fear itself" was not particularly original. French essayist Michel de Montaigne wrote, "The thing I fear most is fear," and Sir Francis Bacon came up with, "Nothing is terrible except fear itself." Closer to home, Henry David Thoreau offered, "Nothing is so much to be feared as fear."

Calvin Coolidge slept, on average, 12 hours every night and insisted on a two-hour nap in the afternoons. His idea of a treat was a nickel cigar or some vanilla pudding.

First Pets

George and Barbara Bush's dog, Millie, became a star after becoming a best-selling "author" while in the White House, and the Clintons made Socks the Top Cat. Presidential pets are a longstanding tradition. George Washington started it all with two pet jackasses, gifts from King Charles III of Spain, as well as four hounds.

Thomas Jefferson's grizzly bear was a gift from Meriwether Lewis (of Lewis and Clark fame) and lived at Monticello. The mockingbird he trained himself followed him around, it was reported, more like an affectionate house cat than a bird. William McKinley, however, went one better. He taught his parrot to whistle "Yankee Doodle." Caroline

Kennedy's childhood pony was named Macaroni, although it's doubtful she was aware of McKinley's parrot's theme song.

Taft's cow, Pauline, and Zachary Taylor's horse, Whitey, were allowed to graze on the White House lawn. Woodrow Wilson kept a flock of 18 sheep there. It was during the war years, and he wanted to set a good example for the country. Having the sheep crop the grass saved money. The sheep were shorn, and the wool was sold at a fundraising auction to benefit the Red Cross. It fetched $52,823. Not baaaad. He also had a pet ram named Old Ike that was partial to eating chewing tobacco.

Fido, that generic nom de canine, comes from the Latin word *fidus*, meaning "faithful." The ubiquity of the name can be traced to a yellow mutt owned by the sons of Abraham and Mary Todd Lincoln. Fido never lived in the White House, but he became famous because of a photograph taken of him, and the popularity of the name spread.

While FDR's beloved Fala received special attention from the press, Richard Nixon's Checkers has a speech named for him, and Lyndon B. Johnson's beagle, Him, was allowed to attend his master's inaugural parade. (Her must have been acting up.) LBJ caught flak from animal rights people when he was photographed holding his dogs by their ears.

After Warren Harding's death, newsboys from around the country donated pennies to honor the late president. The 19,134 pennies they collected were melted down to make a statue of Harding's beloved dog, Laddie Boy. The statue now resides in the Smithsonian.

➤ The Presidential Keel

The closest thing we have to a presidential yacht has been the *Honey Fitz*. Commissioned by Sewell L. Avery, chairman of the board of Montgomery Ward (1931–1955), and originally named the *Lenore*, in honor of his wife, the 88-ton yacht was a familiar sight cruising on Lake Michigan in the 30s. The boat was expropriated by the government in World War II, and Avery never forgave then-president Roosevelt.

After a stint in the Coast Guard as *CG-92004*, the yacht was assigned to the navy yard in Washington, D.C., in 1945. While Harry Truman preferred the larger yacht at his disposal, the 244-foot *Williamsburg*, the *Lenore II*, as the vessel was renamed, was still used to shuttle the Secret Service men who accompanied Truman on his cruises.

Dwight Eisenhower thought the *Williamsburg* "too rich for my blood" and retired it in favor of the *Lenore II*. Renaming it *Barbara Anne* for one of his granddaughters, he had it refurbished and overhauled for the first family's enjoyment.

It was John F. Kennedy, though, who derived special pleasure from the yacht, renamed the *Honey Fitz* (in honor of Rose Fitzgerald Kennedy's father). Jacqueline Kennedy had it redecorated, and the family regularly enjoyed Potomac cruises and ocean-faring holidays aboard ship.

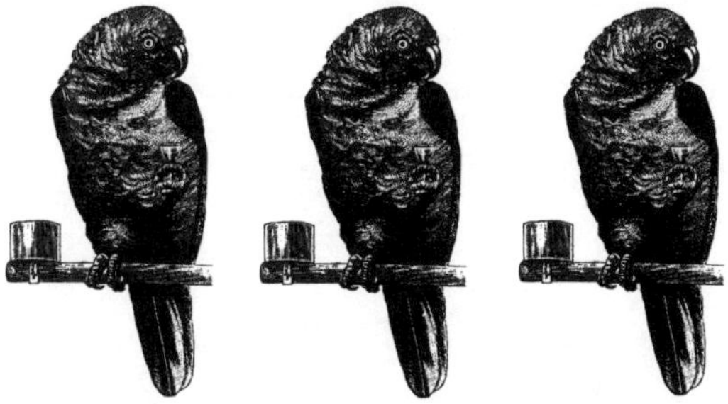

Lyndon Johnson liked to serve lavish Tex-Mex dinners aboard the *Honey Fitz*. Richard Nixon renamed the yacht yet again for his wife, Patricia, but hankered for a larger vessel and put it up for sale in 1970.

Joseph Keating bought the historic yacht, renaming it the *Presidents*, and set about remodeling it to recapture its appearance when Kennedy was at the helm. He has also made the main salon a gallery of the presidents who have been associated with the yacht.

Today the yacht, known again as the *Honey Fitz*, is mostly used by private groups for cruises, weddings, and glamorous events and is often seen docked in the shadow of the World Financial Center in New York City.

Close Seconds

The stories about the office of Vice President of the United States and those who have served as second-in-command have too long been relegated to historical footnote. Attention is due. But, like Canada, little is known or remembered about American veeps. Time to change all that.

Take, for example, the expression "What this country really needs is a good five-cent cigar." The author was Thomas R. Marshall, Wilson's veep, who was being bored to tears during a Senate debate in 1915.

What's a veep to do? Article 2 of the U. S. Constitution addresses this. Amendment 12 covers how a president and vice president are chosen and Amendment 20 states the length of terms they (along with senators) may serve. Amendment 25 explains the procedure and order of succession if a president is disabled.

Following is a list of the Presidents, their Veeps, and the candidates they defeated. How many could you name?

Year Elected	President	Vice President	Losing Candidates
1996	William Clinton (D)	Al Gore	Robert Dole (R) Ross Perot (Ind)
1992	William Clinton (D)	Al Gore	George Bush (R)
1988	George Bush (R)	Danforth Quayle	Mike Dukakis (D)

1984	Ronald Reagan (R)	George Bush	Walter Mondale (D)
1980	Ronald Reagan (R)	George Bush	Jimmy Carter (D) John Anderson (Ind)
1976	Jimmy Carter (D) Gerald Ford (R)	Walter Mondale Nelson Rockefeller	Gerald Ford (R)
1972	Richard Nixon (R)	Spiro Agnew	George McGovern (D) John Schmitz (American Independent)
1968	Richard Nixon (R)	Spiro Agnew	Hubert Humphrey (D) George Wallace (AI)
1964	Lyndon Johnson (D)	Hubert Humphrey	Barry Goldwater (R)
1960	John Kennedy (D)	Lyndon Johnson	Richard Nixon (R)
1956	Dwight Eisenhower (R)	Richard Nixon	Adlai Stevenson (D)
1952	Dwight Eisenhower (R)	Richard Nixon	Adlai Stevenson (D)
1948	Harry Truman (D)	Alben Barkley	Thomas Dewey (R) Strom Thurmond (States Rights) Henry Wallace (P)
1944	Franklin Roosevelt (D)	Harry Truman	Thomas Dewey (R)
1940	Franklin Roosevelt (D)	Henry Wallace	Wendell Wilkie (R)
1936	Franklin Roosevelt (D)	John Nance Garner	Alf Landon (R)
1932	Franklin Roosevelt (D)	John Nance Garner	Herbert Hoover (R)
1928	Herbert Hoover (R)	Charles Curtis	Al Smith (D)
1924	Calvin Coolidge (R)	Charles Dawes	John Davis (D) Robert La Follette (Pr)
1920	Warren Harding (R)	Calvin Coolidge	James Cox (D)
1916	Woodrow Wilson (D)	Thomas Marshall	Charles Hughes (R)
1912	Woodrow Wilson (D)	Thomas Marshall	Theodore Roosevelt (Pr) William Taft (R)
1908	William Taft (R)	James Sherman	William J. Bryan (D)
1904	Theodore Roosevelt (R)	Charles Fairbanks	Alton Barker (D)
1900	William McKinley (R)	Theodore Roosevelt	William J. Bryan (D)
1896	William McKinley (R)	Garret Hobart	William J. Bryan (D)
1892	Grover Cleveland (D)	Adlai Stevenson	Benjamin Harrison (R)
1888	Benjamin Harrison (R)	Levi Morton	Grover Cleveland (D)
1884	Grover Cleveland (D) Chester Arthur (R)	Thomas Hendricks no veep	James G. Blaine (R)
1880	James Garfield (R)	Chester Arthur	Winfield Hancock (D)
1876	Rutherford Hayes (R)	William Wheeler	Samuel Tilden (D)
1872	Ulysses Grant (R)	Henry Wilson	Horace Greeley (D)

1868	Ulysses Grant (R) Andrew Johnson (R)	Schuyler Colfax no veep	Horatio Seymour (D)
1864	Abraham Lincoln (R)	Andrew Johnson	George McClelan (D)
1860	Abraham Lincoln (U)	Hannibal Hamlin	Stephen Douglas (D) John Breckenridge (D) John Bell (Constitutional Union)
1856	James Buchanan (D)	John Breckinridge	John C. Fremont (R) Millard Fillmore (Amer)
1852	Franklin Pierce (D) Millard Fillmore (W)	William King no veep	Winfield Scott John Hale (Free Soil)
1848	Zachary Taylor (W)	Millard Fillmore	Lewis Cass (D)
1844	James Polk (D) John Tyler	George Dallas no veep	Henry Clay (Nat. Rep.)
1840	William H. Harrison (W)	John Tyler	Martin Van Buren (D)
1836	Martin Van Buren (D)	Richard Johnson	William H. Harrison (Whig)
1832	Andrew Jackson (D)	Martin Van Buren	Henry Clay (Nat. Rep.)
1828	Andrew Jackson (D)	John Calhoun	John Quincy Adams (Nat. Rep.)
1824	John Quincy Adams (D)	John Calhoun	Andrew Jackson (none) William H. Crawford (none)
1820	James Monroe (DR)	Daniel Tompkins	John Quincy Adams (none)
1816	James Monroe (DR)	Daniel Tompkins	Rufus King (Fed.)
1812	James Madison (DR)	Elbridge Gerry	DeWitt Clinton (Fed.)
1808	James Madison (DR)	George Clinton	Charles Pinckney (Fed.)
1804	Thomas Jefferson (DR)	George Clinton	Charles Pinckney (Fed.)
1800	Thomas Jefferson (DR)	Aaron Burr	Aaron Burr (DR)
1796	John Adams (Fed.)	Thomas Jefferson	Thomas Jefferson (DR)
1792	George Washington (Fed.)	John Adams	none
1789	George Washington (Fed.)		none

After the vice president, what is the line of succession should the president become incapacitated? Speaker of the House of Representatives; president pro tempore of the Senate; secretary of state; secretary of the treasury; secretary of defense; attorney general; secretary of the interior; secretary of agriculture; secretary of commerce; secretary of labor; secretary of health and human services; secretary of housing and urban development; secretary of transportation; secretary of energy; and secretary of education.

An interesting detail to note: During the president's State of the Union address, all pomp and circumstance are observed. Everyone stands, applauds, and is supposed to show bipartisan support. However, one member of the cabinet does not attend. That one person (chosen at the last moment by lottery) is removed from the premises in case the rest of the chain of command is the victim of foul play or an act of God.

Common LANGUAGE

☛ Get It Strait

It's estimated that more than 300 million people around the globe speak English. There are some 200,000 words in common use. French, for example, has half that in use. That's why we have so many problems expressing ourselves accurately. To wit:

- affect and effect: To affect something is to influence or to pretend. When used as a verb, to effect is to bring something about or to make it happen.

- stationary and stationery: How do you remember that *stationary* means something that doesn't move and *stationery* refers to writing paper and envelopes? The trick is, *stationery* has an *e*, as does the "letter" you write on it.

- stalactite and stalagmite: Geology 101 graduates may have dim recollections of this. *Stalaktos* is Greek for "dripping." Both are icicle-shaped deposits of calcium carbonate, but one hangs down from the ceiling or walls of caves and one "grows" up from the floor. Stalagmite has a *g* in it for ground; stalactite has a *c* for ceiling.

- emigrant and immigrant: The emigrant is the one who leaves his or her country to settle permanently in another country. The emigrant becomes an immigrant, once he or she has entered and settled in that new country. This trick may help you keep them straight: the emigrant leaves (both words have an *e*), while the immigrant is incoming (both words have an *i*).

- principle and principal: A principle is a basic truth, law, or rule. A principal is the person or idea that is most important. Remember: If you have sound principles, the principal will be your pal.

- apogee and perigee: While these two don't come up as much in conversation as the others mentioned, they do pop up in crosswords and on quiz shows. These words have to do with orbits. One refers to the point at which a satellite is closest to the object it is orbiting; the other refers to the most distant point. Another vowel clue will help you remember that the apogee (beginning with *a*) is farther away.

- lie and lay: Another troublesome pair, but you need only remember that *lay* is a transitive verb, while *lie* is intransitive. Not very helpful, you say? Think of it this way: a transitive verb takes a direct object (as in, "Okay, I'm going to lay my cards on the table"). An intransitive verb does not ("I'm feeling a little verklempt—I need to lie down"). Speaking in the past tense does add a bit to the confusion, since the past tense of *lie* is *lay*, and the past tense of *lay* is *laid.* Sounds like a bawdy limerick brewing, doesn't it? But let's let sleeping dogs lie.

George Abbott, the author, playwright, and humorist who passed away in 1994 at the age of 102, was a man who knew his p's and q's. In his 90s, Abbott collapsed on the fairway while playing golf with his wife. She stood over him, pleading, "George, please get up. Don't just lay there." Abbott's eye fluttered open. "Lie there," he corrected.

☛ Left to One's Own Devices

While these literary devices were probably once explained in English class, a refresher course might be in order.

• Similes and metaphors are both comparisons, but similes always contain the word *like* or *as*. An example: "Her lips are like cherries." In a metaphor, the comparison is more direct. To emphasize a point, something becomes something else. For instance, "Her lips were cherries."

• Onomatopoeia (easier to remember what it is than how to spell it) is a word that, when spoken, actually sounds like what it means. *Buzz*, *ululate*, *pop*, and *tintinnabulation* (the ringing of bells).

• When you moan you're so tired you could sleep for a month, you're using hyperbole—gross exaggerations used to underscore a point, made for effect and not to be taken literally. Now give me a cup of coffee the size of Lake Erie so I can snap out of it.

• Oxymorons are not stupid cart-pullers. In an oxymoron, contradictory or incongruous words or phrases are brought together to produce a witty remark such as "the silence was deafening." Some oxymorons are unintentional, as in the case of "jumbo shrimp" or "military intelligence." Indeed, *oxymoron* comes from two Greek words meaning "sharp" and "foolish." Some words are, in themselves, oxymorons. Examples are *bittersweet* and *chiaroscuro* (Italian for "bright-dark").

• Synecdoche is about parts and wholes. In a synecdoche, a part can be used to stand for the whole. In "all hands on deck," for example, "hand" is the part representing "people," the whole. Synecdoches can also be flipped so the whole represents a part, as when "the law" is used to mean a single police officer. Metonymy is a similar rhetorical device (with a bit of the metaphor thrown in), in which a trait or object is used to stand for something with which it is closely associated. The classic example is "the crown" for a monarch; in our democratic society, it becomes "the White House" or "the Oval Office" for the president.

• And while we're on the subject of the presidency, can you identify the literary device used by John F. Kennedy in his inaugural address? "Ask not what your country can do for you, but what you can do for your country" is a chiasmas. This is a technique of inverting the word order of the first phrase in the second of two linked phrases.

- If you think litotes and meiosis are related exclusively to biology, you're wrong. Granted, meiosis is a form of cell division. But, in rhetoric, it's also a kind of understatement that belittles by making something seem less significant than it really is (like referring to a deep cut as "just a little scratch"). Litotes are another convoluting form of understatement, in which a positive is stressed by denying something negative ("This is no small problem").

- "On her fishing trip, my daughter caught a trout and a cold." This is a zeugma, a phrase in which a verb or adjective is used with two or more other words that are not commonly linked.

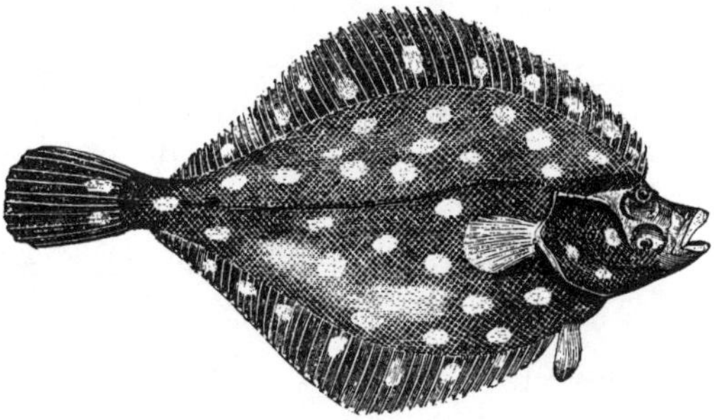

Grammatically Correct

Face it. Grammar is not the subject that makes schoolchildren sit up, pay attention, and beg for more (that's lunch). Diagramming sentences has stripped the gears of many sixth-grade brains, and the I/me quagmire bogs down most English majors.

To help you avoid common grammatical errors you probably never even knew you were making:

- who/whom: Calvin Trillin once said that *whom* was invented to make everyone sound like a butler. Nevertheless, there are times one must use it and use it correctly. Just remember that *who* is the subjective case form (i.e., the subject of the sentence or clause) and *whom* is the objective case form (the object of the verb or preposition). An example: "Who went to the ball game Saturday night?" but "At whom did you throw popcorn Saturday night?" A pertinent quote from George Ade: "'Whom are you?' said he, for he had been to night school."

• I/me: This is another objective versus subjective situation. "Newt and me went to the ball game Saturday night." Why is this ungrammatical (not to mention like hearing nails on a chalkboard for some)? Because you wouldn't say, "Me went to the ball game Saturday night" (unless you provide the voice-over for Cookie Monster). This is another common trap (so common it's in danger of being considered correct): "between you and I" is wrong. It is "between you and me" because *me* is the object of the preposition *between*. Then again, when you greet someone on the phone with "Hi, it's me," you are wrong. Yes, it's you all right, but identify yourself grammatically by saying, "It is I."

• may/can: Another distinction that trips us up is may/can. "Can I please have a piece of candy?" asks your seven-year-old. The "please" is a polite touch and certainly endearing, but the choice of "can" is wrong. *Can* means able to do something. Certainly your child is able to have a piece of candy. What the kid's really asking for is permission to have a piece of candy. Just remember that the children's playground game is "Mother, May I?" not "Mother, Can I?" Whether or not the little one may have that piece of candy is, of course, up to you and how sweet the "please."

• which/that: This is a tough one. The two are often used interchangeably. According to Strunk and White's *Elements of Style*, *that* is the defining (or restrictive) pronoun and *which* is the nondefining (or nonrestrictive) pronoun. A pronoun introducing a restrictive clause does not take a comma, while a pronoun introducing a nonrestrictive clause does. "The VCR that is broken is in the living room." (Defines, in a two-(or-more-)VCR household, which VCR is under discussion.) "The VCR, which is broken, is in the living room." (It's clear this is the only VCR in the house—and forget about taping *The Simpsons* until it's fixed.)

☛ Get It Write

• Brides don't actually walk up or down the aisle. *Aisle* is derived from the French *aile* or "wing," the lateral passages of a church. Brides and grooms walk the central passage.

• *Between* should be used with two, and *among* with more than two. For example, you can only share a candy bar between two people. If there are five of you, it's shared among you, so ya'll better get the big bar.

• *Re* is not an abbreviation for *regarding*, as it is commonly believed to be. Rather, it is a form of the Latin word *res* meaning "matter, thing, or affair." In a business letter, *re* should mean "in the matter of."

• *I.e.* means "that is to say" and comes from the Latin *id est*. This is only used as an abbreviation: using it in full, according to H. W. Fowler, will "convict one of affectation." It should be used to drive home a point and not to introduce an example. To introduce an example, the proper Latin abbreviation is *e.g.* (short for *exempli gratia*, meaning "for instance").

• *Ad hoc* is a Latin phrase that literally means "toward this." It has come to mean something arranged or put together for a particular purpose.

☛ Federal Expressions

• *Hackney*, as in a horse-drawn carriage, comes from the French word *haquenée*, a slow old nag. The shortened version *hack* also refers to a writer who gets the job done without paying much attention to poetry or high literary standards. A *hacker* is someone who tries hard at a sport but, though enthusiastic, is not particularly talented. These days *hacker* also refers to someone knowledgeable about and skilled with computers.

• *Widow's walks* were not designed as a way for the wives of sea captains to watch the horizon for sails. Rather, they provided a way for homeowners to skitter around the rooftop to put out chimney fires.

• *Codger*, meaning an old grumpy guy, comes from Codger's Hall, a London debating society. The name evolved from the Latin expression *cogito ergo sum* (I think, therefore I am).

• England's *Scotland Yard* was so named because the Scottish embassy once occupied the address.

☛ Britspeak

Watching British imports on the telly can really get up your nose, as they say. Though sharing a common language (of sorts), Americans need a dictionary of Briticisms just to "get" what's going on in any BBC production. In the category of cars and driving alone, there are many variations (but first, check out which side of the road you're on):

car trunk—*boot*
tire—*tyre*
gas—*petrol*
diesel—*derv (for diesel engine road vehicle)*
car hood—*bonnet*
main highway between cities—*A-road*
alternative route—*B-road*
flashing light at a crosswalk—*Belisha beacon at a zebra crossing*
intersection marked to warn gridlockers—*box junction*
someone with a learner's permit—*L-driver with an L-plate*
truck—*lorry*
semi—*HGV (heavy goods vehicle)*
speed bump—*sleeping policeman* (really)

In England, pedestrian crosswalks marked with black and white stripes are known as zebra crossings. Some corners where pedestrians may feel especially safe are called pelican crossings. Traffic lights are set to hold traffic while people cross the street. The name has nothing to do with the sea birds. Rather, it's based on PEdestrian LIght CONtrolled crossing.

The most important thing to remember when driving around the British Isles is that a WC (water closet) or loo is our equivalent of a comfort station or toilet.

Parlez-Vous

You say you can't speak French—but you can, little chouchou, and you do every day. Consider how many words in common you and a Parisian already have.

carte blanche—*white card* or complete discretionary power

cause celèbre—*celebrated cause* or an important, notorious, or well-publicized incident

coup d é'tat—forceful overthrow of a government

déjà vu—*already seen* or the sensation of experiencing something experienced before

esprit de corps—*group spirit* or camaraderie

fait accompli—*an accomplished fact* or deed

faux pas—a mistake or social blunder

joie de vivre—*joy of living*

nouveau riche—*new rich*; this carries a pejorative edge for people who have recently come into wealth and are conspicuous consumers

oeuvre—*work* or deed

raison d'être—*reason for being*

sang-froid—*cold-blood* or highly composed or cool

savoir-faire—*to know how to do* with great social confidence

vis-à–vis—*face to face* or compared to

☛ Just a Figure of Speech

• *Tom Swifties,* a fad in the early 1960s, are sentences based upon a punning adverb. "I'm taking flying lessons," she said airily.

• The wonderful term *blurb*—meaning a line printed on a book jacket to entice readers and sell copies—was coined by Gelett Burgess in a speech at the 1907 American Booksellers Convention dinner in New York City. He described his invention as akin to sounds a publisher makes.

• *Freelance* dates back to the Crusades of the 12th century. Warrior knights allied themselves with a landed lord in exchange for property, salary, and a coat of arms. But what if a knight fell out of favor or his sponsor died? The landless and lordless earned a living by offering themselves as mercenaries—lances for hire. Cable: Paladin.

• What is an *epigram*? According to English poet Algernon Swinburne, "A dwarfish whole,/Its body brevity, and wit its soul."

• *Clerihews* are named for Edmund Clerihew Bentley (1875–1956). They are rhyming quatrains featuring irreverent takes on famous folks. For example: Sir Christopher Wren/Said, "I'm going to dine with some men./If anybody calls,/say I'm designing St. Paul's."

• *Pornography* is Greek for "writing of harlots." Porneius is a character from ancient Greek lore whose name means "fornication." The son of Anagnus ("unchaste"), Porneius tried to have his way with Parthenia ("chaste maid"), who, in the end, had her way with him. She ran him through with his own spear. One wag suggested that a group of harlots be referred to as a pride of loins.

• *Anecdote* dates back to Byzantine times. Emperor Justinian, renowned for the Justinian legal code, ruled from A.D. 527 to 565 and kept a journal about the daily doings in court. His observations were written with a keen sense of satire. While it is doubtful Justinian meant for the journal to be read by anyone else, Procopius, a secretary to one of Justinian's generals, published it. Procopius, in a brilliant marketing strategy, titled the collection *Anekdota* meaning "undisclosed and confidential." Hence *anecdote*, a short, factual story akin to those written by Justinian. Yes, this is an anecdote.

Department of Redundancy Department

They do tend to stumble into the middle of a conversation, more as clichés than as clever turns of phrase. But think before you leap to avoid dreaded redundancies. Herewith some redundant phrases most of us have tossed about thoughtlessly:

betwixt and between
each and every
equally as
close proximity
very unique
free gift
revert back
final endgame
opening gambit
consensus of opinion (*consensus* means "a majority of opinions")

Catch a Code

The telegraph, invented by Samuel Finley Breese Morse in 1835, and the Morse code transformed the way the world communicated. By 1838, cables were being laid that could transmit a message in a series of dots and dashes in minutes—no more waiting for the ship to come in or the breathless pony to arrive. It was only in 1994 that the U.S.

Coast Guard stopped routinely monitoring an emergency channel for distress signals in Morse code.

As long as you have a moment, start committing this to memory in case you ever need to tap out a message on a drainpipe.

A .––	J .–––	S ...
B –...	K –.–	T –
C –.–.	L .–..	U ..–
D –..	M ––	V ...–
E .	N –.	W.––
F ..–.	O –––	X –..–
G ––.	P .––.	Y –.––
H	Q ––.–	Z ––..
I ..	R .–.	

period .–.–.–

comma ––..––

question mark ..––..

apostrophe .––––.

quotation marks .–..–.

colon –––...

0 –––––	1 .––––	2 ..–––	3 ...––	4 ....–
5	6 –....	7 ––...	8 –––..	9 ––––.

Mything Persons

Every word has a story, but some of the best come from mythology. Take the word *clue*, for example. In medieval English a clewe (not yet spelled *clue*) was a ball of thread. In Greek mythology, Theseus used a ball of thread given him by the king's daughter, Ariadne, to find his way back through the labyrinth after doing away with the Minotaur. He followed the clue to safety. Others include:

Achilles' heel—This phrase is used to refer to someone or something's weak spot or vulnerability. In Greek myth, Thetis dipped her young son, Achilles, into the River Styx to make him invincible. Unfortunately, she held him by the heel, so it didn't get wet, and this oversight cost him his life. During the Trojan Wars, an arrow struck him in the heel and killed him.

atlas—Atlas was a Titan who attempted to overthrow Zeus, king of the gods. For his treasonous act, he was condemned to support the pillars of heaven for eternity. The 16th-century cartographer Gerhardus Mercator first printed Atlas holding the world on his shoulders to illustrate the first page of his collection of maps. The image was widely imitated, and gradually *atlas* became a generic name for any bound collection of maps.

hygiene—Hygieia was a Greek goddess of health. The daughter of Aesculapius, the god of medicine and healing, she was responsible for maintaining the atmosphere and was capable of warding off pestilence. *Hygiene* is derived from her name.

Janus—According to Roman myth, Janus was the doorkeeper of the universe and could open and close all things. He was often depicted with two faces, one looking to the future and one to the past. The first month of the year is named for him.

nemesis—A Greek goddess of retribution, Nemesis was responsible for the equilibrium of the universe. She meted out both rewards and punishments, but made more lasting impressions with her dark side. Though the word still carries the meaning of retributive justice, the expression "meet one's nemesis" refers to an encounter with a formidable opponent.

protean—Proteus was a minor sea deity who had the gift of prophecy and was able to assume different shapes to elude his enemies. *Protean* can be complimentary (someone who is versatile and flexible) or a bit of a dig (someone who is fickle or changes opinions to best suit selfish ends).

Pygmalion—Picked up by George Bernard Shaw (whose play, in turn, was the basis for the musical *My Fair Lady*), the name was borrowed from an ancient king of Cyprus. A woman-hater, he made his ideal woman by sculpting a statue with which he fell in love. He implored Aphrodite, the goddess of love, to intercede and blow life into the statue. She did, and the king made her his queen.

sword of Damocles—Damocles was a member of the court of Dionysus the Elder. After voicing his envy of the king's wealth and power, Damocles was invited by the king to sample the pleasures of ruling for a day. Damocles eagerly accepted and went to sit on the throne. During a magnificent banquet prepared just for him, he leaned back and noticed a sword directly over his head suspended by a tiny thread. As quickly as he had hopped up onto the throne, he jumped off, realizing that everything had a price. The expression now connotes a constant and imminent danger.

labors of Sisyphus—Sisyphus was a king of Corinth whose criminal acts led to an unusual punishment by the unamused gods. He was sentenced to roll a massive boulder up the side of a mountain, but it would roll down to the bottom each time he got it to the top, and he would have to start again. Hence, a sisyphean task is an effort that is unending and requires enormous exertion.

tantalize—Yet another king who offended the gods, Tantalus was subjected to his own cruel and unusual punishment. In a cave, he was made to suffer the torments of constant hunger and thirst. Luscious fruits grew by his head, just out of reach, and the water in which he stood receded when he tried to drink. He gave us the world *tantalize*, meaning to "tease with the promise of something greatly desired but unattainable."

Make No Myth-take

Here's a list of the major deities in Greek mythology and their Roman counterparts:

Greek	Roman	Areas of Interest and/or Control
Aphrodite	Venus	Goddess of love
Apollo	Apollo	God of light, medicine, and poetry
Ares	Mars	God of war (the moons of the planet Mars are named for his companion Phobos and Deimos, "panic" and "fear")
Artemis	Diana	Goddess of hunting, childbirth, and youth
Athena	Minerva	Goddess of wisdom, war, and arts and crafts
Demeter	Ceres	Goddess of agriculture

Dionysus	Bacchus	God of wine and fertility
Eros	Cupid	God of love
Gaia	Terra	Goddess of the earth
Hades	Pluto	God of the underworld
Hephaestus	Vulcan	God of fire and metalwork
Hera	Juno	Queen of the gods
Hermes	Mercury	Messenger of the gods; also god of commerce and science, and protector of travelers, thieves, and vagabonds
Hestia	Vesta	Goddess of the hearth
Hypnos	Somnus	God of sleep
Poseidon	Neptune	God of the sea
Uranus	Uranus	Father of the Titans
Zeus	Jupiter	King of the gods

Something Is Mything

There are a number of charming myths and legends to explain the origins of various flowers.

narcissus—Narcissus, the poster boy for all-consuming vanity, never noticed the nymphs vying for his attention. The handsome cad also ignored Echo, the mountain nymph who adored him, preferring to spend all his time admiring his own image reflected in a nearby pond. Echo pined until nothing was left of her but her voice (which can still be heard in the mountains). The gods, angry with Narcissus for his vanity and callousness, punished him by turning him into a flower that must always sit by a pool, nodding at its own reflection.

hyacinth—Zephyr, god of the winds, and Apollo, god of the sun, were both fond of Hyacinthus, a prince of Sparta. One day, when Apollo was teaching Hyacinthus to throw a discus, Zephyr was overcome with jealousy. In a rage, he blew the discus back at Hyacinthus, striking him in the head and killing him. The grief-stricken Apollo created the hyacinth from the blood of his beloved friend.

Venus looking-glass (campanula* or *bellflower)—According to Roman legend, Venus, goddess of love and beauty, possessed a magical mirror; whoever looked into the glass saw only beauty reflected back. When Venus misplaced the treasure, a shepherd found it. He was so taken by his new and improved reflection that he refused to return it. Venus dispatched her son, Cupid, to retrieve it. The two struggled, the mirror shattered, and everywhere a sliver fell, a flower grew.

lily of the valley—In 599, St. Leonard, a reclusive member of the court of Clovis of France, received permission from the king to live in a nearby forest to better commune with nature and God. Unfortunately, the forest was also home to a dragon, Temptation, who wasn't keen on sharing his space. Temptation demanded that the intruder leave, but St. Leonard, deep in prayer, didn't hear him. When the dragon burned down his hut, a fierce three-day battle ensued with St. Leonard ultimately slaying the dragon. Where the dragon's blood fell, a poisonous weed grew, but where St. Leonard's blood dropped, the beautiful, sweet-smelling lily of the valley blossomed.

peony—Paeon was a student of Aesculapius, the god of medicine and healing. Leto, mother of the twins Apollo and Artemis, told Paeon of a root growing on Mount Olympus that would ease the pain of childbirth. Paeon decided to harvest the root to use for his patients, but Aesculapius, fearing that his student's medical skill might eclipse his own, swore he'd kill him. Leto intervened and begged Zeus for help. Zeus saved Paeon from the anger of his mentor by turning him into a flower.

primrose—A story about the origin of primroses involves St. Peter, the keeper of the heavenly gates. Upon hearing a rumor that some unsavory types were trying to sneak into heaven through the back door, he dropped his keys. Where they fell, primroses grew. Superstitious folk once thought that the primrose held the power to open locked treasure, perhaps because its cluster of flowers resembles a bunch of keys. The German name for the primrose is *Himmelschusslechen*, or "little keys to heaven."

forget-me-not—After God finished creating the world, He still had the task of naming every creature and plant in it. Anyone who has ever faced the task of naming a newborn knows this is not as easy as it seems. Thinking Himself finished at last, He heard a small voice saying, "How about me?" Looking down, the Creator spied a small flower. "I forgot you once," He said, "but it will not happen again." The forget-me-not was born.

pink dianthus—The first of these flowers were flesh-colored and were called carnations from the Latin *carnatio*, or "flesh." Christian legend has it that carnations sprang up where Mary's tears fell at Calvary.

rose—According to Roman legend, Rhodanthe was a woman of stunning beauty who attracted many men but was interested in none of them. She went to the temple of Diana to avoid her suitors, but they followed her there and broke down the gates to get to her. The enraged goddess Diana turned Rhodanthe into a beautiful rose and her suitors into the thorns.

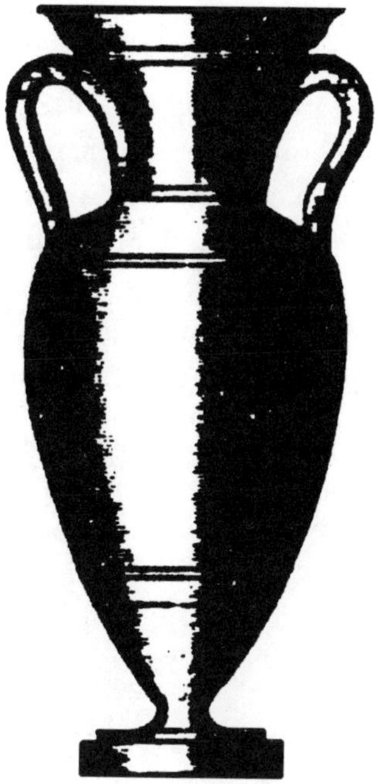

Great White Hope

Not all myths played out in ancient times. In 1994, a miracle happened in the form of Miracle, a white baby buffalo born on the Heider family farm in Wisconsin. The Great Plains Indian tribes exulted, because a white buffalo—or more correctly, bison—is the stuff of myths. It symbolizes hope, rebirth of native culture, and global unity.

Hundreds of people from all over the world made a pilgrimage to see the white calf for themselves and to pay their respects.

The odds of a white buffalo are, according to the National Buffalo Association, about one in six billion. (There are now approximately 200,000 buffalo in North America.) There was one other white buffalo born in this century that we know of. His name was Big Medicine, and he died in 1959 at the age of 36.

The coming of Miracle was especially meaningful to the Cheyenne, who honor white buffalo as a sign of well-being and as messengers of creation. They foretell a new awakening. Just about every Great Plains tribe celebrates the mythic beast. The Rosebud Sioux tell of three hunters who encountered a white calf, which, upon seeing them, turned into a woman. She told the men to go home and await her. They waited for four days, preparing for her arrival. She appeared with a sacred pipe and *Woo'pe*, Sioux laws. The Fox Indians of Wisconsin perform an ancient White Buffalo Dance to empower hunters.

Sweet TALK

Sealed with a Kiss

When trying to wend your way into someone's heart, it's hard to miss if your words are well chosen. Some wonderful love notes have been written by some unlikely people. The author of the sweet reflection "I believe myself that romantic love is the source of the most intense delights that life has to offer" was none other than Bertrand Russell. For some glowing poetry to whip out on Valentine's Day or during a wedding ceremony, consult the classics (they survived for a reason).

In the seventh century, Bhartrihari wrote what is considered to this day some of the most sublime Sanskrit lyric poetry:

Where are you going, winsome maid
Through deepest, darkest night? (he said)
I go to him whom love had made
Dearer to me than life (she said).

Ah, girl, and are you not afraid
For you are all alone? (he said)
The god of love shall be my aid,
Arrows of love fly true (she said).

Andrew Marvell (1621–1678) was an assistant for John Milton and, later, a member of Parliament. He didn't live to see most of his poetic works published and, only in this century, appreciated. From "The Fair Singer":

It had been easie fighting in some plain,
Where Victory might hang in equal choice,
But all resistance against her is vain,
Who has the advantage both of Eyes and Voice,
And all my Forces needs must be undone,
She having gained both the Wind and Sun.

Shakespeare's sonnets offer some of the most exquisite and enduring romantic verse ever written. This is number 116.

Let me not to the marriage of true minds
Admit impediments. Love is not love
Which alters when it alteration finds,
Or bends with the remover to remove;
Oh no! it is an ever-fixed mark
That looks on tempests, and is never shaken;
It is the star to every wandering bark,
Whose worth's unknown, although his height be taken.
Love's not Time's fool, though rosy lips and cheeks
Within his bending sickle's compass come;
Love alters not with his brief hours and weeks,
But bears it out ev'n to the edge of doom:
If this be error, and upon me proved,
I never writ, nor no man ever loved.

Deftly capable of somber religious poems, sermons, and elegies, John Donne (1572–1631) also wrote emotionally charged verse, typified by "The Good-Morrow":

And now good morrow to our waking soules,
Which watch not one another out of feare;

For love, all love of other sights controules,
And makes one little roome, an every where.
Let sea-discoverers to new worlds have gone,
Let maps to other, worlds on worlds have showne,
Let us possesse one world, each hath one, and is one.

Robert Burns, who often composed his poems while humming ancient Scottish ditties, penned the ever-romantic "A Red, Red Rose." You can almost hear the melody:

O my Luve's like a red, red rose
That's newly sprung in June;
O my Love's like the melodie
That's sweetly play'd in tune.

As fair art thou, my bonnie lass,
So deep in luve am I:
And I will luve thee still, my dear,
Till a' the seas gang dry.

Till a' the seas gang dry, my dear,
And the rocks melt wi' the sun;
I will luve thee still, my dear,
While the sands o' life shall run.

Husbands and Wives

Anne Bradstreet is the author of the first volume of original English verse to be published in the New World. This gentle tribute is titled "To My Dear and Loving Husband":

If ever two were one, then surely we,
If ever man were lov'd by wife, then thee.
If ever wife was happy in a man,
Compare with me, ye women, if you can.
I prize thy love more than whole Mines of gold,
Or all the riches that the East doth hold
My love is such that Rivers cannot quench,
Nor ought but love from thee give recompense.
Thy love is such I can no way repay;
The heavens reward thee manifold I pray.
Then while we live, in love let's so persever,
That when we live no more, we may live ever.

Elizabeth Barrett Browning's *Sonnets from the Portuguese* was written for her husband, Robert Browning, and published because Browning felt it would have been inappropriate for him to keep to himself "the finest Sonnets written in any language since Shakespeare." But why Portuguese? "My little Portuguese" was Robert's pet name for his beloved wife. This is Sonnet 43:

How do I love thee? Let me count the ways.
I love thee to the depth and breadth and height
My soul can reach, when feeling out of sight
For the ends of Being and ideal Grace.
I love thee to the level of everyday's
Most quiet need, by sun and candle-light.
I love thee freely, as men strive for Right;
I love thee purely, as they turn from Praise.
I love thee with the passion put to use
In my old griefs, and with my childhood's faith.
I love thee with a love I seemed to lose
With my lost saints,—I love thee with the breath,
Smiles, tears, of all my life!—and, if God choose,
I shall love but thee better after death.

In a letter to Fanny Browne dated July 8, 1819, the poet John Keats wrote, "I love you the more in that I believe you have liked me for my own sake and nothing else. I have met women whom I really think would like to be married to a Poem and be given away by a Novel."

Change of Heart

From Christina Rossetti's "A Birthday":

My heart is like a singing bird
Whose nest is in a watered shoot;
My heart is like an apple-tree
Whose boughs are bent with thickset fruit;
My heart is like a rainbow shell
That paddles in a halcyon sea;
My heart is gladder than all these
Because my love is come to me.

Ardent, indeed. However, it was another Rossetti, Christina's brother, Dante Gabriel Rossetti, who indulged in a quintessentially romantic gesture. In anguish over his young wife's suicide, he took original copies of his poetry and laid them in her arms before her coffin was sealed. He wanted her to go through eternity with these words she had inspired. However, as time passed, the poet came to regret his act, that he had consigned some of his best works to the dust of Elizabeth's grave. He asked for permission to disinter the coffin and retrieve his manuscript. *Poems*, published (with some additions) in 1870, became an instant best-seller.

With Love

Intriguing reflections about love and life can be found in love letters of unexpected authorship.

"I have now come to the conclusion never again to think of marrying; and for this reason, I can never be satisfied with anyone who would be block-head enough to have me," wrote Abraham Lincoln after being rejected by a lady friend.

"There are actually many females in the world, and some among them are beautiful. But where could I find again a face whose every feature, even every wrinkle, is a reminder of the greatest and sweetest memories of my life?" Karl Marx writing about his wife.

Between Men and Women

"The main difference between men and women is that men are lunatics and women are idiots."

—Rebecca West

"Men know that if a woman had to choose between catching a fly ball and saving an infant's life, she would probably save the infant's life, without even considering whether there were men on base."

—Dave Barry

"Men can read maps better than women. 'Cause only the male mind could conceive of one inch equaling a hundred miles."

—Roseanne

"My ancestors wandered lost in the wilderness for 40 years because even in biblical times, men would not stop to ask for directions."

—Elayne Boosler

"Women speak because they wish to speak, whereas a man speaks only when driven to speech by something outside himself—like, for instance, he can't find any clean socks."

—Jean Kerr

"We women are so much more sensible! When we tire of ourselves, we change the way we do our hair, or hire a new cook. Or redecorate the house. I suppose a man could do over his office, but he never thinks of anything so simple. No, dear, a man has only one escape from his old self—to see a different self in some woman's eyes."

—Lucile Watson

"Women were like Russians—if you did exactly what they wanted all the time you were being realistic and constructive and promoting the cause of peace, and if you ever stood up to them you were resorting to cold-war tactics."

—Stanley Duke, in *Stanley and the Women*, by Kingsley Amis

"If men had their way, every woman would lie down a prostitute and get up a virgin."

—Isaac Bashevis Singer

"Never try to impress a woman because if you do she'll expect you to keep to the standard for the rest of your life."

—W. C. Fields

"Give a man a free hand, and he'll try to run it all over you."

—Mae West

"The more I see of men the more I like dogs."

—Madame de Staël

"Woman would be more charming if one could fall into her arms without falling into her hands."

—Ambrose Bierce

"Anyone who says he can see through women is missing a lot."

—Groucho Marx

"All women become like their mothers. That is their tragedy. No man does. That's his."

—Oscar Wilde

"Even the wisest men make fools of themselves about women, and even the most foolish women are wise about men."

—Theodore Reik

"Remember, all men would be tyrants if they could."

—Abigail Adams

"Sometimes I wonder if men and women really suit each other. Perhaps they should live next door and just visit now and then."
—Katharine Hepburn

"Men and women, women and men. It will never work."
—Erica Jong

"At the end of dinner it used to be that the men would retire to the billiard room and the women would go into the parlor. Men and women no longer separate after dinner, however. They now separate after twenty years of apparently happy marriage."
—P. J. O'Rourke

"A little incompatibility is the spice of life, particularly if he has income and she is pattable."
—Ogden Nash

"The important thing in acting is to be able to laugh and cry. If I have to cry, I think of my sex life. If I have to laugh, I think of my sex life."
—Glenda Jackson (attributed)

"To marry is to halve your rights and double your duties."
—Arthur Schopenhauer

"Marriage is a lot like the army: everyone complains, but you'd be surprised at the large number that re-enlist."

—James Garner

"By all means marry; if you get a good wife, you'll become happy. If you get a bad one, you'll become a philosopher."

—Socrates

"I'm glad I'm not a man, for if I were I'd be obliged to marry a woman."

—Madame de Staël

"Many a man in love with a dimple makes the mistake of marrying the whole girl."

—Stephen Leacock

"In biblical times, a man would have as many wives as he could afford. Just like today."

—Abigail Van Buren

"American women hope to find in their husbands a perfection that English women only hope to find in their butlers."

—W. Somerset Maugham

"Marrying a man is a lot like buying something you've been admiring for a long time in a shop window. You may love it when you get it home, but it doesn't always go with everything in the house."

—Jean Kerr

"Do I ever think about divorce? Never! Murder? All the time."

—Dr. Joyce Brothers

On the BOOKS

➾ Garbled Quotes

Like a great many words in the dictionary, famous quotations often become mangled and transform over time. Twelve well-known quotations follow. The trick is to complete each quotation exactly as it came from the originator's mouth or pen. Seems easy, right? Beware, this is not as obvious as it appears.

1. Pride goeth before [______].
2. To [______] the lily.
3. A little [______] is a dangerous thing.
4. A penny for your [______].
5. Music hath charm to sooth the savage [______].
6. Imitation is the sincerest [______] flattery.
7. Ask me no questions and I'll tell you [______].

8. Give him an inch, he'll take [______].
9. Variety's the [______] of life.
10. [______] is the root of all evil.
11. Water, water everywhere, [______] drop to drink.
12. I only regret that I have but [______] for my country.

Answers:

1. Pride goeth before destruction. (Proverbs 16:18)
2. To paint the lily. (William Shakespeare, *King John*)
3. A little learning is a dangerous thing. (Alexander Pope, *Essay on Criticism*)
4. A penny for your thought. (John Heywood, *Proverbs*)
5. Music hath charm to sooth the savage breast. (William Congreve, *The Mourning Bride*)
6. Imitation is the sincerest of flattery. (Charles Caleb Colton, *Lacon*)
7. Ask me no questions and I'll tell you no fibs. (Oliver Goldsmith, *She Stoops to Conquer*)
8. Give him an inch, he'll take an ell. (John Ray, *English Proverbs*)
9. Variety's the very spice of life. (William Cowper, *The Task*)
10. The love of money is the root of all evil. (Timothy 6:10)
11. Water, water everywhere, nor any drop to drink. (Samuel Coleridge, "The Rime of the Ancient Mariner")
12. I only regret that I have but one life to lose for my country. (Nathan Hale)

Bad Girls

Literary bad boys tend to bask in the spotlight, but what about the bad girls? While almost all get their comeuppances eventually (Medea, Delilah, Jezebel, Lady Macbeth, Eve Harrington, and Cruella DeVil spring to mind), it is their naughty deeds that make interesting reading.

• The story of Agave, for example, is from classical mythology and is retold in Euripides' *Bacchae*. She shredded her son, Pentheus, to bits. Granted, she believed he was a lion, but her action was a tad over the top. Alcina, on the other hand, had a bit of the black widow spider in her. She turned her lovers into inanimate objects once she had her pleasure.

• While the actual Lucrezia Borgia was blamed for all sorts of heinous acts and low blows, chances are, as a political target in real life, she wasn't guilty. However, in fictive works her character was exaggerated and she was credited with all sorts of nasty deeds from poisonings to incest. The real-life Marquise de Brinvilliers, however, was a renowned poisoner and probably deserved the execution that ended her life. Speaking of executions, it was Madame Defarge, a character from Charles Dickens's *A Tale of Two Cities*, who compiled a list of traitors to the French Revolution and encoded the names in her knitting. She delighted in watching aristocrats be beheaded.

• Harpies were bad *and* mean. According to Greek myth, the harpies were predatory birds with the faces of women. The daughters of Electra, they were famous for stealing food away from Phineus, who was blind.

• Scylla was also a monstrous creation from the Greeks. Huge, she sported six heads, which were attached to very long necks. Each head was equipped with three rows of sharp, pointed teeth through which she barked and howled. Her spot was the Straits of Messina (separating Italy from Sicily—she sat on the Italian side), where she watched for ships that had strayed too close to one of her gnashing heads. She lends her name to the expression "between Scylla and Charybdis" (or a rock and a hard place). Charybdis was the he-monster who sat on the Sicilian side making life difficult for sailors and swimmers.

Sob Stories

Camille, Anna Karenina, Madame Bovary, Sue Ellen, and Lassie owe much to classic myths, early legends, and ancient ballads. They influenced many great tragedies. Don Quixote took off on his impossible quest, the righting of all wrongs, after reading stories of romance and

chivalry. Racine's plays (the tragedies of Andromache and Titus and Berenice, for example) borrowed from Greek and Roman mythology and, in turn, provided the story lines for many subsequent tales—all great for wallowing. Mini-synopses to bring a tear to your eye:

The true-life love affair of Heloise and Abelard was a truly sad tale. However, it was their exchange of letters after the fact that made them famous. Héloïse, born in 1101, was the niece of Canon Fulbert of Notre Dame and a promising scholar. Her tutor, the philosopher and theologian Pierre Abélard, fell in love with his young student. They were secretly married (as a clergyman, Abélard would have been disgraced and prevented from teaching) after the birth of their son. When Fulbert learned of what he presumed to be Héloïse's seduction, he had Abélard castrated. Héloïse joined a convent and Abélard a monastery. However, their love never diminished, and they exchanged powerfully romantic letters until Abélard's death in 1142. In 1817, their bodies were reburied together.

Lovers joining one another in death is the finale of many a fine tear-jerker. The tragedy is sharpened when one commits suicide mistakenly believing his or her lover is dead. Antigone and Haemon, in Sophocles' tragedy, foretell Romeo and Juliet's sad end by killing themselves rather than be separated by their families. In Shakespeare's telling of another six-handkerchief story, Antony falls on his sword believing Cleopatra dead. He rallies to bestow a last kiss.

His beloved, having lost her man and her empire, allows an asp's bite to end her life.

The story of Aucassin and Nicolette is based upon a 13th-century ballad. Circumstance separates the determined pair time and time again, but they prevail against all odds and are reunited. Another favorite from medieval times is the story of Tristan and Iseult (or Isolde). Tristan is sent by his uncle, King Mark of Cornwall, to bring Iseult, the king's betrothed, to him. On the way, Tristan and Iseult fall in love. They have many adventures, even after Iseult's marriage to King Mark, and when Tristan lies on his deathbed, he sends for Iseult. When she arrives too late, she lies beside Tristan and dies. A mysterious briar links their graves forever.

The Hindu myth of Pururavas and Urvasi has similarities to stories of Apollo and Daphne, Undine and the Knight, and the Little Mermaid. Urvasi is a celestial being who is eager to live as a mortal. She journeys to earth, where she catches the eye as well as the heart of King Pururavas. He courts her, and they agree to marry—*if* Urvasi's ground rules are obeyed. When Pururavas is tricked into breaking one of Urvasi's rules, Urvasi disappears. The king wanders the earth looking for her. Finally, he triumphs and they are united for all eternity.

Choose Your Weapons

The next times your kids morph with weapons flashing or swing their plastic katanas at the dog, introduce them to some really sharp stuff:

- Excalibur was King Arthur's enchanted sword. The name comes from the Latin for "liberated from stone." While one story has Arthur pulling the ancient sword from a stone, thus making him king of England, other versions credit the Lady of the Lake, to whom it was returned upon King Arthur's death.

- Lancelot's sword was called Ar'ondight.

- Durandal (the Inflexible) was the magic sword of Roland. Like Arthurian legends, there are several versions describing the sword's origins, including that it was a gift from Charlemagne (whose own sword was called Flamberge, the Flame-Cutter).

- Tyr, a war god from Nordic mythology, wielded a magic sword that guaranteed him victory in battle.

- Colada was the name of El Cid's battle sword.

Mighty names all, but remember, Davy Crockett named his sure-shootin' rifle Betsy.

Now that's an ORDER

Who's in Charge Here?

The U.S. military is defined by its systems of ranks, orders, badges, salutes, handshakes, uniforms, decorations, medals, and codes. They help to distinguish soldier from sailor, grunt from sergeant, platoon from squad, and, blessedly, John Wayne from Robert Mitchum.

The U.S. military is, of course under the Supreme Command of the President of the United States. The ranking of the members of the U.S. Army is as follows (the identifying insignia are included so you can see who is who when watching parades or war films):

Rank	**Insignia**
General of the Army	5 silver stars fastened in a circle with the U.S. coat of arms in the center
General	4 silver stars
Lieutenant General	3 silver stars
Major General	2 silver stars
Brigadier General	1 silver star
Colonel	silver eagle
Lieutenant Colonel	silver oak leaf
Major	gold oak leaf
Captain	2 silver bars
1st Lieutenant	1 silver bar
2nd Lieutenant	1 gold bar
(Noncommissioned Officers)	
Sergeant Major of the Army	same as Sergeant Major but with 2 stars plus red and white shield on lapel
Command Sergeant Major	3 chevrons above 3 arcs with 5-pointed star with wreath around it in the center
Sergeant Major	3 chevrons above 3 arcs with 5-pointed star in the center
1st Sergeant	3 chevrons above 3 arcs with lozenge in the center
Master Sergeant	3 chevrons above 3 arcs
Platoon Sergeant (or Sergeant 1st Class)	3 chevrons above 2 arcs
Staff Sergeant	3 chevrons above 1 arc
Sergeant	3 chevrons
Corporal	2 chevrons
(Specialists)	
Specialist 7	3 arcs above eagle device
Specialist 6	2 arcs above eagle device

Specialist 5	1 arc above eagle device
Specialist 4	eagle device only

(Other Enlisted Personnel)

Private 1st Class	1 chevron above 1 arc
Private (E-2)	1 chevron
Private (E-1)	none

Warrant Officers

Grade 4	silver bar with 4 enamel black bands
Grade 3	silver bar with 3 enamel black bands
Grade 2	silver bar with 2 enamel black bands
Grade 1	silver bar with 1 enamel black band

Picture yourself at the video arcade. You overhear delighted shouts as your kid wipes out a platoon of aliens. Is this good? Is it better than zapping, say, a brigade or a squadron? Check the list and react accordingly.

Army Units

Squad	in infantry, usually 10 enlisted personnel under a staff sergeant
Platoon	in infantry, 4 squads under a lieutenant
Company	HQ section and 4 platoons under a captain
Battalion	HQ section and 4 or more companies under a lieutenant colonel
Brigade	HQ and 3 or more battalions under a colonel
Division	HQ and 3 brigades with artillery, combat support, and combat service support units under a major general
Army Corps	2 or more divisions with corps troops under a lieutenant general
Field Army	HQ and 2 or more corps with field army troops under a general

Air Force Units

Flight

Squadron

Group

Wing

Air Division

Numbered Air Force

Major Command

The following Navy ranks correspond to the list of Army ranks.

U.S. Navy Rank	Stripes/Stars	U.S. Army Rank
Fleet Admiral	5	General of the Army
Admiral	4	General
Vice Admiral	3	Lieutenant General
Rear Admiral	2	Major General
Commodore	1	Brigadier General

Is a "leftenant" superior to a squadron leader? Is that why Errol never forgave Basil in *The Dawn Patrol*? The British military rankings are, not surprisingly, very similar to those of the United States. However, when World War II heated up and the United States got involved, we needed "brass" that outranked their brass. So the Pentagon came up with four- and five-star generals. Five stars are rare in U.S. military history. Ulysses S. Grant was a three-star general, while George Washington only managed one, until both were awarded their five stars posthumously.

Here's what officers in Her Majesty's Fighting Forces are called:

Royal Navy	Army and Royal Marines	Royal Air Force
Admiral of the Fleet	Field Marshal	Marshal of the R.A.F.
Admiral	General	Air Chief Marshal
Vice Admiral	Lieutenant General	Air Marshal
Rear Admiral	Major General	Air Vice Marshal
Commodore	Brigadier	Air Commodore
Captain	Colonel	Group Captain
Commander	Lieutenant Colonel	Wing Commander
{ Lieutenant Commander	{ Major Captain	{ Squadron Leader Flight Lieutenant
Lieutenant	Lieutenant	Flying Officer
Sublieutenant	Second Lieutenant	Pilot Officer
Midshipman (Lapel)		

➤ Publishing Quandary

The original name chosen for what is now known in the United States as Viking Penguin was to be Half-Moon Press, in honor of Henry Hudson's ship. Rockwell Kent was commissioned to design the emblem but didn't like the look of the English schooner. Instead, he drew a Viking warship. His sketch was so enthusiastically received by the fledgling company that they changed their name to Viking Press.

Why Penguin for a book publisher? The choice was made by the founder's secretary, Joan Coles. Allen Lane was looking for a logo that would suggest "a dignified flippancy"—the overall feeling he wanted for his new list of orange-and-white-jacketed softcovers. Edward Young created the colophon after sketching the penguins at the Regent's Park Zoo in London.

Other animals appearing in publishers' colophons are borzois (Knopf), kangaroos (PocketBooks), owls (Holt), and the dachshund (Tom Dunne Books).

Kindest Cuts of All

Some mighty big literary lions have rewarded the small fry who inspired them:

- Sir James M. Barrie overheard Sylvia Llewelyn-Davies tell her young son to refrain from gobbling up a handful of candy. She warned he'd surely be sick the next day. The boy replied, stuffing in more candy, "Then I shall be sick tonight." Barrie so enjoyed the child's comeback that he incorporated the scene in *Peter Pan* and paid the author of the remark a copyright fee of half a penny every time the play was performed. He ultimately bequeathed the copyright of *Peter Pan* to a children's hospital in London.

- Agatha Christie made a gift of the royalties from her play *The Mousetrap* to her nephew. It's the longest-running play in history.

- Rudyard Kipling gave his original manuscript of *The Jungle Book* to his first child's nanny. When she sold it many years later, it afforded her a very comfortable retirement. And when the author visited his publisher and good friend F. N. Doubleday (whom Kipling nicknamed Effendi from his initials), he spent part of the day entertaining Doubleday's son. He told young Nelson silly stories about how the elephant got his trunk and the leopard his spots. The young and future publisher urged Kipling to write them down in a collection, and they became *The Just So Stories*. Kipling rewarded Nelson with a penny royalty on every copy sold. The collection remains in print, still earning the penny royalty for Doubleday's children. Nelson Jr. splits the literary legacy with his sister, Neltje. The grand total? Anywhere from 15 cents to $4 each year.

- Irving Berlin donated the royalties for "God Bless America" to the Boy Scouts and Girl Scouts of America.

Shipped Strips

Some years ago, Simon & Schuster published a children's book titled, *Dr. Dan the Bandage Man* and, at the last moment, decided to include half a dozen adhesive bandages in each book. Then-publisher Richard Simon had a friend at Johnson & Johnson Company and sent him a succinct telegram: "Please ship two million Band-Aids immediately." The following day, he received a wire back: "Band-Aids on their way. What the hell happened to you?"

Entitlements

Authors and publishers put a great deal of thought into picking titles for their books. So let's stop misquoting them. Herewith the true, original, intended, and complete titles of some popular bits of writing.

- Dante called his trilogy simply *La Commedia.* The "divine" part was added a century after the work's creation by a publisher—perhaps inspired by the engravings by Baldini that accompanied the text.

- The actual title on the title page of Daniel Defoe's *Moll Flanders,* a picaresque novel first published in 1722, is *The Fortunes and Misfortunes of the Famous Moll Flanders, who was born at Newgate, and during a Life of continued Variety for Threescore Years, besides her Childhood, was Twelve Year a Whore, five time a Wife (whereof once to her own Brother), Twelve Year a Thief, Eight Year a Transported Felon in Virginia, at last grew rich, liv'd Honest, and died a Penitent. Written from her own memorandums.* (Granted, this one was enhanced by editing.)

- The Declaration of Independence was originally titled "The Unanimous Declaration of the Thirteen United States of America."

- Charles Darwin's famous text is *On the Origin of Species by Means of Natural Selection, or the Preservation of Favored Races in the Struggle for Life.*

- Kurt Vonnegut's popular novel, while often shortened, is *Slaughterhouse-Five; or, The Children's Crusade: A Duty-Dance with Death.*

- *Vanity Fair, a Novel Without a Hero* is the full and complete title of William Makepeace Thackeray's masterpiece.

• The Kinsey Report (1948) is titled *Sexual Behavior in the Human Male*. "The Kinsey Report," for the author (Alfred Charles Kinsey), must have sounded sexier.

• It's actually *Alice's Adventures in Wonderland*, not *Alice in Wonderland*, for you picky folk who enjoy Lewis Carroll.

• It's *Finnegans Wake* (no apostrophe).

On and Off the Record

Considering what they later did, became famous for, wrote, celebrated, and loathed, it's always entertaining to see what famous folk reveal about themselves in context. For example, Charles Dickens, on a visit to the United States, declared minstrel shows a characteristic form of American entertainment and the greatest contribution to 19th-century theater. Ahem. Other interesting revelations:

Jack Kerouac, while browsing through the British Museum, found a reference to the derivation of his family name, which, it turned out, came from Brittany. Jack's real first name was Jean-Louis. The inscription on the coat of arms was "Work, Love, Suffer."

"A woman, especially, if she have the misfortune of knowing anything, should conceal it as well as she can." So proclaimed Jane Austen.

James Barrie, who created Peter Pan, once said, "I am not young enough to know everything."

"Be polite; write diplomatically; even in a declaration of war one must observe the rules of politeness" is credited to Otto von Bismarck.

Angered by immigration rules, Pearl Buck wrote, "We send missionaries to China so the Chinese can get to heaven, but we won't let them into our country."

Ever whimsical, Lewis Carroll said, "It's a poor sort of memory that only works backwards."

Joseph Conrad wrote, "The belief in a supernatural source of evil is not necessary; men alone are quite capable of every wickedness." Don't tell Stephen King that.

"Everything comes to him who hustles while he waits," said Thomas Alva Edison. Some wags might say that "hustle" is the operative word for Edison, who took credit for many of his employees' inventions and breakthroughs.

Albert Einstein, ever the shy guy, said, "Isn't it strange that I who have written only unpopular books should be such a popular fellow?"

➤ Signed and Sealed

Ever wonder what those seals and awards are stamped onto book jackets in the children's section? A variety of awards are given annually to recognize and honor those who write, illustrate, and publish books for the younger set. These are among the most prestigious:

Christopher Awards. Established in 1970, these are given each year to honor authors and illustrators whose works affirm the highest values of the human spirit, artistic and technical proficiency, and significant degree of public acceptance. The categories include children's fiction, nonfiction, and picture books.

Coretta Scott King Awards. These awards have been given out annually since 1969 to African-American authors and illustrators whose works promote an understanding and appreciation of the culture and contribution of all people to the American Dream. Winners receive a plaque, honorarium, and set of encyclopedias.

Edgar Allan Poe Awards. These awards, accompanied by a ceramic bust of Poe, honor mystery writers in various categories including juvenile mysteries.

John Newbery Awards. One of the oldest prizes, these recognize distinguished contributions to American literature for children. They have been given out by the American Library Association since 1922.

Parents' Choice Awards. The winners are determined by popular vote. Parents nominate family favorites through the Parents' Choice Foundation.

Randolph Caldecott Awards. A gold medal and certificate goes to artist of the year's most distinguished picture books for children. These have been managed by the American Library Association since 1936.

The Long and the Short of It

Some of the longest one-word titles of hardcover best-sellers include:

Reminiscences *by Douglas MacArthur*

Andersonville *by MacKinlay Kantor*

Kaleidoscope *by Danielle Steel*

Civilisation *by Kenneth Clark*

Firestarter *by Stephen King*

Wanderlust *by Danielle Steel*

Megatrends *by John Naisbitt*

Fatherhood *by Bill Cosby*

Chesapeake *by James Michener*

Centennial *by James Michener*

Titles of best-sellers seem to be getting shorter, while the books themselves are getting longer. Here is a list of the shortest best-selling titles:

S *by John Updike (1988)*

V *by Thomas Pynchon (1968)*

K *by Mary Roberts Rinehart (1915)*

It *by Stephen King (1987)*

Me *by Katharine Hepburn (1991)*

Max *by Katherine Cecil Thurston (1905)*

Burr *by Gore Vidal (1981)*

1876 *by Gore Vidal (1976)*

Cujo *by Stephen King (1981)*

Star *by Danielle Steel (1989)*

Sons *by Pearl S. Buck (1932)*

Uh-Oh *by Robert Fulghum (1991)*

Veil *by Bob Woodward (1987)*

Zoya *by Danielle Steel (1988)*

If paperback best-sellers were included in this list, we'd have *Drum*, *Dr. No*, and *1984*, but none of these made the best-seller lists as hardcovers.

The longest title (excluding colons and subtitles) to appear on the *New York Times* best-seller list was *Everything You Always Wanted to Know About Sex (But Were Afraid to Ask)*, by Dr. David Reuben, followed by *When You Look Like Your Passport Photo, It's Time to Go Home*, by Erma Bombeck.

Octogenarians and older authors who have written best-sellers include:

Bessie and Sadie Delaney with *Having Our Say* (100: actually, at 100 years of age the sisters are the only centenarians to make the best-seller list)

George Burns with *Gracie* (a nonagenarian at 92)

Helen H. Santmeyer with "*...and Ladies of the Club*" (88)

Bernard Baruch with *Baruch: My Own Story* (87)

Agatha Christie with *Sleeping Murder* (86) and *Curtain* (85)

Dr. Seuss with *Oh, the Places You'll Go!* (86) and *You're Only Old Once!* (81)

J.R.R. Tolkein with *The Silmarillion* (85)

Douglas MacArthur with *Reminiscences* (84)

Katharine Hepburn with *Me* (83)

Rose Kennedy with *Times to Remember* (83)

Winston Churchill with *The Birth of Britain* (81)

While in their 70s and 80s, James Michener and Louis L'Amour each have had books on the list several times.

RELIGIOUS *Order*

The word *hierarchy* literally means "sacred leader." So it is no accident that the pyramids of the Middle East, South America, and Mexico are shaped the way they are. Like Gothic architecture, all the structures point dramatically heavenward. Symbolically, the laity should make the spiritual effort to be near their god. A massive spire or pyramid immediately reminds people where they stand in the great scheme of things.

Choir of Angels

Angel mania, big in the Middle Ages, has taken flight again in recent years. A popular subject for feature articles, talk shows, and books, seraphim, cherubim, and guardian angels are media darlings.

While many cultures revere angels, the more commonly known appear in folklore. The angel Raziel, for example, helped all mankind by taking pity on Adam and Eve after the apple incident (according to Christian tradition, Satan himself was a fallen angel). After another angel casts the two from the Garden of Eden, Raziel gives Adam a book of knowledge. The tome was entrusted to Enoch and, later, was consulted by Noah for help designing the ark.

In the Roman Catholic Church, October 2 is celebrated as a day to honor the three angels mentioned by name in the Bible. September 29 is the feast day of Michael, Gabriel, and Raphael (the latter being the guardian angel of guardian angels). The archangel Uriel is toasted on July 28 by Ethiopian and Egyptian Orthodox Christians.

In the hierarchy of the church, the angels outrank the apostles and rank just below God Himself. There are levels within the host of angels that indicate their degree of perfection, their nature, and their grace. These levels are called choirs and have nothing to do with singing.

In descending order, the hierarchy of angels is:

First Choir	**Second Choir**	**Third Choir**
Seraphim	Dominations (or Dominions)	Principalities
Cherubim	Virtues	Archangels
Thrones	Powers	Angels

Remember the film *It's a Wonderful Life*? Jimmy Stewart was rescued by his guardian angel after jumping into the icy river. The Catholic Church assures its members that each one has a guardian angel of his or her own. They are chosen from the lower choir, and if they save Jimmy Stewart, presumably they move up a notch.

☛ The Land Down Under

The flipside to the hierarchy of heaven is the kingdom of the devil. In the highly structured world where Lucifer reigns, there are scores of demons and lowlifes who do his bidding. Ancient texts, known as grimoires, are a sort of bible of demonology and the black arts, and describe the hierarchy of hell. Every spirit has secret talents and special abilities that are carefully delineated in the grimoires. Heaven forbid you should send a lock specialist to hypnotize a cat.

As there are several versions of the Bible, so there are different grimoires. The following is a more prevalent list of the most popular evil spirits. Keep in mind that this pecking order is a descending hierarchy; that is, the higher your rank, the more evil you are. There is still some hope for redemption if your rank is low.

The Superior Spirits:

Lucifer—Emperor

Beelzebub—Prince

Astaroth—Grand Duke

Each Superior Spirit has two inferiors who patrol the continents:

Lucifer: Satanchia, Agaliarept—Europe and Asia

Beelzebub: Tarchimache, Fleurety—Africa

Astaroth: Sargatanas, Nebrios—North and South America

Lucifuge Rofocale has control over wealth and treasures. Subordinates: *Beel, Agares, Marbas.*

Satanchia can control wives and maidens to do as he wishes. Subordinates: *Pruslas, Aamon, Barbatos.*

Agaliarept has the faculty to discover arcane secrets in government and unveils most sublime mysteries, a useful skill in Washington. He commands the second Legion of Spirits. Subordinates: *Buer, Gusoyn, Botis.*

Fleurety has the power to perform any labor at night and can cause hailstorms. He controls a huge army of spirits. Subordinates: *Bathsin, Pursin, Eligar.*

Sargatanas has the power to make anyone invisible, to transport himself anywhere, to open all locks, and to reveal whatever is taking place in private houses. A less useful skill is his ability to teach all the arts of shepherds. He commands several brigades of spirits. Subordinates: *Zoray, Valefar, Faraii.*

Nebrios has the power to inflict evil on whomsoever he will; reveals every virtue of metals, minerals, vegetables, and animals. In the infernal hierarchies, Nebrios is one of the greatest necromancers, or one who predicts the future by communicating with the dead, a skill that would seem to go with the territory. Subordinates: *Ayperos, Naberis, Glassyalabolas.*

The World According to Dante

In *The Divine Comedy*, Dante delineated the levels of Paradise, Hell, and Purgatory according to the classifications of sins and based upon the writings of Aristotle and Cicero. Dante wrote of three types of sin: Incontinence, Violence, and Fraud (or Malice). He then subclassified these into seven circles of Hell: four of Incontinence, one of Violence, and two of Fraud.

These are categories of unethical behavior, to which Dante added two circles of wrong belief: Unbelief (Limbo) and Mischief (Heresy). These make up the total of nine circles of Hell. To the Vestibule of the Futile he assigned those who had no faith or good works to recommend them.

Dante divided Purgatory into seven Cornices whereon the seven Capital Sins were purged.

Upper Purgatory

- Disordered Love of God
  - Cornice 7—Lustful
  - Cornice 6—Gluttonous
  - Cornice 5—Covetous

Middle Purgatory

  - Cornice 4—Slothful

Lower Purgatory

- Love of Neighbor's Harm (Love Perverted)
  - Cornice 3—Wrathful
  - Cornice 2—Envious
  - Cornice 1—Proud

Peter's Gate

- Three Steps
  - 3—Satisfaction

2—Contrition

1—Confession

Ante-Purgatory holds those who died unprepared. After a brief period of time, a sort of detention, they will eventually be admitted into Purgatory to wash away their sins and ascend to Paradise.

Terrace 2

Indolent

Unshriven

Preoccupied

Terrace 1

the Excommunicate

Finally, Paradise was divided into seven heavens, a celestial ladder, and then three more heavens.

First heaven: Moon—where Angels dwell

Second heaven: Mercury—Archangels

Third heaven: Venus—Principalities

Fourth heaven: Sun—Powers

Fifth heaven: Mars—Virtues

Sixth heaven: Jupiter—Dominations

Seventh heaven: Saturn—Thrones

Celestial Ladder

Eighth heaven: fixed stars—Cherubim

Ninth heaven: Primum Mobile—Seraphim

Tenth heaven: Empyrean

☛ Meanwhile Back on Earth

The Catholic Church has sustained itself as an institution for an impressively long time, and its rigid structure may be partly responsible. The pope is the supreme authority in Catholicism, with the cardinals in the second most important position. The pope is chosen by the cardinals, but, surprisingly, does not have to be a cardinal himself when selected.

Pope—the supreme authority

Cardinal—a prince of the Catholic Church; collectively, the College of Cardinals; ranks:

1. Cardinal Bishop (there are six living in Rome)
2. Cardinal Priest (usually Bishops or Archbishops)
3. Cardinal Deacons

Archbishop—title given to a bishop who governs one or more dioceses or districts

Bishop—head of a diocese or district

Monsignor—an honorary title

Priest—usually has jurisdiction over a parish

Deacon—first of the major orders but lowest in the hierarchy

Abbot, guardian, prior, and rector are titles given to the "superiors" of religious orders for men, such as the Jesuits or Franciscans.

In the past, initiates to a religious order had to go through several stages before taking final vows and becoming full members. A hopeful would be tested while moving up the ladder from postulate to novitiate. Obedience, poverty, and chastity were the three evangelical counsels of perfection.

As an example, those who aspired to join the Benedictines centuries ago had to be serious-minded (not just looking for free meals and an easy escape from the plague). The Rule of Saint Benedict was to test applicants' motives to see "whether they came from God." An applicant found himself knocking on the gates of the monastery for a very long time, and if he persevered for "four or five days... then let admittance be granted to him and let him stay at the guest house for a few days." One can only hope that he was also give ice for his swollen hand.

☛ And the Art of Zen

Zen Buddhism is based upon a belief that life is a continuous process of learning and seeking perfection. Ironically, the emphasis is on meditation, training, and development of the inner qualities. A true student of Zen will reach divine freedom and knowledge without any conspicuous effort.

Zen teaches that there are six worlds (or *Lokas*) that stand for the states of mind produced by greed, hate, and delusion:

Heaven

Humans

Animals

Asura

Hungry Ghosts

Hell

Lokas are classically drawn in a circular design with a snake (hate), a pig (greed), and a cock (delusion) chasing one another in the center. Lokas are states of mind that result from ignorance and materialism, as opposed to actual places one endures in life or goes to in death.

☛ It Was All So Simple Then

The ancient Greeks had a simpler worldview. Plato theorized that the universe was a Great Chain of Being wherein all things fell into a series of gradations arranged hierarchically below the gods, who sat at the summit of Mount Olympus. The Great Chain of Being was layered this way:

Gods

Angels

Man

Animals

Plants

Rocks (and other inorganic material)

Whereas man was separated from the angels and the gods by his unfortunate tendency toward mortality, he was blessed with an intellect, which kept him above flora, fauna, and geological formations.

LIFE *on* EARTH

Terra Firma

You may have spent a lot of your childhood digging for China, but you probably bypassed the geology offerings in your college course catalog. You may not know, therefore, that geologists divide the earth into three zones:

Lithosphere: all solids from the earth's surface to the earth's center

Hydrosphere: all surface water

Atmosphere: the multilayered gaseous envelope that surrounds the earth's surface

They then divide the planet Earth into the following sections, innermost to outermost:

Section	Miles Below the Surface
Inner Core	3,200–3,958
Outer Core	1,800–3,200
Lower Mantle	560–1,800
Upper Mantle	9–560
Crust	0–9

If the earth begins to move under your feet and you haven't a seismograph handy for a Richter scale measurement, you'll be glad to know that there is an alternative. It's called the Mercalli intensity scale, and it's based on the description of the quake as opposed to an actual measurement of its energy and force.

I. Detectable by experienced observers when lying down
II. Detectable by a few; delicately poised objects may move
III. There is some vibration; still unnoticed by many
IV. Felt by most indoors; some moderate vibrations
V. Felt by almost everyone; unstable objects will move
VI. Felt by everyone; strong vibrations and heavy objects will move
VII. Very strong vibrations; weak buildings damaged
VIII. General damage in all but quake-proof buildings; objects overturned
IX. Buildings shifted from foundations; collapse; some ground cracks
X. Serious ground fissures; larger buildings damaged or destroyed
XI. Few if any structures will survive—catastrophic
XII. Total devastation; vibrations strong enough to distort vision

After that number XII Mercalli earthquake hits, it will, of course, be important to understand the following geological distinctions:

Fragment	Diameter (mm)
Boulder	more than 256
Cobble	64–256
Pebble	4–64
Granule	2–4

Weather or Not

Everyone complains about weather forecasters, but nobody seems to do much about them. Perhaps if we were all better decoders of their cryptic terminology, their forecasts would seem more accurate. Then again, maybe not.

"Wind" is defined by the U.S. Weather Bureau as "horizontal motion of the air past a given point." Then things pick up speed:

Light wind—Speed is 6 knots or less

Gust—Sudden surge in wind speed to more than 16 knots with a variation of 9 knots or more between peak and lull

Squall—Sudden surge in wind by at least 16 knots and rising to 32 knots or more and lasting for at least one minute

Wind shift—Change in wind direction of 45 degrees or more that takes place in less than 15 minutes

Sir Francis Beaufort, an Englishman, devised a scale to measure the strength of the wind. In 1805, he drew up what is known, aptly, as the Beaufort scale, and it is still in use when modern instruments are unavailable (presumably having been blown into the next county). Some hairsetting gels resist number 12 on the Beaufort scale.

Beaufort Number	mph	Knots	International Description	Specifications
0	less than 1	less than 1	Calm	Calm; smoke rises vertically
1	1–3	1–3	Light air	Direction of wind shows by smoke drift, but not by wind vanes
2	4–7	4–6	Light breeze	Wind felt on face; leaves rustle; vanes moved by wind
3	8–12	7–10	Gentle breeze	Leaves and small twigs in constant motion; wind extends light flags
4	13–18	11–16	Moderate	Raises dust, loose paper; small branches move
5	19–24	17–21	Fresh	Small trees begin to sway; crested wavelets form on inland water
6	25–31	22–27	Strong	Large branches in motion; umbrellas used with difficulty
7	32–38	28–33	Near gale	Whole trees in motion; inconvenience felt walking against wind
8	39–46	34–40	Gale	Breaks twigs off trees; impeded progress
9	47–54	41–47	Strong gale	Slight structural damage occurs
10	55–63	48–55	Storm	Trees uprooted; considerable damage occurs
11	64–72	56–63	Violent storm	Widespread damage
12	73–82	64–71	Hurricane	Devastation

The National Hurricane Center further defines hurricanes by what is known as the Saffir-Simpson scale:

Tropical storm	39–73 mph
Hurricane	
Category 1	74–95 mph
Category 2	96–110 mph

Category 3	111–130 mph
Category 4	131–155 mph
Category 5	over 155 mph

By the way, storms are named when winds reach the tropical storm level of 39 mph. In the past 40 years, 1995 ranks as the busiest season for Atlantic storms; 21 storms were named, greatly exceeding the record 14 posted in 1991.

Since 1953, when the practice of assigning names to storms began, a number of names have been retired; the National Hurricane Center reports that names of "killer" hurricanes are not used again. Camille, in 1969, was the most intense U.S. storm, with sustained winds of 155 miles per hour when it slammed into the coast of Louisiana and Mississippi, while the deadliest storm was Audrey, which killed 390 people in Louisiana and Texas.

The following is a list of the names and the years of these devastating storms. Something to keep in mind, perhaps, when offering baby-naming suggestions?

Agnes	*1972*	**Celia**	*1970*	**Frederic**	*1979*
Alicia	*1983*	**Cleo**	*1964*	**Gilbert**	*1988*
Allen	*1980*	**Connie**	*1955*	**Gloria**	*1985*
Andrew	*1992*	**David**	*1979*	**Gracie**	*1959*
Anita	*1977*	**Diana**	*1990*	**Hattie**	*1961*
Audrey	*1957*	**Diane**	*1955*	**Hazel**	*1954*
Betsy	*1965*	**Donna**	*1960*	**Hilda**	*1964*
Beulah	*1967*	**Dora**	*1964*	**Hugo**	*1989*
Bob	*1991*	**Edna**	*1954*	**Inez**	*1966*
Camille	*1969*	**Elena**	*1985*	**Ione**	*1955*
Carla	*1961*	**Eloise**	*1975*	**Janet**	*1955*
Carmen	*1974*	**Fifi**	*1974*	**Joan**	*1988*
Caro	*1954*	**Flora**	*1963*	**Klaus**	*1990*

What's the difference between moderate and heavy precipitation? Is it time for a raincoat, or will an umbrella suffice? How do you make the distinction between scattered and broken clouds? And if you have your head in the clouds, just how high is it? Let the U.S. Weather Bureau explain it all to you.

Intensity of Precipitation (other than drizzle) on Rate-of-Fall Basis:

Very Light—scattered drops or flakes that do not completely wet or cover an exposed surface regardless of duration

Light—trace to 0.10 inch per hour; maximum 0.01 inch in six minutes

Moderate—0.11 inch to .30 inch per hour; more than 0.01 inch to 0.03 inch in six minutes

Heavy—more than 0.30 inch per hour; more than 0.03 inch in six minutes

Intensity of Drizzle on Rate-of-Fall Basis:

Very Light—scattered drops that do not completely wet an exposed surface, regardless of duration

Light—trace to 0.01 inch per hour

Moderate—more than 0.01 inch to 0.02 inch per hour

Heavy—more than 0.02 inch per hour

Intensity of Drizzle and Snow with Visibility as Criterion:

Very Light—scattered flakes or droplets that do not completely cover or wet an exposed surface, regardless of duration

Light—visibility of 5⁄8 statute mile or more

Moderate—visibility of less than 5⁄8 statute mile but more than 5⁄16 statute mile

Heavy—visibility of less than 5⁄16 statute mile

Sky Cover Classifications

Clear—cloudless or sky cover is less than 0.1

Scattered—0.1–0.5 at and below the level of a layer aloft

Broken—0.6–0.9 at and below the level of a layer aloft

Overcast—1.0 at and below the level of a layer aloft

Partly Obscured—1.0 or more but not all of the sky is hidden by surface-based obscuring phenomenon (such as smoke or fog)

Obscured—sky is completely hidden by surface-based obscuring phenomenon

Type of Cloud	Height in Feet
Cirrus	16,500–45,000
Cirrocumulus	1,500–6,500
Cirrostratus	16,500–45,000
Altocumulus	16,500–45,000
Cumulus	6,500–23,000
Stratocumulus	surface to 1,500
Cumulonimbus	1,500–6,500
Stratus	1,500–6,500

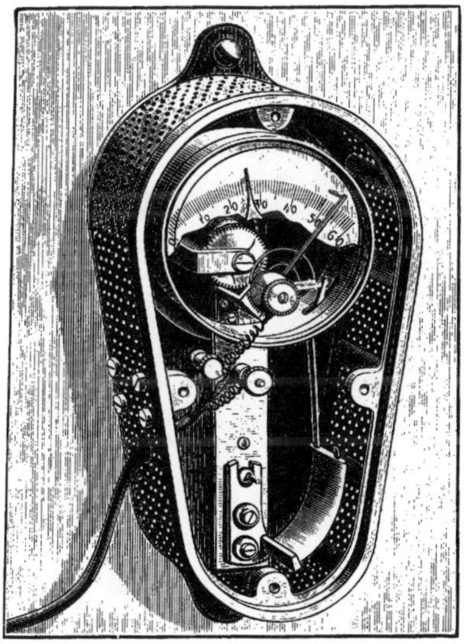

You are contemplating spending the day on a friend's boat, so you listen to the nautical weather report on the radio. The announcer tells you the sea is "phenomenal." Great! You hop into your car and drive three hours to the marina only to find your friend mourning the tiny splinters of what was once her boat. What happened? Phenomenal, in sea parlance, has a bit of a different meaning.

Code Figure	Description of Sea	Maximum Height of Waves in Feet
0	calm–glassy	0
1	calm–rippled	0–1
2	smooth–wavelets	1–2
3	slight	2–4
4	moderate	4–8
5	rough	8–13
6	very rough	13–20
7	high	20–30
8	very high	30–45
9	phenomenal	45 and over

GOD SAVE *the* QUEEN OR KING

➢ Rule Brittania

The antics of the members of the House of Windsor keep Fleet Street journalists and photographers busy. Imagine the tabloid headlines for Henry VIII, who switched wives (Catherine of Aragon, Anne Boleyn, Jane Seymour, Anne of Cleves, Catherine Howard, and Catherine Parr) and religions with merry abandon. Three of his children actually sat on the throne.

Edward VI (his only son, with Jane Seymour) ruled under regents and was forced to name Lady Jane Grey his successor before he died at age 16. She managed to hold onto the throne for nine days. Mary Tudor, Henry's daughter with Catherine of Aragon, won Council's approval to proclaim herself queen and later had Jane beheaded. She ruled until being ousted by her half-sister Elizabeth, the daughter of Anne Boleyn with Henry.

House of Normandy

William I (the Conqueror), by defeating Harold II, 1066–1087

William II, third son of William I, 1087–1100

Henry I, youngest son of William I, 1100–1135

House of Blois

Stephen, grandson of William I and Count of Blois, 1135–1154

House of Plantagenet

Henry II, grandson of Henry I, 1154–1189

Richard I (the Lion-Heart), third son of Henry II, 1189–1199

John, youngest son of Henry II, 1199–1216

Henry III, son of John, 1216–1272

Edward I, son of Henry III, 1272–1307

Edward II, son of Edward I, 1307–1327

Edward III, son of Edward II, 1327–1377

Richard II, grandson of Edward III, 1377–1399

House of Lancaster

Henry IV, grandson of Edward III, 1399–1413

Henry V, son of Henry IV, 1413–1422

Henry VI, son of Henry V, 1422–1461 (deposed)

House of York

Edward IV, great-great-grandson of Edward III, 1461–1470, 1471–1483

Edward V, son of Edward IV, 1483 (murdered in Tower of London)

Richard III, brother of Edward IV, 1483–1485

House of Tudor

Henry VII, descendant of Edward III, 1485–1509

Henry VIII, son of Henry VII, 1509–1547

Edward VI, son of Henry VIII, 1547–1553

Mary I, daughter of Henry VIII, 1553–1558

Elizabeth I, younger daughter of Henry VIII, 1558–1603

House of Stuart

James I (James VI of Scotland), descendant of Henry VII, 1603–1625, first to call himself King of Great Britain

Charles I, son of James I, 1625–1649

Commonwealth and Protectorate

Council of State, 1649–1653

Oliver Cromwell, Lord Protector, 1653–1658

Richard Cromwell, son of Oliver, Lord Protector, 1658–1659

House of Stuart (Restored)

Charles II, son of Charles I, 1660–1685

James II, younger son of Charles I, 1685–1688

William III, grandson of Charles I, ruled jointly with Mary II, daughter of James II, 1689–1694; ruled alone, 1694–1702

Anne, younger daughter of James II, 1702–1714

House of Hanover

George I, great-grandson of James I, 1714–1727

George II, son of George I, 1727–1760

George III, grandson of George II, 1760–1820

George IV, son of George III, 1820–1830

William IV, third son of George III, 1830–1837

Victoria, granddaughter of George III, 1837–1901

House of Saxe-Coburg and Gotha

Edward VII, eldest son of Victoria, 1901–1910

House of Windsor (family name changed during World War I)

George V, son of Edward VII, 1910–1936

Edward VIII, son of George V, 1936 (abdicated to marry the woman he loved)

George VI, second son of George V, 1936–1952

Elizabeth II, daughter of George VI, 1952–

Highland Reel

Macbeth seized the kingdom of Scotland from Duncan I in 1040 and was in turn killed by Duncan's son Malcolm III. Malcolm's wife, Margaret, a Saxon princess, introduced the English language. Her son Edgar moved the court to Edinburgh. He was succeeded by his brothers Alexander I and David I. Malcolm IV, David's grandson, was next on the throne, followed by his brother William the Lion in 1165, William's son Alexander II in 1214, and Alexander's son Alexander III in 1249. His successor was his granddaughter Margaret, who died when only eight years old. Robert the Bruce came to power in 1306 and was succeeded by his only son, David II. Robert II, grandson of Robert the Bruce, began the Stuart line, ascending to the throne in 1371. After him, the order was:

Robert III, son of Robert II, 1390–1406

James I, son of Robert III, 1406–1437

James II, son of James I, 1437–1460

James III, son of James II, 1460–1488

James IV, son of James III, 1488–1513

James V, son of James IV, 1513–1542

Mary, daughter of James V, became queen when she was seven days old in 1542 and was crowned in 1543. Married to Francis (son of Henry II of France), Mary continued to rule after his death in 1560. She was eventually imprisoned and then beheaded by Elizabeth I in 1567. Mary's son with Lord Darnley became James VI of Scotland and, upon Elizabeth's death, James I of England, uniting the two thrones.

Russian Around

Beginning with the tsars of Muscovy, the Russian rulers are as follows:

Ivan III, 1462–1505

Basil III, 1505–1533

Ivan IV (the Terrible), 1533–1584

Fëdor I, 1584–1598

Boris Godunov, 1598–1605

Fëdor II, 1605

Demetrius, 1605–1606

Basil IV, 1606–1610

Wladyslaw, (a Polish prince), 1610–1613

Mikhael Romanov, 1613–1645

Alexis I, 1645–1676

Fëdor III, 1676–1682

Ivan V and Peter I (the Great), 1682–1689

Peter I (alone, declaring himself emperor in 1721), 1689–1725

Catherine I, widow of Peter I, 1725–1727

Peter II, grandson of Peter I, 1727–1730

Anna, niece of Peter I, 1730–1740

Ivan VI, great-grandson of Ivan V, 1740–1741

Elizabeth, daughter of Peter I, 1741–1762

Peter III, grandson of Peter I, 1762 (deposed)

Catherine II (the Great), consort of Peter III, 1762–1796

Paul I, son of Catherine II, 1796–1801

Alexander I, son of Paul I, 1801–1825

Nicholas I, brother of Alexander I, 1825–1855

Alexander II, son of Nicholas I, 1855–1881 (assassinated)

Alexander III, son of Nicholas I, 1881–1894

Nicholas II, last tsar of Russia, 1894–1917

➢ Louis, Louis

Some of the men named Louis who wore the French crown were given interesting sobriquets (that's nicknames, not fuel for a barbecue grill):

Louis I (778–840) was known as Louis the Debonair and the Pious

Louis II (846–879) the Stammerer

Louis VI (966–987) the Lazy

Louis VII (1121–1180) the Fat

Louis VIII (1187–1226) the Lion

Louis X (1289–1316) the Quarrelsome

Louis XII (1462–1515) Father of the People

Louis XIV (1638–1715) the Sun King

Louis XV (1710–1774) the Beloved

Louis XVII (1785–1795?) the Lost Dauphin

China Shop

The dynasties of China beginning with Kublai Khan (1216-1294):

Yüan dynasty 1271–1368

Ming dynasty (reunified China) 1368–1644

Ch'ing (Manchu) dynasty 1644–1912

Within the Manchu dynasty, the rulers were:

Shun Chih 1644–1661

K'ang-hsi 1661–1722

Yung Chêng 1722–1735

Ch'ien Lung 1735–1796

Chia Ch'ing 1796–1820

Tao Kuang 1821–1851

Hsien Fêng 1851–1861

T'ung Chi 1862–1875

Kuang Hsü 1875–1908

Hsüan T'ung 1908–1912

Provincial rulers and warlords fought among themselves until 1949, when the People's Republic of China was founded with Mao Zedong as chairman of the Central People's Administrative Council of the Communist Party.

The LAST WORD

Some of the sweetest words appear on stone. Herewith a selection of epitaphs (the word is from the Greek for "writing on a tomb"), including the sublime and silly.

Poet ***John Gray*** wrote for his own tomb in Westminster Abbey:

Life is a jest and all things show it
I thought so once, but now I know it

John Keats, who died and is buried in Rome, wanted simply "Here lies one whose name was writ on water." But, knowing how stung the young poet had been by London critics before his death, Keats's friend Joseph Severn added an explanatory preface to the stone—"This grave contains all that was Mortal of a young English Poet Who on his Death Bed in the Bitterness of his Heart at the Malicious Power of his Enemies Desired these words to be engraven on his Tomb Stone"—and the date, which was February 23, 1821.

Edgar Allan Poe's epitaph echoes one of his most famous refrains, "Quoth the Raven, nevermore."

Thomas Wolfe's is taken from *Look Homeward, Angel*: "The last voyage, the longest, the best."

Joseph Conrad's comes from Spenser's *The Faerie Queen*:

Sleep after toyle, port after stormie seas,
Ease after warre, death after life, does greatly please.

As a young man, ***Benjamin Franklin*** suggested for his headstone

The Body of
B. Franklin, Printer
(Like the cover of an old book,
Its contents torn out,
And stript of its Lettering and Gilding)
Lies here, Food for Worms.
But the Work shall not be Lost;
For it will (as he believ'd) appear once more,
In a new and more elegant Edition
Corrected and amended
By the Author.

Hans Christian Andersen left detailed plans for his funeral. He asked a friend who was composing the funeral march to keep in mind, "Most of the people who will walk after me will be children, so make the beat keep time with little steps."